THE
SCHOOL MATHEMATICS PROJECT

When the SMP was founded in 1961, its objective was to devise radically new mathematics courses, with accompanying GCE syllabuses and examinations, which would reflect, more adequately than did the traditional syllabuses, the up-to-date nature and usages of mathematics.

The first stage of this objective is now more or less complete. *Books 1–5* form the main series of pupil's texts, starting at the age of 11 + and leading to the O-level examination in 'SMP Mathematics', while *Books 3 T, 4* and *5* give a three-year course to the same O-level examination. (*Books T* and *T4*, together with their Supplement, represent the first attempt at this three-year course, but they may be regarded as obsolete.) *Advanced Mathematics Books 1–4* cover the syllabus for the A-level examination in 'SMP Mathematics' and in preparation are five (or more) shorter texts covering the material of various sections of the A-level examination in 'SMP Further Mathematics'. There are two books for 'SMP Additional Mathematics' at O-level. Every book is accompanied by a Teacher's Guide.

For the convenience of schools, the SMP has an arrangement whereby its examinations are made available by every GCE Examining Board, and it is most grateful to the Secretaries of the eight Boards for their co-operation in this. At the same time, most Boards now offer their own syllabuses in 'modern mathematics' for which the SMP texts are suitable.

By 1967, it had become clear from experience in comprehensive schools that the mathematical content of the SMP texts was suitable for a much wider range of pupil than had been originally anticipated, but that the presentation needed adaptation. Thus it was decided to produce a new series, *Books A–H*, which could serve as a secondary-school course starting at the age of 11 +. These books are specially suitable for pupils aiming at a CSE examination; however, the framework of the CSE examinations is such that it is inappropriate for the SMP to offer its own examination as it does for the GCE.

The completion of all these books does not mean that the SMP has no more to offer to the cause of curriculum research. The team of SMP writers, now numbering some thirty school and university mathematicians, is continually testing and revising old work and preparing for new. At the same time, the effectiveness of the SMP's work depends, as it always has done, on obtaining reactions from active teachers—and also from pupils—in the classroom. Readers of the texts can therefore send their comments to the SMP in the knowledge that they will be warmly welcomed.

Finally, the year-by-year activity of the SMP is recorded in the annual Director's Reports which readers are encouraged to obtain on request to the SMP Office at Westfield College, University of London, London N.W. 3.

The S.M.P. texts are based on the original contributions of

*A. B. Bolt	*D. A. Hobbs	P. G. T. Lewis
P. G. Bowie	S. W. Hockey	T. D. Morris
H. M. Cundy	*D. J. Holding	D. A. Quadling
J. H. Durran	G. Howlett	G. D. Stagg
L. E. Ellis	A. Hurrell	*A. R. Tammadge
A. G. Gallant	T. A. Jones	*J. V. Tyson
C. C. Goldsmith	M. J. Leach	J. S. T. Woolmer
B. J. W. Heath		

and are edited by A. G. Howson, assisted by H. N. R. Moore.

Those primarily concerned with this book are indicated by the asterisk.

Many other schoolteachers have been directly involved in the further development and revision of the material and the Project gratefully acknowledges the contributions which they and their schools have made.

THE
SCHOOL
MATHEMATICS
PROJECT

BOOK 3
[METRIC]

CAMBRIDGE
AT THE UNIVERSITY PRESS
1971

Published by the Syndics of the Cambridge University Press
Bentley House, 200 Euston Road, London NW1 2DB
American Branch: 32 East 57th Street, New York, N.Y. 10022

© Cambridge University Press 1967

Library of Congress Catalogue Card Number: 66–73798

ISBN: 0 521 07670 6

First edition 1967
Metricated 1970
Reprinted 1971

Printed in Great Britain
at the University Printing House, Cambridge
(Brooke Crutchley, University Printer)

PREFACE

With Book 3 the S.M.P. O-level course passes the half-way mark. By now most of the topics to be studied at O level have been introduced and the emphasis now begins to be placed on the interrelations that exist between the various topics. For example, matrices, which were first encountered in Book 2, are now used to illumine the study of topology, transformation geometry, relations and inverse functions.

The first chapter does introduce a new topic—for in it we consider probability for the first time. This is a perpetually fascinating subject and one that every pupil should meet before he leaves school. Apart from basic arithmetic, no mathematics is more likely to be of practical use than probability and statistics—for even this sentence contains its special language! Statistics was first introduced in Book 2 and in Chapter 13 we return to it, this time from a more quantitative point of view.

In Chapter 2 we look once again at transformation geometry. The transformations of reflection, rotation and translation were met in Books 1 and 2. Now we consider them together, investigating the properties they have in common and seeing how they combine. In this chapter the emphasis shifts from the geometrical figure to the transformation, and the results obtained and the experience gained are more relevant to later work on matrices, functions and groups than to work on pure geometry.

Work on geometry of a more traditional kind is to be found in Chapters 5, 7 and 15. In these chapters we consider the circle and its properties, simple three-dimensional geometry and the engaging topic of loci and envelopes. Chapter 12 is a mixture of 'ancient and modern' for in it we use the geometrical transformation of shearing as a spring-board for studying the areas and volumes of simple figures. This chapter also prepares the way for a study of general affine transformations and extends work on the description of transformations by matrices.

Matrices are studied in detail in Chapter 3 and thereafter appear on many occasions. In Chapter 6 we use them to investigate networks, relations and even pools-forecasting. This chapter takes up again several topological ideas mentioned earlier including Euler's relation for polyhedra and the four-colour problem and hints at a number of industrial and commercial applications of matrix theory. Further up-to-date applications of mathematical techniques are described in Chapters 8 and 14. The simple introduction to the practice of linear programming contained in Chapter 8 has a two-fold purpose—to show how mathematics is applied in the outside world and to present standard work on linear algebra in an entertaining and engrossing manner. Chapter 14 serves a double purpose too. Here we try to demonstrate what a computer can do and how it does it, but a second aim is to show how problems are broken down into series of simple logical steps.

The preface to Book 2 referred to the problems of the teaching of algebra and the necessity for striking a just balance between the acquisition of manipulative techniques and the study of basic concepts. The S.M.P. views on this are further developed in Chapters 10 and 11 in which it will be noted that we, at this stage, are still mainly concerned with concepts such as function, identity and inverse.

Finally we consider two traditional topics. In Chapter 4, we study rates of change—a Stage A approach to differentiation—in a fairly traditional manner. In Chapter 9, however, trigonometry is not tackled in a traditional way; here we have made a deliberate attempt to divorce trigonometry from triangles and instead have endeavoured to show the practical importance of the study of wave forms.

As with previous books in this series, answers to exercises are not printed at the end of the book but are contained in the companion Teacher's Guide which gives a chapter-by-chapter commentary on the pupil's text.

ACKNOWLEDGEMENTS

The drawings in this book are by Cecil Keeling.

The Project is grateful to English Electric and to Elliott Automation for supplying the photographs of computers reproduced in Chapter 14 and also to the Oxford and Cambridge Schools Examination Board for permission to make use of examples from the S.M.P. Elementary Mathematics examinations.

We are much indebted to the Cambridge University Press for their co-operation and help at all times in the preparation of this book.

The Project owes a great deal to its secretary, Miss A. J. Freeman, and to Miss M. Z. Andrews and Mrs C. Young for their typing in connection with this book.

CONTENTS

Preface   *page* v

1 Probability   1

2 Isometries   12

3 Matrices   27

4 Rates of Change   49

Revision Exercises   62

5 The Circle   67

6 Networks   88

7 Three-Dimensional Geometry   110

8 Linear Programming   121

Revision Exercises   135

9 Waves   141

10 Functions and Equations   154

11 Identity and Inverse   180

12 Shearing   195

Revision Exercises   219

13 Statistics   224

14 Computers and Programming   241

15 Loci and Envelopes   261

Puzzle Corner   277

Revision Exercises   282

Index   290

A NOTE ON METRICATION

With the 1970 reprint of this book, some changes have been made in the notation and units used.

(i) All quantities of money have been expressed in pounds (£) and new pence (p).

(ii) All measures have been expressed in metric units. The fundamental units of the Système International (that is the metric system to be used in Great Britain) are the metre, the kilogram and the second. These units have been used in the book except where practical classroom considerations or an estimation of everyday practice in the years to come have suggested otherwise.

(iii) The notation used for the abbreviations of units and on some other occasions conforms to that suggested in the British Standard publications PD 5686: 1967 and BS 1991: Part 1: 1967.

Where units and numbers have been changed in the texts, the corresponding changes in the Teacher's Guides have been listed in a small leaflet which will be available with the present Guides. Changes involving notation only will not be so listed. The contents of the leaflet will be incorporated into the Teacher's Guides when they are next reprinted.

1

PROBABILITY

It is remarkable that a science which began with the consideration of games of chance should be elevated to the rank of the most important subjects of human knowledge.

LAPLACE

1. PROBABILITY

'It is extremely unlikely that a Third Division team will win the F.A. Cup.'

'There's a fifty-fifty chance of a coin landing head upwards when it is tossed.'

'John has a better chance of reaching the final of the school tennis tournament than Brian.'

'The odds are on Russia beating America to the Moon.'

In all these statements there is a comparison of possible future events and the chance that one is more likely than another. We make these comparisons by using words and phrases such as: 'almost certain', 'extremely unlikely', 'a good chance', 'probable', 'evens' and so on. For many purposes these phrases are sufficient, but where a comparison has to be made which involves a payment of money, whether in betting on horses or calculating the fire insurance to be paid on a house, it is necessary to be more exact.

(*a*) What are the chances of your school football team winning the next home match? (Very good, good, reasonable, poor.)

Before being able to answer this question what facts must you consider?

(*b*) If you look at a page of a book written in English, which of the following is the most likely:

that there are (i) more '*e*'s than '*p*'s,

(ii) about the same number of '*e*'s as '*p*'s,

(iii) more '*p*'s than '*e*'s?

How did you decide upon the correct alternative?

Can you give a number to say how much more likely one letter is than the other?

(*c*) If you kept a note of the registration numbers of passing cars, would you expect to see a 3 in the tens place more often than a 9?

(*d*) How would you rate your chances of playing for the school tennis team before you leave? (Good, reasonable, poor, nil.)

(*e*) What is the chance of throwing a '5' with a die?

(*f*) In which of the following would you be most likely to have an accident while travelling from Plymouth to Glasgow:

(i) a car; (ii) a train; (iii) a boat; (iv) a plane?

Before being able to answer these questions you needed to draw on some of your past experiences. To make any worthwhile judgement on the outcome of a football match it is useful to know the recent results of the two teams, whether either team has players out because of injury, what are the strong points and the weak points of each team, and so on. The more information of this kind you have, the better will be your estimate of your team's chances. However, in this situation you can never be very exact because there are so many things to consider which defy measurement.

The numbers of '*e*'s and '*p*'s in a book lend themselves far more easily to measurement and it is soon clear, from counting, that the number of '*e*'s far exceeds the number of '*p*'s. To make any more exact statement such as "there are 20 times as many '*e*'s as '*p*'s", although tempting, would have little value.

Compare the ratio of '*e*'s to '*p*'s in four separate paragraphs.

When an experiment can be repeated many times under the same conditions, such as tossing a penny or throwing a die, it is possible to be more exact.

In an experiment a die was thrown 72 times and the results recorded as in Figure 1. The same die was then thrown 240 times with the results shown in Figure 2.

Exercise A

1. In the first experiment described above, 6 was scored twice as often as 3. Does this mean that the chances of throwing a '6' with the die are twice as good as those of throwing a '3'?

2

Score		Frequency	Score	Frequency
1	LHT LHT IIII	14	1	40
2	LHT LHT II	12	2	39
3	LHT III	8	3	44
4	LHT LHT III	13	4	38
5	LHT IIII	9	5	37
6	LHT LHT LHT I	16	6	42

| Fig. 1 | Fig. 2 |

2. In the second experiment each of the scores 1, 2, 3, 4, 5, 6, came up approximately 40 times each out of 240 throws.

(*a*) Is this what you would expect?

(*b*) Approximately how many times would you expect to score 5 out of 6000 throws?

3. Would you expect exactly two '3's to turn up with twelve throws of a die? If not, why not?

4. Toss two pennies and note whether 2 heads, 1 head or 0 heads occur. Repeat this experiment (*a*) 10 times, (*b*) 50 times, (*c*) 100 times. Plot the results as frequency diagrams in each case.

(i) What do you deduce about the relative chances of obtaining a head and a tail to 2 heads from the results of (*a*), (*b*) and (*c*)? Which result is most reliable?

(ii) What fraction of the experiments gives 2 heads in (*c*)?

(iii) Approximately how many times would you expect 2 heads to occur if you tossed the two pennies 1000 times?

5. If 3 coins are tossed, what is the chance that they will all turn up heads? Answer this experimentally by finding what fraction of the trials you carry out produces 3 heads.

6. A match-box contains 3 red beads and 2 yellow beads which, apart from their colour, are identical. An experiment is performed by shaking the box, then, without looking, opening the box and removing a bead. The colour of the bead is recorded and the bead returned to the box. This is repeated 60 times. Approximately what fraction of the beads taken out would you expect to be yellow? Carry out this experiment using Smarties or beads in a match-box and see if the results agree with your estimate.

7. Put a selection of beads of different colours in a match-box. Use 7 beads and preferably no more than 3 colours (e.g. 2 red, 4 yellow, 1 blue). Exchange your box with a neighbour, and, by repeating the experiment described in Question 6, try to determine the contents of the box.

8. In playing games such as Monopoly it is usual to throw two dice together and total the score indicated on them. What possible scores are there?

Is the chance of scoring 2 the same as that of scoring 8? Throw a pair of dice 200 times and keep a record of the total scored each time. Plot your results as a frequency diagram. Does it appear that the chances of some scores occurring are better than others? What fraction of your trials gave a score of (*a*) 2, (*b*) 4, (*c*) 7?

2. EXPERIMENTAL PROBABILITY

In 1654 a gambler, the Chevalier de Méré, asked a French mathematician, Blaise Pascal, to help him in deciding how to share the stake money in a game of dice. Pascal discussed the problem with Fermat, another eminent mathematician, and in solving the problem they started the theory of probability. Today the theories that were developed from a game of dice are used extensively in economics, industry, science and sociology.

To understand how these mathematicians measured the chances of a particular event happening, consider Figure 2, which records the results obtained from throwing a die. The die was thrown 240 times and, in these trials, the '5' turned up 37 times. This leads us to expect that if the same die were thrown 480 times the '5' would turn up about 74 times. We assume, in other words, that the proportion of '5's which occur remains about the same. The validity of this assumption depends on our taking a large number of trial throws for, as you will have seen from the questions you have answered, with a small number of throws almost anything can happen. (For instance, a penny tossed 3 times might easily land head upwards each time but no one would be foolish enough to deduce from this that it would never land tail uppermost.)

The proportion of '5's which occur after a large number of trials is expressed as a fraction and called the *experimental probability* that the '5' will turn up if the die is thrown again.

In the experiment being discussed this experimental probability is $\frac{37}{240}$.

What is the experimental probability of scoring: (a) 2, (b) 3, (c) 1?

What is the experimental probability that *either* a '1' *or* a '4' will turn up?

What is the experimental probability that a '6' does *not* turn up?

If the probability of drawing a heart from a hand of playing cards is 1, what do you deduce?

What is the probability that a die will turn up a '7'?

If a coin is tossed 1000 times and lands head uppermost 1000 times, what is the probability that if tossed again it will land head uppermost? What do you deduce about the coin?

Use the following definition of experimental probability to answer the questions in Exercise B:

$$\text{Experimental probability} = \frac{\text{the number of trials in which the event happens}}{\text{the total number of trials that have taken place}}.$$

Exercise B

1. Choose any number between 1 and 400. Look up the hymn with this number in your school hymn book and note how many verses it has. Do this for 60 trials and record your results.

4

(*a*) What is the experimental probability that a hymn chosen at random from the book will have: (i) 4 verses, (ii) 2 verses, (iii) more than 6 verses?

(*b*) Can you suggest any other way of working out the probability of selecting a hymn with 2 verses?

2.

Distance (km)	Less than 500	500 to 1000	1000 to 1500	More than 1500
Frequency	125	257	328	90

A large tyre manufacturer kept a record of the distance at which a particular kind of cycle tyre needed to be replaced. The table shows the results from 800 samples. What is the probability that if you buy a tyre of this kind:

(*a*) it will need to be replaced before it has covered 500 km;

(*b*) it will last more than 1000 km;

(*c*) it will need to be replaced after it has covered somewhere between 500 and 1500 km?

3. In a game of Whist the first player leads with a Jack of Spades while the second player plays a 2 of Hearts. What is the probability that the second player has no Spades?

4. Deal yourself a hand of 13 cards face down. Draw a card from the hand and note its suit. Return the card to the hand. Shuffle the cards in the hand and repeat the process 40 times.

(*a*) What is the experimental probability of drawing:

(i) a Heart,   (ii) a Spade?

(*b*) Compare your experimental probability with the proportion of (i) Hearts and (ii) Spades in your hand. What do you deduce?

5. Roll a 5p piece onto a chess board and note whether it comes to rest lying inside a square or not. Do this a large number of times and find the experimental probability that a 5p piece rolled on the chess board comes to rest inside a square.

6. Draw a set of parallel lines across a piece of paper so that the lines are all 3 cm apart. Drop a matchstick (or pin) onto the paper and note whether it crosses a line or not. Repeat this (*a*) 10 times, (*b*) 50 times, (*c*) 150 times. What is the experimental probability in each case of a matchstick falling between the lines? If you repeated the experiment 1000 times, approximately how many times would the matchstick fall between the lines?

7. Find out the birthdays of the pupils in your year at school and from this give the experimental probability that any pupil picked out from your year has a birthday in March.

8. Throw two dice together and note the total thrown. By repeating this a large number of times find the experimental probability for each of the possible scores. In playing a game of Monopoly a boy finds that he will be 'safe' if he scores either 3, 4, 5, 6 or 10. What is the probability that he will be (*a*) 'safe', (*b*) not 'safe'?

9. Find experimentally the probability of obtaining exactly 3 heads when 5 pennies are tossed.

10. Write the names of three of your friends and yourself on pieces of paper and put them in a hat. Find experimentally the probability that if you draw two pieces of paper from the hat, you will find:

(*a*) your name and the name of your oldest friend,

(*b*) your name and one other.

5

11. What is the experimental probability that a word picked out of an English Dictionary has more than 4 letters? Compare your result with that obtained using a French Dictionary.

12. Throw a die 50 times, recording the number of '6's which occur. Calculate the experimental probability of throwing a '6'. Repeat for 100, 150, 200 (and as many as you have time for) throws. Graph the function

$$\text{number of throws} \to \text{experimental probability}.$$

3. EXPECTED PROBABILITY

In the last section you were able to determine the chance of an event happening by carrying out a series of experiments. It is likely that someone else carrying out the same experiments might obtain a different value for the probability although they are usually approximately the same. Often it is possible to deduce the chance of an event occurring by quite different means.

Consider a die which consists of a perfectly symmetrical cube. Because of its symmetry (unless it is loaded!) it is reasonable to say that the chance of a '1' turning up is the same as that of a '2' turning up and so on. There are six ways in which a die can land and, since these are equally likely, the chance that any particular one of them will turn up is 1/6. This is the *expected probability* of throwing a particular number with a die and the experimental probability usually approximates to it.

Let us look more closely at this example. The set of the possible outcomes of throwing a die is

$$\mathscr{E} = \{1, 2, 3, 4, 5, 6\}.$$

Suppose that we are interested in the probability of throwing either a '2' or a '3'. The set of outcomes we are interested in is

$$S = \{2, 3\}.$$

Then the *expected probability* is defined as

$$\frac{\text{the number of elements in } S}{\text{the number of elements in } \mathscr{E}}.$$

Thus the expected probability of throwing either a '2' or a '3' is $\frac{2}{6} = \frac{1}{3}$. This is usually written

$$p(S) = \frac{n(S)}{n(\mathscr{E})} = \frac{2}{6} = \frac{1}{3},$$

where $p(S)$ denotes the expected probability of event S, and $n(S)$ and $n(\mathscr{E})$ denote the *number of elements* in S and $\mathscr{E}$ respectively.

Example 1

Consider the probability of cutting a pack of playing cards and obtaining an ace. In this case the set of possible outcomes is

$$\mathscr{E} = \{\text{the 52 cards in a pack of playing cards}\}$$

and the event we are interested in is

    $S = \{$ace of Hearts, ace of Clubs, ace of Diamonds, ace of Spades$\}$.

The probability of obtaining an ace is

$$p(S) = \frac{n(S)}{n(\mathscr{E})} = \frac{4}{52} = \frac{1}{13}.$$

Earlier in the chapter when throwing two dice together you were probably surprised to find that the chance of scoring say 7 is considerably more than scoring 12. This is where intuition leads us astray. Suppose, for argument's sake, that you have a red die and a blue die. In how many different ways can they land when thrown together?

To help in answering this, consider the number of ways in which the blue die can land when the red die, which has already been thrown, (a) shows a '1', (b) shows a '2', (c) shows a '3', ..., (f) shows a '6'.

These possibilities can be neatly represented on graph paper as in Figure 3. Each cross represents a possible outcome. The circled cross, for example, represents a '5' on the red die and a '4' on the blue die. This can conveniently be represented as the ordered pair (5, 4).

What does (4, 5) represent?

Make a copy of Figure 3 and mark on it the ordered pairs (2, 3), (3, 1) and (6, 6). What do these represent in terms of the dice?

How many of the crosses represent a trial in which the total score is 7? (For example, (2, 5).)

What is the probability of scoring 7 when throwing 2 dice?

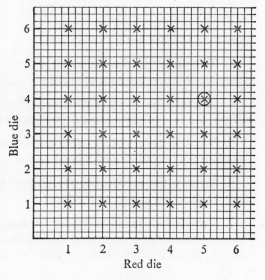

Fig. 3

Example 2

Calculate the expected probability of scoring 5 with two dice.

    $\mathscr{E} = \{$the different ways in which 2 dice can land$\}$,

    $S = \{(4, 1), (3, 2), (2, 3), (1, 4)\}$.

Hence the expected probability of scoring 5 is

$$p(S) = \frac{n(S)}{n(\mathscr{E})} = \frac{4}{36} = \frac{1}{9}.$$

Example 3

A boy is chosen at random from Anthony, Brian, Colin, Donald, Dennis and Eric. What is the probability that the boy who is chosen has a name beginning with D?

$$\mathscr{E} = \{\text{Anthony, Brian, Colin, Donald, Dennis, Eric}\},$$
$$S = \{\text{Donald, Dennis}\}.$$

Hence the probability that the boy chosen has a name beginning with D is

$$p(S) = \frac{n(S)}{n(\mathscr{E})} = \frac{2}{6} = \frac{1}{3}.$$

Exercise C

1. What is the expected probability of a prime number turning up when a die is thrown once?

2. A penny and a 5p piece are tossed together. Calculate the probability that:
(a) they will both turn up heads,
(b) they will not both turn up heads.

3. Two dice are thrown together. Calculate the probabilities of each of the possible scores occurring. What is the sum of these probabilities?

4. In a raffle for a box of chocolates 324 tickets are sold. What is the probability that you will win the box of chocolates if you have bought 3 tickets?

5. What is the set of possible outcomes when a penny and a die are tossed together? Calculate the probability of a head and a number greater than 4 turning up.

6. What is the expected probability of selecting a picture card from a pack of playing cards by selecting a card at random?

7. Two dice are made as regular tetrahedra and have the numbers 1, 2, 3, 4 on their faces. Using ordered pairs of numbers, make a list of the possible outcomes when they are thrown together. What is the probability that the two numbers which turn up have a *product* equal to 12?

8. The names of Andrew, Betty, Christine and David are put in a hat to select two representatives for an inter-form competition. Make a list of all the possible pairs of names that could be drawn from the hat. What are the probabilities of drawing:
(a) Andrew and David; (b) a boy and a girl;
(c) a pair which includes Betty; (d) a pair which does not include David?

9. A football match can end in 3 ways; the home team can win (W), draw (D), or lose (L). List the 9 different ways in which the results of two matches can end. Assuming that there is an equal chance of W, D or L for each match, calculate the probabilities that:
(a) both matches end in a draw; (b) no match is drawn.

10. In a game of cards a tie is often decided by each player drawing a card from the pack in turn and the person who draws the highest valued card is said to have won. If the first person

draws the '9 of Diamonds', what is the probability that the second player will draw a higher card?

11. (a) What is the set of possible outcomes when 3 pennies are tossed together?

(b) Calculate the probability that the outcome is: (i) 3 heads, (ii) 2 heads and a tail, (iii) a head and 2 tails, (iv) 3 tails.

(c) What is the probability that no heads occur?

(d) What is the probability of 4 heads?

(e) In an experiment, 3 pennies were tossed 80 times. Of these trials 3 heads occurred together on 8 occasions. Do you think this is evidence that the coins are biased?

12. The *odds* of an event happening is the *ratio*

probability of the event happening: probability of the event not happening.

For example, the *odds* of 2 heads turning up when 2 coins are used is

probability of 2 heads: probability of not 2 heads

$$= \tfrac{1}{4} : \tfrac{3}{4}$$
$$= 1 : 3.$$

Give the odds when 3 pennies are tossed of obtaining:

(a) 3 heads;   (b) 2 heads and a tail;   (c) a head and 2 tails;
(d) 3 tails;   (e) at least one head;   (f) more than one tail.

4. RANDOM SELECTION

The phrase 'at random' was used in the previous section. It is very easy to introduce bias into a random selection as you will see in some of the following examples.

(a) Look back at Example 3 on p. 8. How would you choose one of the boys *at random*?

Can you think of methods based on:

(i) drawing from a 'hat',   (ii) throwing a die,   (iii) any other ways?

(b) Ask a friend to name a number at random between 5 and 12.

In theory all numbers between 5 and 12 have an equal probability of being named, but in practice which number might be named most frequently?

(c) You want to select three pupils at random from your school for a survey about travel to school. What is wrong with going to the school entrance a few minutes before school begins and selecting a group of three who are coming in together?

(d) A firm of porridge oat manufacturers wanted to find out how popular porridge was for breakfast.

They opened a London telephone directory at random and contacted everyone on that page. They found that 80 % had porridge for breakfast.

Can you explain what had gone wrong with their random sample?

Exercise D

1. You want to predict the result of the local elections and to do this you go into the main street at 11 a.m. on a Monday morning and interview people on the pavement. Will you have a random sample?

2. 'Last night $3\frac{1}{4}$ million people watched the big fight on television.'
How would this information be obtained?

3. A firm which manufactures dish-washing machines wants to know what percentage of the population uses their machines. They do this by selecting people at random from a telephone directory. Have they introduced bias into their sample?

4. 'In a random sample of 10 housewives, 9 preferred Whoosh to any other detergent.'
What questions would you want to ask the advertisers about the randomness of their sample and about their method of obtaining this information?

5. The arrangement of numbers in Figure 4 is called a Latin Square. Notice that each number appears once and only once in every row and column.

1	2	3	4
2	4	1	3
3	1	4	2
4	3	2	1

Fig. 4

Make up a different arrangement satisfying this condition. How would these patterns help a farmer who wished to test the effects of 4 different fertilizers on a crop of wheat?

6. (a) What is the connection between the two tables in Figure 5?
   (b) (i) In how many ways do exactly 2 heads occur when 3 pennies are tossed?
     (ii) How many of the decimal numbers from 0 to 7 have two '1's in their binary representation?

Ways in which 3 pennies can land			Binary numbers		
3rd	2nd	1st	Fours	Twos	Units
T	T	T	0	0	0
T	T	H	0	0	1
T	H	T	0	1	0
T	H	H	0	1	1
H	T	T	1	0	0
H	T	H	1	0	1
H	H	T	1	1	0
H	H	H	1	1	1
(a)			(b)		

Fig. 5

10

7. By comparing the patterns of the two tables in Figure 5 make similar tables with four columns showing the connection between the ways in which 4 pennies can land, and the binary representation of the decimal numbers from 0 to 15.

(*a*) In how many ways do exactly 2 heads occur when 4 pennies are tossed?

(*b*) What is the probability of at least 3 heads occurring when 4 pennies are tossed?

8. Using your answer to Question 7, invent a method for finding a random number between 0 and 15.

Extend this method to find random numbers between

$$(a) \ 0 \text{ and } 63; \qquad (b) \ 0 \text{ and } 511.$$

9. The table in Figure 6 shows the number of outcomes when different numbers of pennies are tossed. By extending the results of Questions 6 and 7 complete a copy of the table.

Number of pennies tossed	Number of heads showing						Total number of outcomes
	0	1	2	3	4	5	
1	1	1	0	0	0	0	2
2							
3			3				8
4		4					
5				10			

Fig. 6

10. The table in Question 9 is closely related to Pascal's triangle of numbers which you met in Book 2.

(*a*) Use your knowledge of the connections between the numbers in Pascal's triangle to write down the number of ways in which: 0 heads, 1 head, 2 heads, 3 heads, 4 heads, 5 heads and 6 heads can occur when 6 pennies are tossed.

(*b*) When 6 pennies are tossed what is the probability of obtaining (i) at least 4 heads; (ii) fewer than 4 heads?

2-2

2

ISOMETRIES

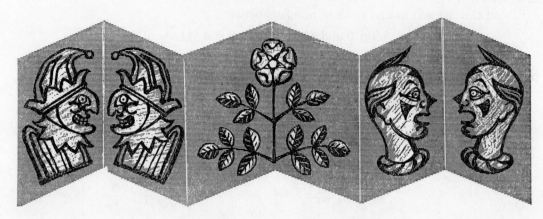

Plus ça change....

ALPHONSE KARR, *Les Guepes*

1. POTATO PRINTING

Figure 1 shows the pattern of the blue parts of an inaccurately drawn Union Jack. If you cut a potato in half and carve it with a penknife, it is easy to produce a block that will enable you to print triangles with the aid of an ink pad (see Figure 2).

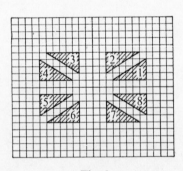

Fig. 1

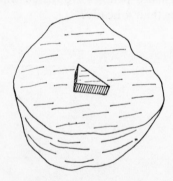

Fig. 2

Will you be able to print all the triangles in Figure 1 with the block shown in Figure 2? If not, which of the numbered triangles would it print, and how many more potato blocks would be required? Describe them.

Consider very simple movements of the block from one position to another and try to describe these movements in terms of the transformations (*a*) rotation, (*b*) reflection or (*c*) translation. Can the block be moved in a way that corresponds to each of these transformations? If not, which is impossible?

If the potato printing were to be automated, you would have to give the machine exact instructions. Having printed triangle 1, it would need to be told what movement to make before printing 2, 3 or whichever triangle you wanted it to print next. Discuss what instructions would be required for △1 → △2; △2 → △5; △5 → △6; what will have to happen before the remaining triangles can be printed? Discuss a suitable sequence for them.

2. COMBINING TRANSFORMATIONS

You will have discovered in the last section that the familiar transformations—rotation, reflection and translation—are the ones that correspond to the movements of a triangle from one position to another. Why have we not mentioned enlargement? Rotations, reflections and translations are all *isometries* (Greek; *isos*-equal, *metron*-measure). Discuss the meaning of this word.

Before proceeding, we shall find discussion easier if we draw the flag again on a larger scale (Figure 3). The simplest transformation that will move the printing block from 1 to 2 (or map △1 onto △2) is a rotation of 180° about the point (5, 3). Is there any other simple transformation that will map △1 onto △2?

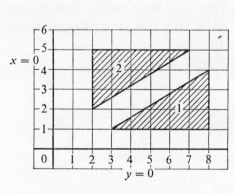

Fig. 3

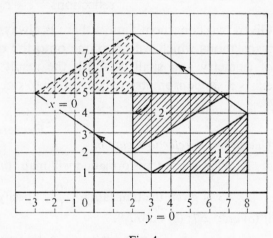

Fig. 4

It is plain that there are many *pairs* of transformations that will map △1 onto △2. For instance, the translation specified by the vector $\begin{pmatrix} -6 \\ 4 \end{pmatrix}$, followed by a rotation of 180° about the vertex at (2, 5) will do this (see Figure 4). What translation will be needed to complete the transformation if we start with a rotation of 180° about the

13

vertex $(3, 1)$? If we start with a translation of $\begin{pmatrix} -6 \\ 1 \end{pmatrix}$, is there a rotation which will then map the image of triangle 1 onto triangle 2? If so, specify it. Discuss whether the same pairs of transformations will work if applied the other way round (that is, are they commutative?).

Summary

An isometry maps a figure onto another figure that is identical as far as lengths and angles are concerned. Such figures are called *congruent*. The congruence may be

(*a*) *direct*, or (*b*) *opposite*, see Figure 5.

(*a*) Direct (*b*) Opposite

Fig. 5

The isometries we have met are:

$$\left.\begin{array}{l} \text{translations} \\ \text{rotations} \end{array}\right\} \rightarrow \text{direct isometries,}$$

reflections $\rightarrow$ opposite isometries.

Given two congruent figures there is always a sequence of rotations, reflections and translations which will map one onto the other. (We shall later meet a fourth type of isometry and shall establish the result that given two congruent figures there exists a single isometry which will map one onto the other.)

Exercise A

Questions 1–5 refer to Figure 6.

1. What single transformation will map: (*a*) $\triangle 3$ onto $\triangle 7$; (*b*) $\triangle 3$ onto $\triangle 8$?

2. $\triangle 3$ is given the translation $\begin{pmatrix} 10 \\ 0 \end{pmatrix}$. Specify the second transformation which will map it (*a*) onto $\triangle 7$; (*b*) onto $\triangle 8$.

3. $\triangle 4$ is reflected in the line $x = 0$. State with reasons whether its image can be translated onto: (*a*) $\triangle 8$; (*b*) $\triangle 7$.

4. Specify a pair of translations which will map $\triangle 7$ onto $\triangle 4$. Try to find two further pairs. How many such pairs are there? Do you need the diagram to help you specify them?

5. $\triangle 8$ can be mapped onto $\triangle 3$ by means of a pair of rotations. If the first one maps $\triangle 8$ onto $\triangle 7$, specify each rotation. Will the same rotations performed in the reverse order have the same effect?

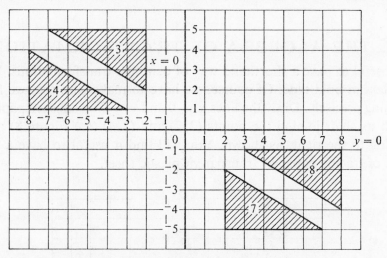

Fig. 6

6. What translation must be given to △4 so that its image coincides with the image of △7 under the translation $\begin{pmatrix} 2 \\ 6 \end{pmatrix}$?

Use your answer to find a pair of translations under which △7 → △4.

D7. Is it *ever* possible for:
(*a*) a rotation followed by a reflection to be equivalent to a translation;
(*b*) a translation followed by a rotation to be equivalent to a reflection;
(*c*) a reflection followed by another reflection to be equivalent to a rotation?

Questions 8–12 refer to Figure 7.

8. What single transformation, if any, will map

(*a*) △2 onto △7;   (*b*) △2 onto △1;
(*c*) △2 onto △8?

9. △2 is given a 90° rotation *clockwise* about *O*. Specify the second transformation needed to map its image onto △7.

D10. Discuss whether it is possible to map any particular triangle of Figure 7 onto any other: (*a*) by translations only; (*b*) by reflections only.

11. △8 is given a 180° rotation about (6, 1). Specify if possible a second transformation which will map its image: (*a*) onto △7; (*b*) onto △2.

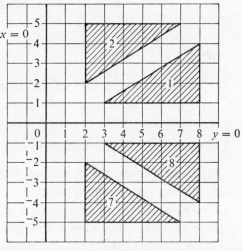

Fig. 7

12. △2 is reflected in its longest side. Discuss which further triangles its image can now be mapped onto by a single rotation and how you would find the centre of such a rotation.

15

3. THE ALGEBRA OF TRANSFORMATIONS

It is very useful to have a shorthand way of denoting transformations. We shall use capital letters in bold type. Of course, we have to make sure that we have defined their meaning precisely. Draw the lines $x = 0$ and $y = 0$ on squared paper. Draw the flag F with its shaft joining the points $(2, 2)$ and $(2, 4)$ (see Figure 8) and with the flag pointing to the right, as shown. You will find it useful to have a tracing of F on a piece of tracing paper or transparent plastic sheet.

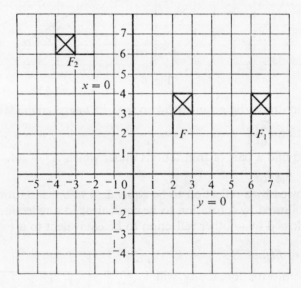

Fig. 8

Let us denote a rotation of $90°$ in an anticlockwise direction about $(0, 0)$ by **P**. The image of F under this will be denoted by **P**(F). Mark **P**(F) on your squared paper.

Let us denote the translation $\begin{pmatrix} 4 \\ 0 \end{pmatrix}$ by **T**. If we now carry out the transformation **T** on **P**(F), we denote the resulting image by **TP**(F)—an abbreviation for **T(P**(F)**)**. Mark this on your squared paper. What single transformation maps F onto **TP**(F)?

Copy F_1 and F_2, two images of F shown in Figure 8, onto your paper. (Neither of them should coincide with **P**(F) or **TP**(F).) Describe the single transformations that map F onto: (a) F_1; (b) F_2. How could you map F_1 by a single transformation onto F_2?

Sometimes we are interested only in the transformation and not in the particular figure which is being transformed. We then write the letter only, without anything in brackets after it. Describe again the single transformation that has the same result

16

as the combined transformation **TP**. Call this **R**. Discuss the meaning of the sentence **TP** = **R**, taking particular care to explain the precise meaning of the relation ' =' in this context.

Specify the transformations **J** and **K** if the images **J**(F) and **KJ**(F) are as shown in Figure 9. Describe **L** if **KJ** = **L**. What do you find about **JK**(F)?

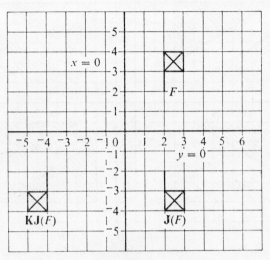

Fig. 9

Summary

We use capital letters in bold type to denote transformations. If **A** and **B** are transformations and P is a figure or object, then:

(a) **A**(P) denotes the image of P under the transformation **A**;

(b) **BA**(P) denotes the image of **A**(P) under the transformation **B**.

The object may be omitted. **BA** = **C** means that transformation **B** applied *after* transformation **A** is equivalent to the single transformation **C**.

Exercise B

Questions 1–6 refer to Figure 10. Use tracing paper to help find the answers.

1. Let **A** denote a rotation of 180° about (5, 3), **B** denote a rotation of 180° about (5, ⁻3) and **C** denote the translation $\binom{10}{6}$.

State which of the following are true, which false:

(a) **A**(△1) = △2;   (b) **A**(△2) = △1;
(c) **C**(△5) = △1;   (d) **C**(△4) = **A**(△8).

2. With the same data state which of the following are true, which false:

(a) **AC**(△6) = △2;   (b) **BC**(△6) = △2;   (c) **CB**(△7) = **A**(△3);
(d) **AB**(△6) can be mapped onto △1 by a single translation.

3. Let **X** denote reflection in the line $x = 0$, **Y** denote reflection in the line $y = 0$, and let **A**, **B** and **C** have their previous meanings. Copy and complete the following:

(a) $\mathbf{X}(\triangle 4) = \qquad$; (b) $\mathbf{Y}(\quad) = \triangle 2$;

(c) $\mathbf{XB}(\quad) = \triangle 5$; (d) $\qquad (\triangle 2) = \triangle 8$.

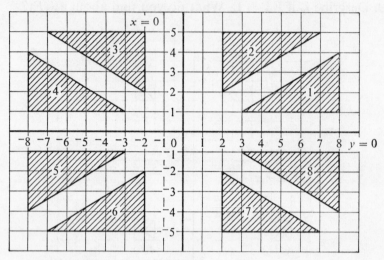

Fig. 10

4. *Powers of a transformation.* If **C** still has the same meaning, what does **CC** mean? What will be the coordinates of the right-angled vertex of the image of $\triangle 1$ under the transformation **CCC**? Suggest a shorter notation for **CC** and **CCC**. What do you think **C**⁴ should mean?

5. With the above notation state which of the following are true, which false:

(a) $\mathbf{A}^2(\triangle 2) = \triangle 8$; (b) $\mathbf{X}^2(\triangle 4) = \mathbf{Y}^2(\triangle 4)$; (c) $\mathbf{C}^2(\triangle 6) = \mathbf{C}(\triangle 1)$.

6. *The identity transformation.* This is the 'transformation' which moves nothing. Some call it the 'stay-put' transformation.

(*Note*: 'identical' means 'exactly the same'.)

We denote this transformation by the letter **I**. Which of the following describe the identity transformation for the pattern in Figure 10?:

(a) The translation $\binom{0}{0}$.

(b) Rotation through 180° about the pattern's centre of symmetry.

(c) Rotation through 360° about the pattern's centre of symmetry.

(d) Rotation through 360° about a vertex of one of the triangles.

(e) Reflection in one of the two lines of symmetry.

7. Let **X** denote reflection in $x = 0$, **Y** denote reflection in $y = 0$ and **H** denote a rotation of 180° about O. Simplify the following:

(a) $\mathbf{H}^2$; (b) $\mathbf{XY}$; (c) $\mathbf{HX}$; (d) $\mathbf{H}^4$; (e) $\mathbf{X}^2\mathbf{Y}^2\mathbf{H}^2$.

8. If **R** is *any* operation what can you say about **RI**? Simplify:

(a) $\mathbf{IR}$; (b) $\mathbf{RI}^2$; (c) $\mathbf{I}^4\mathbf{R}^2$.

9. Let **L** denote the translation $\begin{pmatrix} 4 \\ 5 \end{pmatrix}$ and **M** the translation $\begin{pmatrix} -3 \\ 6 \end{pmatrix}$. Specify translations **E** and **F** such that:

(a) **LM** = **E**;   (b) **LF** = **M**.

Find **G** given that **EFG** = **I**.

10. Let M_1 denote reflection in $x = 1$, M_2 denote reflection in $x = 2$, and so on. Let P be the point $(2, 2)$. Mark on a diagram the points P, $M_1(P)$, $M_2(P)$, $M_3(P)$. Discuss whether $M_2 = I$. If a is a number other than 1, is it possible to find a such that $M_1 = M_a$?

11. Figure 11 shows a diagram of the feet of a dancer. The feet are denoted by L and R. Describe the transformations which will most simply take the feet from position (a) to position (b).

12. Let **Q** denote a rotation of 240° about (−1, 2). Find the smallest value of z for which $\mathbf{Q}^z = \mathbf{I}$. What other values of z satisfy this equation?

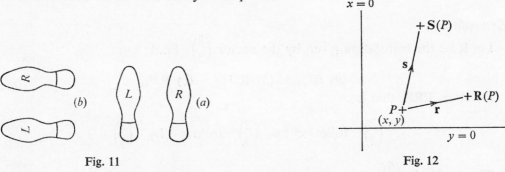

Fig. 11   Fig. 12

4. TRANSLATIONS COMBINED

So far we have considered various mixtures of our three isometries in a rather unsystematic way. Let us now take a more careful look at some of the possible combinations. You have already combined translations in Book 2, Chapter 7, using the *vector* notation. Let us see how this links with the transformations we have been considering.

Suppose **R** denotes the translation specified by vector **r**, **S** that specified by vector **s**, and P is the point (x, y). Typical positions for P, **R**(P) and **S**(P) might be as shown in Figure 12. (The vectors **r** and **s** might be, say,

$$\begin{pmatrix} 3 \\ 1 \end{pmatrix} \quad \text{and} \quad \begin{pmatrix} 1 \\ 3 \end{pmatrix},$$

but since we want to talk in general terms we shall not specify them.) Copy Figure 12, not taking any special vectors for **r** and **s** and mark **RS**(P). Where is **SR**(P)?

If **T** is a third translation, is **RST** a translation? How can you tell at a glance whether it is possible for one figure to be mapped onto another by one or more translations? Are **RTS**, **TRS**, etc., the same as **RST**? How many different arrangements for these three transformations can you find? Sketch the effect of these transformations on a point P—of what does the resulting diagram remind you?

5. INVERSE TRANSFORMATIONS

If an object F is mapped by a one-to-one transformation $\mathbf{A}$ onto the image F', then there will always be a second transformation which will map F' onto F. This is called the *inverse* of $\mathbf{A}$. It is written $\mathbf{A}^{-1}$. Since transforming and then returning to the starting position is the same as 'staying put', we see that

$$\mathbf{A}^{-1}\mathbf{A} = \mathbf{I}.$$

What can you say about $\mathbf{A}\mathbf{A}^{-1}$?

If $\mathbf{R}$ is a translation, what can you say about $\mathbf{R}^{-1}$? If $\mathbf{S}^{-1}$ is a translation, what can you say about $\mathbf{S}$?

Example 1

Let $\mathbf{R}$ be the translation given by the vector $\begin{pmatrix} 2 \\ 3 \end{pmatrix}$. Find:

$$(a)\ \mathbf{R}^3; \qquad (b)\ \mathbf{R}^{-1}; \qquad (c)\ \mathbf{R}^{-3}.$$

(a) $\mathbf{R}^3 = \mathbf{RRR}$, that is

$$\begin{pmatrix} 2 \\ 3 \end{pmatrix} \text{ followed by } \begin{pmatrix} 2 \\ 3 \end{pmatrix} \text{ followed by } \begin{pmatrix} 2 \\ 3 \end{pmatrix}.$$

This is clearly $\begin{pmatrix} 6 \\ 9 \end{pmatrix}$.

(b) $\mathbf{R}^{-1}$ brings you back to your starting point after $\begin{pmatrix} 2 \\ 3 \end{pmatrix}$, it is therefore $\begin{pmatrix} -2 \\ -3 \end{pmatrix}$.

(c) $\mathbf{R}^{-3}$ has not been defined, but a sensible meaning would be 'the transformation which combined with $\mathbf{R}^3$ brings you back to your starting point'. It is therefore $\begin{pmatrix} -6 \\ -9 \end{pmatrix}$. Note that it is also $(\mathbf{R}^{-1})^3$, that is,

$$\begin{pmatrix} -2 \\ -3 \end{pmatrix} \text{ followed by } \begin{pmatrix} -2 \\ -3 \end{pmatrix} \text{ followed by } \begin{pmatrix} -2 \\ -3 \end{pmatrix}.$$

Summary

The identity or stay-put transformation leaves every point of a figure unchanged. It is denoted by $\mathbf{I}$.

Given a transformation $\mathbf{A}$, the transformation which undoes the effect of $\mathbf{A}$ is called the *inverse* of $\mathbf{A}$. It is written $\mathbf{A}^{-1}$.

Exercise C

1. If $\mathbf{T}$ denotes 'translate across the page from left to right through 2 units', describe:

$$(a)\ \mathbf{T}^2; \qquad (b)\ \mathbf{T}^3; \qquad (c)\ \mathbf{T}^4; \qquad (d)\ \mathbf{T}^{-1}; \qquad (e)\ \mathbf{T}^{-3}.$$

What do you think $\mathbf{T}^0$ should mean? (Compare 2^0 which you met in Book 2, Chapter 9.)

2. Let S denote the translation $\binom{2}{3}$ and T the translation $\binom{-1}{1}$. Write down the co-ordinates of the points onto which (0, 0) is mapped under the transformations:

(a) ST;   (b) TS;   (c) T²;   (d) S⁻¹;

(e) T⁻²;   (f) TST;   (g) STS⁻¹.

3. Let X denote the translation $\binom{0}{1}$ and Y the translation $\binom{1}{0}$. Write down the coordinates of the image of the point (1, 1) under the transformations;

(a) X²;   (b) Y³;   (c) X⁻²;   (d) XYXY;   (e) X²Y²;

(f) X⁻³Y³;   (g) X⁴Y;   (h) X⁻⁴Y⁻⁵;   (i) XᵃYᵇ?

4. Draw a letter L by joining the points (2, 6), (1, 2) and (4, 1).

(a) Write down the single translation that will map it onto the letter L joining (⁻3, 3), (⁻4, ⁻1) and (⁻1, ⁻2).

(b) Write down a pair of translations that will effect the same transformation as that in (a).

(c) Write down a triple of translations that will also effect the same transformation.

(d) Write down the coordinates of the image of the first L under the translation $\binom{5}{5}$.

(e) If the first letter L is translated so that (1, 2) maps onto (3, ⁻2), find the images of the other vertices.

5. It is given that $\mathbf{a} = \binom{3}{4}$ and $\mathbf{b} = \binom{-2}{1}$;

also that A is the translation associated with **a** and B the translation associated with **b**. If P is the point (⁻1, ⁻2), give the coordinates of the points A(P) and B(P). If **c** = 2**a** + 3**b** and C is the translation associated with **c**, find C(P).

6. If $\mathbf{m} = \binom{8}{9}$, what is ⁻m?

Suggest a notation to denote the translation associated with **m**. How would you then describe the translation associated with ⁻m?

7. Let K denote the translation $\binom{6}{-4}$. Copy Figure 13 and plot K⁻¹(S) where S denotes the square shown. If **k** is the vector associated with the translation **K**, mark vectors 2**k** and 2.⁻**k** on your diagram. How would you denote the translations associated with (a) 2**k**; (b) 2.⁻**k**?

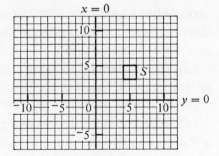

Fig. 13

D8. The transformation

R₁ is a translation through $\binom{1}{0}$,

R₂ through $\binom{2}{0}$,

R₃ through $\binom{3}{0}$,

and so on. If O is the origin, plot the points R₁(O), R₂R₁(O), R₃R₂R₁(O), R₄R₃R₂R₁(O), and calculate the coordinates of R₁₀R₉...R₃R₂R₁(O). (The dots indicate that all the intermediate

21

R's are to be thought of as being there.) Where is the point $R_1 R_2 R_3 \ldots R_9 R_{10}(O)$? After how many transformations R will the x-coordinate of the image of O be at least 100?

9. Discuss the meaning of $(T^{-1})^{-1}$ where T is any translation.

6. REFLECTION IN PARALLEL LINES

We shall now consider the combination of reflections. We begin with the easiest case. In Figure 14 the flag has been reflected in parallel lines m_1 and m_2. The flag P and three of its images have been numbered 1, 2, 3, 4. We shall write M_1 to denote reflection in the line m_1 and M_2 to denote reflection in the line m_2.

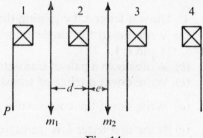

Fig. 14

(a) Copy Figure 14 fairly closely. Which distances have to be equal to those marked d and e? Take care over the position of 4. Label the appropriate images $M_1(P)$, $M_2(P)$, $M_1 M_2(P)$, $M_2 M_1(P)$. You will have to draw one further image. Which one? Label it 5.

The images of objects under reflections are, of course, congruent to each other. The original P has the flag on the right of the pole, so does one of the images in Figure 14 (which?). P and this image are directly congruent. The other images have the flag on the left of the pole. These are oppositely congruent to P.

(b) What single transformation will map 3 onto oppositely congruent 4? Will the same transformation map 4 onto 3? Give it an appropriate letter and suffix. What happens if you perform this transformation twice on 3? What is the inverse of this transformation?

(c) What single transformation will map 1 onto its directly congruent image 3? Is there any connection between the distance needed to describe this transformation and the distances d and e?

(d) Specify exactly the single transformation that will map 1 onto its directly congruent image 5. What is the distance between the images involved?

(e) Are there more images of P than those you have drawn? How many?

(f) Repeated reflection in two parallel lines produces a pattern that can be used for a frieze as shown in Figure 15. Copy this diagram, or better, make up a frieze of this type for yourself starting with your own basic pattern (or *motif*). How many parallel mirror-lines need there be? Can you put them where you like? Mark them on your diagram. It is obvious that this pattern can also be produced by repeated translations. What is the connection between the distance between the mirrors and the distance through which the motif has to be translated?

Fig. 15

Exercise D

1. P is the point $(3, 1)$. The mirror-line m_1 is $x = 0$, and m_2 is $x = 4$. M_1 denotes reflection in m_1 and M_2 reflection in m_2. Give the coordinates of:

    (a) $M_1(P)$;   (b) $M_2(P)$;   (c) $M_1 M_2(P)$;   (d) $M_2 M_1(P)$.

Describe the single transformations equivalent to $M_1 M_2$ and to $M_2 M_1$. How are these connected?

2. (a) Draw two parallel lines m_1 and m_2 as shown in Figure 16 and a triangle A between them. Construct the triangles $M_1(A)$, $M_2 M_1(A)$, $M_1 M_2 M_1(A)$, etc. Discuss what the pattern will look like if it is continued. Would it be satisfactory for a frieze? (You are advised to make a template by cutting a triangle out of thin card.)

    (b) Repeat Question 2a using a triangle that cuts one of the lines, as in Figure 17. Is your answer the same?

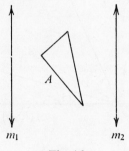

Fig. 16

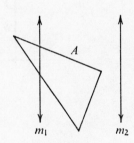

Fig. 17

3. Make a pleasing pattern using two parallel mirror-lines, and a triangle that cuts them both.

4. The point $(^-2, 0)$ is mapped onto $(5, 0)$ after being reflected in a line and then reflected again in a parallel line. Find possible equations of the lines. How many pairs are there? How will they lie with respect to the points (that is, are they both between the points, or one between them and one outside, etc.)?

5. Make an accurate drawing and use it to help you to write down the equation of the mirror-line of the reflection which maps $(4, 2)$ onto $(^-4, ^-2)$.

6. A girl's face is about 40 cm from a mirror. In order to see the back of her hair she holds another mirror nearly parallel to the first and 30 cm behind her head. How far from her eyes does the back of her head appear to be? (Make a reasonable estimate for the dimensions of her head.)

23

7. REFLECTIONS IN INTERSECTING LINES

Copy Figure 18. Let **P** denote reflection in p and **Q** denote reflection in q. S denotes the sword shown. (Note that the important part of it is the straight line representing blade and handle, the hilt and guard are optional extras and can be added afterwards, freehand.)

Construct **P**(S) and **QP**(S). What single transformation will map S onto **QP**(S)? To specify it precisely you will need to measure an angle. What relation does this angle appear to have to the angle between p and q?

Construct **Q**(S) and **PQ**(S) as well. What single transformation maps S onto **PQ**(S)? Does the angle involved appear to have any relation to the angle you measured previously? Do **PQ** and **QP** map S onto the same image?

What is the connection between all this and Figure 9 (p. 17)? In that example you noted that **JK** = **KJ**. Can you see why **J** and **K** are commutative whereas **P** and **Q** are not?

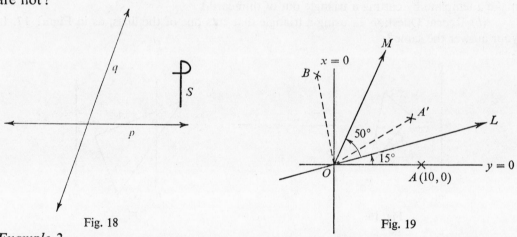

Fig. 18   Fig. 19

Example 2

The line OL passes through the origin O and makes an angle of $15°$ with $y = 0$. OM is another line through O and $\angle LOM$ is $50°$. The point $A(10, 0)$ is reflected in OL and its image is reflected in OM, giving B. Find angle $\angle AOB$.

In Figure 19 let A' be the reflection of A in OL, then
$$\angle LOA' = \angle AOL = 15°;$$
$$\Rightarrow \angle AOA' = 30°.$$
Since $\qquad \angle LOM = 50°$ and $\angle LOA' = 15°$, $\angle A'OM = 35°$.
But B is the reflection of A' in OM so that
$$\angle MOB = \angle A'OM = 35°.$$
$$\Rightarrow \angle A'OB = \angle A'OM + \angle MOB = 70°,$$
$$\Rightarrow \angle AOB = \angle AOA' + \angle A'OB = 30° + 70° = 100°.$$

24

Exercise E

1. Let X denote reflection in $x = 0$, P be the point $(3, {}^-2)$, $P_1 = X(P)$, $P_2 = X^2(P)$, and so on. Plot P, P_1 and P_2. Discuss the position of P_n.

2. Draw a flag F whose shaft joins the points $(2, 1)$ and $(3, 4)$. Construct its image after reflections in the lines $y = 1$, $y = 2$, $y = 3$ and $y = 4$. What do you find? What can you say about the set of images of a figure under a set of reflections in parallel lines?

3. Copy Figure 20. Let M_1 denote reflection in the line m_1, and so on. Construct $M_1(F)$ and $M_2 M_1(F)$.

Draw lines m_1' and m_2' parallel to m_1 and m_2 respectively. Construct $M_1'(F)$ and $M_2'(F)$. How are $M_2 M_1(F)$ and $M_2' M_1'(F)$ related? Discuss why you will obtain a similar result if you construct $M_2 M_1'(F)$ and $M_2' M_1(F)$. State a general principle.

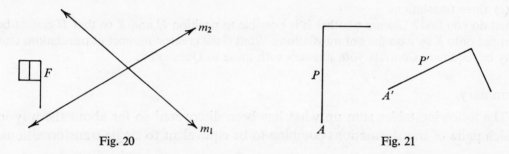

Fig. 20   Fig. 21

4. Let X denote reflection in $x = 0$, Y denote reflection in $y = 0$, and A denote reflection in $x = y$. Describe the transformations:

(a) YX;   (b) AY;   (c) YA;   (d) AXY (be careful!).

5. Copy Figure 19. Make it large enough to have plenty of room to label angles. With the data of Example 2 of Section 7, take the point $A(10, 0)$ and reflect it in OM, and then reflect its image in OL to give D. Find $\angle AOD$. What connection has this with $\angle AOB$?

D6. Discuss the following *theorem*, which is the generalization of Example 2 and Question 5:

The product of reflections in two intersecting lines m_1 and m_2, in that order, is a rotation about their point of intersection through twice the angle from m_1 to m_2.

Discuss also how it can be proved and what special cases arise.

D7. If M_1, M_2 are reflections in two intersecting lines, describe the transformations $M_1 M_2 M_2 M_1$ and $(M_1 M_2)^{-1}$. If $M_1 M_2 = M_2 M_1$, what can you say about the lines?

8. (a) In Figure 21 the figure P has been reflected in *two* straight lines v and w respectively and its image is P'. Do you think the lines v and w are parallel? Copy Figure 21 and construct the mirror-line v of the reflection which maps A onto A'. Construct also the image of P under this reflection and discuss how you can now reflect it onto the final position P'. Hence construct the line w. Are these the only possible positions for lines v and w? Use tracing paper to construct the fixed point O of the rotation which maps P onto P'. What connection has O with v and w?

(b) Consider any convenient pair of directly congruent figures, A and B. Can A be mapped onto B by a single reflection? By a double reflection? (Consider the construction

3   25   SM 3

in part (*a*).) Does it make any difference if *A* and *B* are in parallel positions so that they can be related by a translation?

(*c*) Answer the questions in (*b*) with respect to a pair of oppositely congruent figures.

D9. Sketch a pair of congruent flags *F* and *G* such that *G* is the image of *F* under

(*a*) a single reflection; (*b*) two reflections; (*c*) three reflections.

Discuss whether it is possible to place *F* and *G* in such a way that *F* cannot be mapped onto *G* by a product of reflections. What is the greatest number of reflections that may be required? In which case is there only one set of positions of the mirror-lines?

D10. Sketch a pair of congruent flags *H* and *K* in such a way that *K* is the image of *H* under

(*a*) a single translation;
(*b*) two translations;
(*c*) three translations.

What do you find? Discuss whether it is possible to position *H* and *K* so that *H* cannot be mapped onto *K* by a product of translations. What is the greatest number of translations that may be required? Contrast your answers with those to Question 9.

Summary

The following tables sum up what has been discovered so far about the way in which pairs of transformations combine to be equivalent to single transformations.

TABLE 1. *Translations*

2nd TRANSFORMATION ⟍ 1st TRANSFORMATION	TRANSLATION through t_2	TRANSLATION through $^-t_1$
TRANSLATION through t_1	TRANSLATION through $t_1 + t_2$	IDENTITY

TABLE 2. *Reflections*

2nd TRANSFORMATION ⟍ 1st TRANSFORMATION	REFLECTION in same line *m*	REFLECTION in line parallel to *m*	REFLECTION in line perpendicular to *m*	REFLECTION in line at angle $\theta°$ with *m*
REFLECTION in line *m*	IDENTITY	TRANSLATION through twice distance between lines	ROTATION of half-turn about point of intersection of lines	ROTATION through $2\theta°$ about point of intersection of lines

26

3
MATRICES

Man is a tool-using animal—without tools he is nothing, with tools he is all.

CARLYLE, *Sartor Resartus*

1. MATRICES

(*a*) When we were considering networks in Book 2, we found that it was possible to describe them by means of a *matrix*. In this chapter we shall find that matrices have many other uses. You will remember that the network in Figure 1, for example, can be represented by the matrix

$$\begin{pmatrix} 1 & 1 & 1 \\ 0 & 0 & 2 \\ 1 & 1 & 0 \end{pmatrix}.$$

What does the number 2 in the matrix represent?

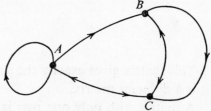

Fig. 1

On many occasions a large quantity of numerical data has to be stored for use and very often this data can be most conveniently arranged in a matrix form.

27

For example, the list below might be displayed in the packing department of Messrs Freak Bean's Biscuit Factory to help the workers assembling Christmas Gift Boxes.

	Type of biscuit			
Box	Choco- late	Thin Wine	Short- bread	Lincoln Cream
Holly Berries	8	10	6	4
Sleigh Bells	12	0	15	9
Reindeer Special	16	8	12	10

Such an array of numbers is a coded set of instructions for the packers, who will soon get to know what each row and each column refers to; all they need is the matrix

$$\begin{pmatrix} 8 & 10 & 6 & 4 \\ 12 & 0 & 15 & 9 \\ 16 & 8 & 12 & 10 \end{pmatrix}.$$

This matrix has 3 *rows* and 4 *columns*, but matrices can come in varying shapes and sizes. Because of this it is convenient to have a convention enabling us to describe the shape of a matrix: we say that the above matrix is 3×4 (read as 'three by four') and this is known as the *order* of the matrix.

(*b*) Describe the orders of the following matrices:

$$\text{(i)} \begin{pmatrix} 1 & 3 & 2 \\ 5 & 1 & 6 \end{pmatrix}; \quad \text{(ii)} \begin{pmatrix} 2 & 1 & 4 \\ 0 & -1 & 0 \\ 1 & 3 & -5 \end{pmatrix}; \quad \text{(iii)} \begin{pmatrix} 6 & 0 \\ 1 & -2 \\ 3 & 5 \end{pmatrix};$$

$$\text{(iv)} \begin{pmatrix} 5 \\ 7 \\ 0 \end{pmatrix}; \quad \text{(v)} \begin{pmatrix} -4 & 6 \\ 0 & 1 \end{pmatrix}; \quad \text{(vi)} \begin{pmatrix} 3 & 8 & 1 & 4 \end{pmatrix}.$$

(*c*) Which of the above matrices would one call *square*?

The biscuit packers could, of course, have been given the information they required in a table in which the rows referred to the different types of biscuit and the columns to the boxes. This would have resulted in the matrix

$$\begin{pmatrix} 8 & 12 & 16 \\ 10 & 0 & 8 \\ 6 & 15 & 12 \\ 4 & 9 & 10 \end{pmatrix}.$$

This matrix gives exactly the same information as the previous one; nevertheless, it is a different matrix.

A matrix with only one row is called a *row matrix*. Similarly, a matrix with one column is called a *column matrix*. It is no accident that the same notation is used for a column matrix and a column vector: you will see that they have the same properties.

28

Exercise A

1. Make up matrices having order:

   (a) 3×5;   (b) 4×2;   (c) 2×4;   (d) 3×1;   (e) 1×4;   (f) 2×2.

2. A firm of manufacturers of radio parts sells a number of 'do-it-yourself' kits for the amateur radio constructor. They market a kit called the Beginner's Bijou with 3 valves, 2 coils, 1 speaker, 7 resistors and 5 capacitors; another, the Straight Eight has 8 valves, 6 coils, 2 speakers, 25 resistors and 24 capacitors, while the Super Sistor has 6 transistors, 8 coils, 1 speaker, 23 resistors and 16 capacitors. Tabulate this information in a 3×6 matrix.

3. Susan, Bridget and Jennifer decide to make their own dresses for a party. Susan's pattern needs $4\frac{1}{2}$ m of velvet, 4 m of binding, a 35 cm zip-fastener and 3 buttons. Bridget's has a separate jacket; her dress and jacket need $1\frac{1}{2}$ m of velvet, 5 m of nylon, $1\frac{1}{2}$ m of binding, a 20 cm zip-fastener and no buttons. Jennifer favours a shift: $2\frac{1}{2}$ m of velvet, 2 m of binding and no zip-fastener or buttons will be needed. State their requirements in matrix form.

4. Five shops hold the following stocks of 'pop' records. Shop A has 60 L.P.s, 87 E.P.s and 112 singles; shop B has 103 L.P.s, 41 E.P.s and 58 singles; shop C only stocks L.P.s and has 72 of them. Shop D is selling off and has 23 E.P.s and a dozen singles left. Shop E specializes in E.P.s and singles and has 275 records in stock, of which 157 are singles. List the stocks in matrix form.

5. The following information was extracted from a cookery book:
Shrewsbury Biscuits: 125 g butter, 125 g sugar, 200 g flour, 1 egg.
Shortbread Biscuits: 500 g flour, 300 g butter, 200 g sugar, 2 eggs.
Lincoln Biscuits: 250 g flour, 250 g sugar, 125 g butter, 1 egg.
Bannocks: 500 g butter, 250 g sugar, 1 kg flour.
Easter Biscuits: 125 g sugar, 125 g butter, 250 g flour, 1 egg.
American Biscuits: 500 g flour, 100 g butter, 30 g sugar, 2 eggs.
(N.B. Should you want to make the biscuits, such items as baking powder, salt, ginger, spoonfuls of milk, have been omitted.)

   (a) Tabulate this data in a 6×4 matrix and add another column to give the total mass of raw materials for each kind of biscuit.

   (b) Calculate another 6×4 matrix, giving the mass of each ingredient in grams (to the nearest 10 g) per kilogram of biscuits.

   (Assume that an egg has a mass of 60 g and there is no loss in mass in cooking.)

6. Write down the *direct-route* matrices corresponding to the networks in Figure 2.

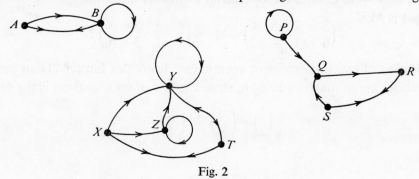

Fig. 2

29

7. Draw the network corresponding to the direct-route matrix

$$\begin{pmatrix} 2 & 2 & 1 \\ 1 & 0 & 1 \\ 0 & 1 & 1 \end{pmatrix}.$$

Why are direct-route matrices always *square*?

2. MATRIX ADDITION

Throughout the football season newspapers publish league tables: here is an extract from one of them.

Team	Home matches				Away matches			
	Played	Won	Lost	Drawn	Played	Won	Lost	Drawn
Liverpool	9	6	2	1	6	4	2	0
Manchester Utd.	7	4	1	2	9	5	3	1
Chelsea	8	4	3	1	6	3	1	2

(a) Write down a 3×4 matrix representing the results of the home matches and a similar matrix for the away matches.

Use these two matrices to write down a third 3×4 matrix relating to the results of *all* the matches played.

To answer this last problem you will have had to add together the numbers in the corresponding positions of the matrices relating to home and away matches. This process, whereby two matrices of the same order are combined to form a third by adding corresponding elements, is known as matrix addition.

If, for example,

$$A = \begin{pmatrix} 2 & 3 \\ -1 & 0 \\ 4 & 5 \end{pmatrix} \quad \text{and} \quad B = \begin{pmatrix} 1 & 7 \\ 2 & 6 \\ 9 & 0 \end{pmatrix},$$

then $A+B$ is defined to be

$$\begin{pmatrix} 2+1 & 3+7 \\ -1+2 & 0+6 \\ 4+9 & 5+0 \end{pmatrix} = \begin{pmatrix} 3 & 10 \\ 1 & 6 \\ 13 & 5 \end{pmatrix}.$$

Notice that matrices are denoted by capital letters in bold type A, B, ..., and that we use the sign + to denote the operation of matrix addition.

(b) What is M if

$$\begin{pmatrix} 3 & 2 & 5 & 0 \\ 6 & -1 & 4 & 2 \end{pmatrix} + M = \begin{pmatrix} 6 & 3 & 5 & 4 \\ 7 & 2 & 3 & -6 \end{pmatrix}?$$

The addition of two displacement vectors (see Book 2, Chapter 7) can be thought of as a special case of matrix addition, since the law of combination is the same. For example,

$$\begin{pmatrix} 3 \\ 2 \end{pmatrix} + \begin{pmatrix} -5 \\ 6 \end{pmatrix} = \begin{pmatrix} -2 \\ 8 \end{pmatrix}.$$

Exercise B

1. The four houses of a co-educational school are named after the planets: Mars, Pluto, Saturn and Venus. The way in which first-form boys and girls were allocated to these houses is described by the following matrices:

$$
\begin{array}{cc}
\begin{array}{c} \\ \text{Boys} \\ \text{Girls} \end{array} &
\begin{array}{cccc} \text{M} & \text{P} & \text{S} & \text{V} \\ \left(\begin{matrix} 3 & 2 & 5 & 5 \\ 4 & 6 & 2 & 4 \end{matrix}\right) \end{array}
\end{array}
\quad
\begin{array}{cccc} \text{M} & \text{P} & \text{S} & \text{V} \\ \left(\begin{matrix} 5 & 4 & 2 & 1 \\ 4 & 3 & 5 & 5 \end{matrix}\right) \end{array}
\quad
\begin{array}{cccc} \text{M} & \text{P} & \text{S} & \text{V} \\ \left(\begin{matrix} 3 & 6 & 3 & 4 \\ 3 & 2 & 6 & 5 \end{matrix}\right) \end{array}
$$
$$
\qquad \text{Form 1 A} \qquad\qquad \text{Form 1 B} \qquad\qquad \text{Form 1 C}
$$

(*a*) Calculate from these matrices a 2×4 matrix describing the allocation of boys and girls by houses in the first form as a whole.

(*b*) Which house has the largest number of:

(i) boys;   (ii) girls;   (iii) first-formers?

2. In the first match of the cricket season Brown bowled 12 overs, of which 4 were maidens, and he took 3 wickets for 25 runs. In the second match he took 5 wickets in 17 overs, of which 3 were maidens, for 51 runs.

Exhibit these figures as 1×4 matrices and obtain a 1×4 matrix representing Brown's bowling performance for the two matches combined.

3. A milkman sells 3 kinds of milk; red top, silver top and gold top. As he makes his way down Topsham Road he notes:

$$
\begin{array}{c}
\text{No. 1} \quad\ \text{No. 2} \quad\ \text{No. 3} \quad\ \text{No. 4} \\
\begin{array}{c} \text{Gold} \\ \text{Silver} \\ \text{Red} \end{array}
\left(\begin{matrix} 0 \\ 2 \\ 1 \end{matrix}\right)
\quad
\left(\begin{matrix} 2 \\ 0 \\ 0 \end{matrix}\right)
\quad
\left(\begin{matrix} 1 \\ 1 \\ 1 \end{matrix}\right)
\quad
\left(\begin{matrix} 2 \\ 1 \\ 2 \end{matrix}\right).
\end{array}
$$

(*a*) What single matrix represents his deliveries to these four houses?

(*b*) What matrix represents the amount of milk bought weekly by the housewife at No. 1 if her daily order remains the same throughout the week?

4. Let
$$
\mathbf{A} = \begin{pmatrix} 2 & 5 \\ 0 & 1 \end{pmatrix}, \quad \mathbf{B} = \begin{pmatrix} 3 & 1 \\ 2 & 5 \end{pmatrix} \quad \text{and} \quad \mathbf{C} = \begin{pmatrix} 1 & -1 \\ 2 & 0 \end{pmatrix}.
$$

(*a*) Calculate   (i) $\mathbf{A}+\mathbf{B}$;   (ii) $\mathbf{B}+\mathbf{C}$;   (iii) $\mathbf{C}+\mathbf{A}$.

(*b*) Give the matrices which you think represent:

(i) $2\mathbf{A}$;   (ii) $3\mathbf{C}$;   (iii) $2\mathbf{A}+\mathbf{B}$;   (iv) $\mathbf{B}-\mathbf{C}$.

5. If $\mathbf{A}$, $\mathbf{B}$ and $\mathbf{C}$ are any three matrices having the same order, does
(*a*) $\mathbf{A}+\mathbf{B} = \mathbf{B}+\mathbf{A}$ (that is, is matrix addition commutative?),
(*b*) $\mathbf{A}+(\mathbf{B}+\mathbf{C}) = (\mathbf{A}+\mathbf{B})+\mathbf{C}$ (that is, is matrix addition associative?)?
Give examples to illustrate your answer.

6. Let
$$
\mathbf{P} = \begin{pmatrix} 3 & 2 \\ 5 & -1 \\ 4 & 0 \end{pmatrix} \quad \text{and} \quad \mathbf{Q} = \begin{pmatrix} 5 & 7 \\ -6 & 4 \\ 2 & -9 \end{pmatrix}.
$$
Find a matrix $\mathbf{R}$ such that
$$
\mathbf{P}+\mathbf{Q}+\mathbf{R} = \begin{pmatrix} 0 & 0 \\ 0 & 0 \\ 0 & 0 \end{pmatrix},
$$
a zero matrix.

7. If
$$\begin{pmatrix} 3 & -2 & -5 \\ 1 & 4 & 6 \end{pmatrix} + \begin{pmatrix} a & b & c \\ d & e & f \end{pmatrix} = \begin{pmatrix} 4 & a & b \\ c & d & e \end{pmatrix},$$

find the values of a, b, c, d, e and f.

Summary

1. A matrix is a rectangular array of numbers. For example,

$$\begin{pmatrix} 3 & 0 & -6 & 3 \\ 2 & 2 & 0 & 1 \\ -5 & 1 & 7 & 4 \end{pmatrix}.$$

2. The *order* of a matrix is said to be $m \times n$ when the matrix has m *rows* and n *columns*. The matrix above, for example, is said to have order 3×4.

In particular a $1 \times n$ matrix is called a *row* matrix,

an $m \times 1$ matrix is called a *column* matrix,

and an $n \times n$ matrix is called a *square* matrix.

3. Two matrices *having the same order* are *added* by adding their corresponding elements. For example, if

$$\mathbf{A} = \begin{pmatrix} 3 & 2 & 0 \\ 0 & 1 & -5 \end{pmatrix} \quad \text{and} \quad \mathbf{B} = \begin{pmatrix} -1 & 4 & 6 \\ 2 & 7 & 1 \end{pmatrix},$$

then
$$\mathbf{A} + \mathbf{B} = \begin{pmatrix} 2 & 6 & 6 \\ 2 & 8 & -4 \end{pmatrix}.$$

Addition of matrices having different orders is not defined. Also, if

$$\mathbf{C} = \begin{pmatrix} 1 & 3 & 3 \\ 1 & 4 & -2 \end{pmatrix} \quad \text{then we write} \quad \mathbf{A} + \mathbf{B} = 2\mathbf{C}.$$

4. A zero matrix is any matrix in which all the elements are zero.
5. Matrix addition is commutative and associative, that is

$$\mathbf{A} + \mathbf{B} = \mathbf{B} + \mathbf{A} \quad \text{and} \quad (\mathbf{A} + \mathbf{B}) + \mathbf{C} = \mathbf{A} + (\mathbf{B} + \mathbf{C}).$$

3. COMBINING ROW AND COLUMN MATRICES

You have seen already how information can be displayed in a matrix and how it is often meaningful to add such matrices together. There are many circumstances, however, in which it is convenient to combine matrices in a different way as the following examples illustrate.

Example 1

On Guy Fawkes' Day, John went to his local toy shop and bought: 10 bangers at 1p each, 3 fountains at 2p each; 2 Catherine wheels at 4p each and 6 rockets at 3p each.

(*a*) How much did John spend on fireworks?

In this example two kinds of numerical information are given: the numbers of fireworks bought, and the cost of each kind of firework. This information could conveniently be displayed by means of the two row matrices:

$$(10 \quad 3 \quad 2 \quad 6) \qquad \text{and} \quad (1 \quad 2 \quad 4 \quad 3),$$

the first relating to the numbers of fireworks, and the second to the prices.

To find out how much John paid for fireworks it is necessary to calculate

$$10 \times 1 + 3 \times 2 + 2 \times 4 + 6 \times 3 = 42.$$

Thus we have combined the order matrix and the price matrix to give a single number representing the cost and we could write this as

$$(10 \quad 3 \quad 2 \quad 6) * (1 \quad 2 \quad 4 \quad 3) = 42,$$

or, because it is essentially a bill, use column matrices and write

$$\begin{pmatrix} 10 \\ 3 \\ 2 \\ 6 \end{pmatrix} * \begin{pmatrix} 1 \\ 2 \\ 4 \\ 3 \end{pmatrix} = 42.$$

There are obviously several ways in which we might write the two matrices but, so that no confusion arises, a convention has been agreed upon. The convention (apparently a compromise between the two suggestions above, but really a form that can be given many applications) is to write the first matrix as a row and the second matrix as a column:

$$(10 \quad 3 \quad 2 \quad 6) \begin{pmatrix} 1 \\ 2 \\ 4 \\ 3 \end{pmatrix} = (42).$$

Notice that no symbol is used between the matrices and that the number 42 is thought of as a 1×1 matrix. This is called the *product* of the two matrices.

(*b*) When Rosemary bought her fireworks she bought 6 fountains, 4 Catherine wheels and 5 rockets.

Express Rosemary's order as a 1×3 matrix and combine it with a 3×1 price matrix to give the total cost of her fireworks.

33

An alternative way of writing the bill for Rosemary's purchases would be

$$(0\ \ 6\ \ 4\ \ 5)\begin{pmatrix}3\\2\\4\\3\end{pmatrix} = (43),$$

where the fact that she bought no bangers is indicated by the 0 in the row matrix.

(c) Why would it be silly to write

$$(6\ \ 4\ \ 5)\begin{pmatrix}1\\2\\4\\3\end{pmatrix}$$

Example 2

In a local football league, the results of two keen rivals, Pinhoe Pirates and Whipton Whippets, are:

	W	L	D
Pinhoe Pirates	5	2	3
Whipton Whippets	7	2	1.

2 points are awarded if a match is won, 0 points if it is lost and 1 point if it is drawn. Write the points scheme as a column matrix and use it to find the total points obtained by each team.

Using the conventional notation we have:

Pinhoe Pirates $\qquad (5\ \ 2\ \ 3)\begin{pmatrix}2\\0\\1\end{pmatrix} = (5\times2+2\times0+3\times1) = (13);$

Whipton Whippets $\quad (7\ \ 2\ \ 1)\begin{pmatrix}2\\0\\1\end{pmatrix} = (7\times2+2\times0+1\times1) = (15).$

Exercise C

1. Calculate:

(a) $(1\ \ 3\ \ -2)\begin{pmatrix}4\\6\\5\end{pmatrix};$

(b) $(3\ \ -1)\begin{pmatrix}-2\\-10\end{pmatrix};$

(c) $(5\ \ 0)\begin{pmatrix}0\\-6\end{pmatrix};$

(d) $(5\ \ 2\ \ 3\ \ 4)\begin{pmatrix}1\\0\\-1\\6\end{pmatrix};$

(e) $(3\ \ 0\ \ 1\ \ 4)\begin{pmatrix}1\\1\\1\\1\end{pmatrix}.$

2. In a traffic census on the Putney Flyover, a check was made on the people carried by 200 cars. This was at a time when most people could be assumed to be driving to work. The

result was that: 96 of the cars carried only the driver, 39 carried 2 people, 34 carried 3 people, 22 carried 4 people, 6 carried 5 people, and 3 carried 6 people.

(*a*) Using this information write down a row matrix and a column matrix whose product gives the total number of people carried by the 200 cars.

(*b*) What was the average number of people per car? Comment.

3. The way in which the First XV scored in the first 3 matches of the season is shown in the following table:

	Tries	Con- versions	Penalty goals
Match 1	5	1	3
Match 2	3	2	1
Match 3	2	0	3

3 points are awarded for a try, 2 for a conversion and 3 for a penalty goal.

(*a*) Write down the points scheme as a column matrix and hence write down three matrix products to show the points scored by the team in each match.

(*b*) The scores of the team's opponents were:

Match 1	4	3	2
Match 2	2	0	4
Match 3	3	1	1

Which matches did the First XV win?

4. A breakfast cereal, Corny Crisps, is sold in three sizes: small, family, and large. The mass of cereal contained in these packets is 300 g, 420 g, and 600 g respectively and to a shopkeeper they cost 5p, 6p, and 8p.

(*a*) Express these facts as column matrices, one for mass and one for cost.

(*b*) A shopkeeper orders 20 small, 40 family and 30 large packets. Write down the mass of cereal ordered as a product of two matrices and work it out.

How much did the order cost the shopkeeper?

(*c*) Which size is the better buy?

5. In athletics matches between two schools it is usual to have 2 competitors from each school in each event and to award points for 1st, 2nd, 3rd and 4th places. Matches are often so keenly contested that a change in the way the points are awarded will give a different final result. One match between Town School and County School gave the following individual results:

	1st	2nd	3rd	4th
Town School	(8	3	6	7)
County School	(4	9	6	5)

(*a*) Add these two row matrices together and explain the result.

(*b*) Why is the sum of the components in each matrix 24?

(*c*) The home team, Town School, arranged that: 5 points should be awarded for a first, 3 points for a second, 1 point for a third, and nothing for a fourth. Express this points scheme as a column matrix and calculate each team's score. Which team won?

(*d*) Travelling home in the bus after the match, the captain of County School team felt that they had been very unlucky to lose by so much so he worked out the match score on the basis of: 4 points for a first, 3 points for a second, 2 points for a third and 1 point for a fourth. What did he discover?

6. An American girl buys 2 kg sugar, 3 kg flour, 1 kg butter, and 4 kg rice; the prices per kg being sugar 45 ¢, flour 24 ¢, butter 75 ¢ and rice 60 ¢.

(a) Write down the order matrix and the price matrix. Find their product and state the meaning of your answer.

(b) If all the prices are increased by one-third, write down the new price matrix. She saves money the next week by buying half the quantities. Calculate by how much her total bill is decreased.

7. Use the matrices $(5 \quad 4)$ and $\begin{pmatrix} 3 \\ 2 \end{pmatrix}$

to make up some problems in which the matrices represent prices and purchases.

8. Let
$$U = (2 \quad 3), \quad V = (-1 \quad 4) \quad \text{and} \quad W = \begin{pmatrix} 3 \\ -1 \end{pmatrix}.$$

(a) Calculate UW, VW and $U+V$ and show that $UW+VW = (U+V)W$.

(b) By first calculating $3U+5V$, $3UW$ and $5VW$ show that $(3U+5V)W = 3UW+5VW$.

9. Find the value of x if:

(a) $(3 \quad x)\begin{pmatrix} 5 \\ 1 \end{pmatrix} = (18)$;

(b) $(x \quad 7)\begin{pmatrix} 4 \\ x \end{pmatrix} = (22)$;

(c) $(-2 \quad x \quad 4)\begin{pmatrix} x \\ 3 \\ 5 \end{pmatrix} = (15)$;

(d) $(x \quad 3 \quad 0)\begin{pmatrix} x \\ 0 \\ 4 \end{pmatrix} = (16)$.

10. In spring-board diving championships a diver is given a mark out of 10 for each dive he performs and this mark is then multiplied by a number (called its tariff) which depends upon the difficulty of the dive. If a diver performs a 1·8 tariff dive, for example, and the judges award him 7 marks his score will be $7 \times 1\cdot8 = 12\cdot6$. The tables below give the details of a recent competition up to the fourth dive. Calculate the order of the competitors at this stage. (Use your slide rule.)

Marks awarded in each dive

	I	II	III	IV
Adrian	8	9	9	7
Brian	7	8	6	5
Charles	7	7	5	9
David	6	9	7	6
Edward	8	8	7	8
Frank	9	6	7	7

Tariffs for each dive

	A	B	C	D	E	F
I	1·4	1·5	1·3	1·6	1·5	1·2
II	1·6	1·4	1·7	1·4	1·6	1·5
III	1·5	1·9	1·9	2·0	1·9	1·7
IV	1·7	2·1	1·4	1·8	2·0	1·9

4. MATRIX MULTIPLICATION

Let us return to the example in the last section in which John and Rosemary went to buy fireworks and let us suppose that, in addition, Andrew bought 5 bangers, 5 fountains and 8 rockets. Their purchases can be displayed in matrix form as follows:

$$
\begin{array}{cccc}
 & \text{B} & \text{F} & \text{C.W.} & \text{R} \\
\begin{array}{c}\text{John}\\ \text{Rosemary}\\ \text{Andrew}\end{array}
\begin{pmatrix}
10 & 3 & 2 & 6 \\
0 & 6 & 4 & 5 \\
5 & 5 & 0 & 8
\end{pmatrix}.
\end{array}
$$

Using the notation of the last section, we can calculate the cost of fireworks for each person from the products:

$$
\text{John} \qquad (10 \ \ 3 \ \ 2 \ \ 6)\begin{pmatrix}1\\2\\4\\3\end{pmatrix} = (42),
$$

$$
\text{Rosemary} \qquad (0 \ \ 6 \ \ 4 \ \ 5)\begin{pmatrix}1\\2\\4\\3\end{pmatrix} = (43),
$$

$$
\text{Andrew} \qquad (5 \ \ 5 \ \ 0 \ \ 8)\begin{pmatrix}1\\2\\4\\3\end{pmatrix} = (39).
$$

However, since the price matrix in each case is the same, we can combine these three statements and write:

$$
\begin{array}{c}\text{John}\\ \text{Rosemary}\\ \text{Andrew}\end{array}
\begin{pmatrix}
10 & 3 & 2 & 6 \\
0 & 6 & 4 & 5 \\
5 & 5 & 0 & 8
\end{pmatrix}
\begin{pmatrix}1\\2\\4\\3\end{pmatrix} =
\begin{pmatrix}42\\43\\39\end{pmatrix}.
$$

Late on Guy Fawkes' Day, the shopkeeper reduced his prices so as to avoid having any fireworks left. The new prices were bangers $\frac{1}{2}$p; fountains 1p; Catherine wheels 3p; and rockets 2p.

(a) Write down two matrices which, when combined, would give the cost of John's, Rosemary's and Andrew's purchases had they bought their fireworks at these lower prices. Calculate the product of these matrices.

The arithmetic involved in solving this problem, together with the earlier part of the example, could be neatly represented by the product

$$
\begin{array}{c}
\\
\\
\text{John} \\
\text{Rosemary} \\
\text{Andrew}
\end{array}
\quad
\begin{array}{cccc}
\text{B} & \text{F} & \text{C.W.} & \text{R}
\end{array}
\quad
\overbrace{\begin{array}{cc}\text{1st} & \text{2nd}\end{array}}^{\text{Prices}}
\quad
\overbrace{\begin{array}{cc}\text{1st} & \text{2nd}\end{array}}^{\text{Cost}}
$$

$$
\begin{pmatrix} 10 & 3 & 2 & 6 \\ 0 & 6 & 4 & 5 \\ 5 & 5 & 0 & 8 \end{pmatrix}
\begin{pmatrix} 1 & \frac{1}{2} \\ 2 & 1 \\ 4 & 3 \\ 3 & 2 \end{pmatrix}
=
\begin{pmatrix} 42 & 26 \\ 43 & 28 \\ 39 & 23\frac{1}{2} \end{pmatrix}.
$$

We have now progressed from forming the product of a row and a column matrix to forming the product of two relatively large matrices. This has been done by extending our convention in a straightforward manner.

This method of combining two matrices is often called *multiplication* and this extended use of the word is not contradictory, for by thinking of ordinary numbers as 1×1 matrices we obtain the expected result.

For example,
$$(3)(5) = (15) \quad \text{and} \quad 3 \times 5 = 15.$$

(Compare also matrix *addition*, for $(3) + (5) = (8)$.)

In working out the product of two matrices the rows of the left-hand matrix are combined with the columns of the right-hand matrix.

For example, to calculate the product of
$$
\mathbf{A} = \begin{pmatrix} 3 & 2 & -1 \\ 0 & -2 & 4 \end{pmatrix}
\quad \text{and} \quad
\mathbf{B} = \begin{pmatrix} 6 & 0 & 1 \\ 0 & 2 & 3 \\ 1 & 5 & 1 \end{pmatrix},
$$

first combine the first row of $\mathbf{A}$ with successive columns of $\mathbf{B}$ to give

$$
\begin{pmatrix} 3 & 2 & -1 \\ 0 & -2 & 4 \end{pmatrix}
\begin{pmatrix} 6 & 0 & 1 \\ 0 & 2 & 3 \\ 1 & 5 & 1 \end{pmatrix}
=
\begin{pmatrix} 17 & -1 & 8 \\ & & \end{pmatrix},
$$

and then the second row of $\mathbf{A}$ with successive columns of $\mathbf{B}$ to complete the product:

$$
\begin{pmatrix} 3 & 2 & -1 \\ 0 & -2 & 4 \end{pmatrix}
\begin{pmatrix} 6 & 0 & 1 \\ 0 & 2 & 3 \\ 1 & 5 & 1 \end{pmatrix}
=
\begin{pmatrix} 17 & -1 & 8 \\ 4 & 16 & -2 \end{pmatrix}.
$$

The product
$$
\begin{pmatrix} 3 & 2 & -1 \\ 0 & -2 & 4 \end{pmatrix}
\begin{pmatrix} 6 & 0 & 1 \\ 0 & 2 & 3 \\ 1 & 5 & 1 \end{pmatrix}
$$

is denoted by $\mathbf{AB}$ and we say that we have multiplied $\mathbf{B}$ *on the left* by $\mathbf{A}$ *or* that we have multiplied $\mathbf{A}$ *on the right* by $\mathbf{B}$.

(b) If the matrix
$$A = \begin{pmatrix} 3 & 5 & 2 \\ 1 & -1 & 4 \end{pmatrix}$$

can be multiplied on the left by a matrix **B**, why must matrix **B** have only 2 columns?

(c) If a matrix **C** can be multiplied on the left by **A**, how many rows must it have?

You will have seen from answering these questions that two matrices can only be multiplied if the matrix on the left has as many columns as the matrix on the right has rows. When this is the case the matrices are said to be *compatible* for multiplication.

(d) Let
$$P = \begin{pmatrix} 2 & 5 \\ 0 & 1 \end{pmatrix} \quad \text{and} \quad Q = \begin{pmatrix} 3 & 1 \\ 2 & 4 \\ 0 & 5 \end{pmatrix}.$$

Which of **PQ** and **QP** are possible products? Work out the one that is.

(e) If **R** is a 5×3 matrix and **S** is a 3×2 matrix, what is the order of **RS**?

Exercise D

1. Calculate the following products:

(a) $\begin{pmatrix} 2 & 0 & 3 \\ 1 & 4 & 1 \end{pmatrix} \begin{pmatrix} 6 \\ -2 \\ 3 \end{pmatrix}$;

(b) $(2 \ \ 1) \begin{pmatrix} 8 & -3 & 2 \\ -1 & 0 & 1 \end{pmatrix}$;

(c) $(1 \ \ 3 \ \ 4) \begin{pmatrix} 2 & 5 \\ 0 & 3 \\ 1 & 2 \end{pmatrix}$;

(d) $\begin{pmatrix} 3 & 0 & 1 \\ 5 & 7 & 0 \\ -1 & 0 & 2 \end{pmatrix} \begin{pmatrix} 5 \\ 1 \\ 2 \end{pmatrix}$;

(e) $\begin{pmatrix} 3 & 1 & 0 & 1 \\ 2 & 0 & 5 & -2 \end{pmatrix} \begin{pmatrix} 3 \\ 2 \\ 2 \\ 5 \end{pmatrix}$;

(f) $(2 \ \ 3) \begin{pmatrix} 5 & 0 & 1 \\ 1 & 4 & 2 \end{pmatrix} \begin{pmatrix} 1 \\ 2 \\ 1 \end{pmatrix}$.

2. (a) A coal merchant started out on his rounds with 1000 kg of Gloco, 400 kg of Phurnacite and 1250 kg of coal. If these fuels cost 160p, 200p, and 180p respectively for 100 kg, what was his load worth?

(b) His first five deliveries are represented by the columns of the matrix

$$\begin{pmatrix} 150 & 0 & 0 & 200 & 500 \\ 50 & 0 & 50 & 100 & 0 \\ 0 & 250 & 200 & 500 & 0 \end{pmatrix} \begin{matrix} \text{Gloco} \\ \text{Phurnacite} \\ \text{Coal} \end{matrix}$$

Write the prices of fuel, (per kilogram) as a row matrix and use its product with the above matrix to give the bill for each of the five deliveries.

(c) The next four orders in the coal merchant's order book are

$$\begin{pmatrix} 100 & 100 & 50 & 100 \\ 50 & 0 & 150 & 100 \\ 100 & 200 & 150 & 200 \end{pmatrix} \begin{matrix} \text{G} \\ \text{P} \\ \text{C} \end{matrix}$$

Which two of these can be completed without reloading?

3. In a triangular athletics match between the schools A, B and C, points were awarded as follows: 1st, 6; 2nd, 4; 3rd, 3; 4th, 2; 5th, 1.

The individual results are shown by the matrix

$$
\begin{array}{c}
 \\
A \\
B \\
C
\end{array}
\begin{array}{ccccc}
\text{1st} & \text{2nd} & \text{3rd} & \text{4th} & \text{5th} \\
\begin{pmatrix} 4 & 2 & 3 & 2 & 6 \\ 2 & 5 & 4 & 4 & 3 \\ 4 & 3 & 3 & 4 & 1 \end{pmatrix}
\end{array}.
$$

(a) Write the points scheme as a column matrix and calculate the scores of each team.

(b) Which team would have won if the points scheme had been: 1st, 8; 2nd, 5; 3rd, 3; 4th, 2; 5th, 1?

4. A housewife went shopping to buy $1\frac{1}{2}$ kg of butter, 1 kg of cheese and 3 kg of sugar. In her local stores these were priced at 46p, 30p and 20p per kilogram respectively, but at the supermarket in a nearby town they could be bought at 32p, 22p and 15p per kilogram. How much would she save by going to town if her bus fare is 25p return?

Write the order as a row matrix and represent the prices as the columns of a 3×2 matrix.

5. A factory produces 3 types of portable radio sets called Audio 1, Audio 2 and Audio 3. Audio 1 contains 1 transistor, 10 resistors and 5 capacitors, while Audio 2 contains 2 transistors, 18 resistors and 7 capacitors, and Audio 3 contains 3 transistors, 24 resistors and 10 capacitors.

Arrange this information in matrix form and find the factory's weekly consumption of transistors, resistors and capacitors, if its weekly output of sets is 100 of Audio 1, 250 of Audio 2 and 80 of Audio 3.

6. 'Bildit' is a constructional toy with standard parts called Flats (F), Pillars (P), Blocks (B), Rods (R) and Caps (C). It is boxed in sets, numbered 1 to 4. Set 1 has 1 flat, 4 pillars, 8 blocks, 14 rods and 2 caps. Set 2 has 2 flats, 10 pillars, 12 blocks, 30 rods and 4 caps. Set 3 has 4 flats, 24 pillars, 30 blocks, 60 rods and 10 caps. Set 4 has 10 flats, 40 pillars, 72 blocks, 100 rods and 24 caps. Tabulate this information in a matrix with sets in rows and parts in columns.

The manufacturers get an order for 20 of set 1, 25 of set 2, 10 of set 3 and 6 of set 4. Writing this as a matrix, arrange a suitable multiplication to find the numbers of each part that will be needed.

7. (a) With the data of Question 6, suppose flats cost 6p each, pillars 4p, blocks 1p, rods 2p, and caps 3p. Write a matrix for these costs and use it to find the cost of the various sets.

(b) What is the total cost of the order? Can you express this as a product of the three matrices?

8. Let $\mathbf{A} = \begin{pmatrix} 0 & 1 & 0 \\ 0 & 0 & 1 \\ 1 & 0 & 0 \end{pmatrix}$, $\mathbf{B} = \begin{pmatrix} 0 & 0 & 1 \\ 1 & 0 & 0 \\ 0 & 1 & 0 \end{pmatrix}$, $\mathbf{C} = \begin{pmatrix} 1 & 0 & 0 \\ 0 & 1 & 0 \\ 0 & 0 & 1 \end{pmatrix}$;

$$
\mathbf{X} = \begin{pmatrix} 2 \\ 4 \\ 6 \end{pmatrix} \quad \text{and} \quad \mathbf{Y} = (1 \quad 3 \quad 5).
$$

(a) Find the products $\mathbf{AX}$, $\mathbf{BX}$, $\mathbf{CX}$, $\mathbf{YA}$, $\mathbf{YB}$ and $\mathbf{YC}$. What do you notice about the components of the products?

40

(b) Find a matrix **D** for which

$$\mathbf{D}\begin{pmatrix} 2 \\ 4 \\ 6 \end{pmatrix} = \begin{pmatrix} 2 \\ 6 \\ 4 \end{pmatrix}.$$

What is the value of **YD**?

9. Find x and y if

$$(x \quad y)\begin{pmatrix} 2 & 3 \\ 0 & 1 \end{pmatrix} = (6 \quad 10).$$

10. Perform the following multiplications:

(a) $\begin{pmatrix} 2 & 5 \\ 3 & 2 \end{pmatrix}\begin{pmatrix} 1 & 0 \\ 2 & -1 \end{pmatrix}$;

(b) $\begin{pmatrix} 4 & 3 \\ 0 & -1 \end{pmatrix}\begin{pmatrix} 1 & 2 & 0 \\ 0 & 3 & 4 \end{pmatrix}$;

(c) $\begin{pmatrix} 5 & -1 & 3 \\ 0 & 2 & 1 \end{pmatrix}\begin{pmatrix} 7 & 2 & 0 \\ 0 & 3 & 1 \\ 1 & 4 & 1 \end{pmatrix}$;

(d) $\begin{pmatrix} 3 & 1 \\ 2 & -1 \\ 0 & 2 \end{pmatrix}\begin{pmatrix} 0 & 2 \\ 4 & 1 \end{pmatrix}$;

(e) $\begin{pmatrix} 1 & 0 & 0 \\ 0 & 1 & 0 \\ 0 & 0 & 1 \end{pmatrix}\begin{pmatrix} 5 & 6 & -8 \\ 2 & 4 & 1 \\ 0 & 3 & 9 \end{pmatrix}$;

(f) $(3 \quad 1 \quad 5)\begin{pmatrix} 7 & 2 \\ 1 & 4 \\ 0 & 1 \end{pmatrix}\begin{pmatrix} 3 & 0 \\ 0 & 2 \end{pmatrix}$.

11. (a) What is the order of matrix **B**, if

$$(3 \quad 4 \quad 2)\,\mathbf{B} = (2 \quad 1 \quad 0 \quad 3 \quad 6)?$$

(b) If **P** is a 3×4 matrix and **Q** is such that both the products **PQ** and **QP** are possible, what is the order of **Q**?

(c) When a 3×4 matrix is multiplied by a 4×7 matrix what is the order of the product?

12. Take $\quad\quad \mathbf{A} = \begin{pmatrix} 3 & 0 \\ 0 & 3 \end{pmatrix}, \quad \mathbf{B} = \begin{pmatrix} 0 & 2 \\ -1 & 1 \end{pmatrix}, \quad \mathbf{C} = \begin{pmatrix} 1 & 2 \\ 3 & 4 \end{pmatrix}$

and work out **BC** and **A(BC)**. Now work out **AB** and **(AB)C**. Does **A(BC)** = **(AB)C**?
Is it true that **AB** = **BA** and **BC** = **CB**?

13. If matrices of the form

$$\begin{pmatrix} p_1 & 0 \\ 0 & p_2 \end{pmatrix}$$

are called P matrices and matrices of the form

$$\begin{pmatrix} 0 & q_1 \\ q_2 & 0 \end{pmatrix}$$

are called Q matrices, what form is the product of:
(a) a P matrix and a P matrix;
(b) a P matrix and a Q matrix (does the order matter?);
(c) a Q matrix and a Q matrix?

Summary

1. A row matrix and a column matrix with the same number of elements can be combined to form a *product* by multiplying their corresponding components and adding. $\quad (a \quad b \quad c)\begin{pmatrix} x \\ y \\ z \end{pmatrix} = (ax + by + cz).$

2. The product **C** of two matrices **A** and **B** is defined when **A** has as many columns as **B** has rows. If **A** is $m \times n$ and **B** is $n \times p$, then the matrices are said to be *compatible* for multiplication and the product matrix **C** is of order $m \times p$.

$$\underset{m \times \underline{n} \;\; \underline{n} \times p}{\textbf{A} \quad \textbf{B}} = \underset{m \times p}{\textbf{C}}$$

3. To form the product of two matrices the rows of the matrix on the left are combined in turn with the columns of the matrix on the right.

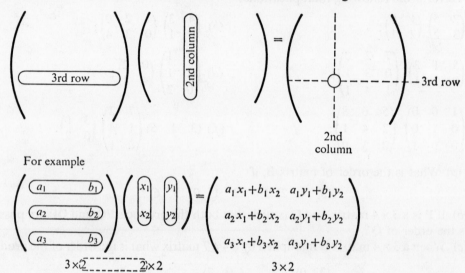

For example

$$\begin{pmatrix} a_1 & b_1 \\ a_2 & b_2 \\ a_3 & b_3 \end{pmatrix} \begin{pmatrix} x_1 & y_1 \\ x_2 & y_2 \end{pmatrix} = \begin{pmatrix} a_1 x_1 + b_1 x_2 & a_1 y_1 + b_1 y_2 \\ a_2 x_1 + b_2 x_2 & a_2 y_1 + b_2 y_2 \\ a_3 x_1 + b_3 x_2 & a_3 y_1 + b_3 y_2 \end{pmatrix}$$

$$3 \times 2 \qquad\qquad 2 \times 2 \qquad\qquad\qquad 3 \times 2$$

5. MATRICES AND TRANSFORMATIONS

One of the most important applications of the idea of a matrix, and one which provides many useful illustrations, is to the geometry of transformations. Consider the translation **T** defined by the displacement vector $\begin{pmatrix} 5 \\ 3 \end{pmatrix}$. Figure 3 shows a triangle *ABC* and its image under **T**.

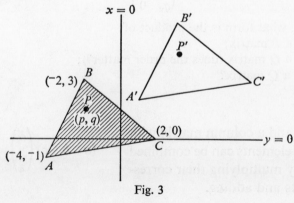

Fig. 3

(*a*) What are the coordinates of A', B' and C'?

(*b*) What are the coordinates of P'?

This translation can be represented by the two mappings

$$x \to x+5 \quad \text{and} \quad y \to y+3,$$

which indicate clearly that the x coordinate has been increased by 5 and the y coordinate increased by 3.

Using matrix notation, however, we can streamline this by combining the two mappings to give the single matrix mapping

$$\mathbf{T}: \begin{pmatrix} x \\ y \end{pmatrix} \to \begin{pmatrix} x+5 \\ y+3 \end{pmatrix}.$$

(*c*) The following mapping defines a reflection:

$$\mathbf{M}: \begin{pmatrix} x \\ y \end{pmatrix} \to \begin{pmatrix} y+3 \\ x-3 \end{pmatrix}.$$

By taking specific values for x and y and plotting the corresponding object and image points on a graph, find the position of the mirror-line of this reflection.

For example, the point (4, 6) is mapped onto the point (9, 1), since under $\mathbf{M}$

$$\begin{pmatrix} 4 \\ 6 \end{pmatrix} \to \begin{pmatrix} 6+3 \\ 4-3 \end{pmatrix} = \begin{pmatrix} 9 \\ 1 \end{pmatrix}.$$

The coordinates of a point, for example, $D(5, 4)$, can be written as the elements of a column matrix, in this case, $\begin{pmatrix} 5 \\ 4 \end{pmatrix}$. This should remind you of the displacement (or column) vectors which you met in Chapter 7 of Book 2. We can, in fact, think of this column matrix as a column vector describing the displacement $\mathbf{OD}$ of D from the origin (see Figure 4). When vectors are used in this way to determine the position of a point in the plane they are called *position vectors*.

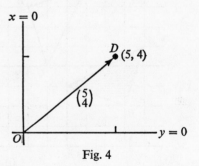

Fig. 4

Exercise E

1. Copy Figure 5 onto graph paper and on it draw the images of S under the following transformations:

(*a*) $\begin{pmatrix} x \\ y \end{pmatrix} \to \begin{pmatrix} x \\ -y \end{pmatrix}$;
  (*b*) $\begin{pmatrix} x \\ y \end{pmatrix} \to \begin{pmatrix} -y \\ x \end{pmatrix}$;
  (*c*) $\begin{pmatrix} x \\ y \end{pmatrix} \to \begin{pmatrix} -\frac{1}{2}x \\ -\frac{1}{2}y \end{pmatrix}$;

(*d*) $\begin{pmatrix} x \\ y \end{pmatrix} \to \begin{pmatrix} x-5 \\ y-4 \end{pmatrix}$;
  (*e*) $\begin{pmatrix} x \\ y \end{pmatrix} \to \begin{pmatrix} x-2y \\ y+3 \end{pmatrix}$.

Where possible describe the transformations geometrically.

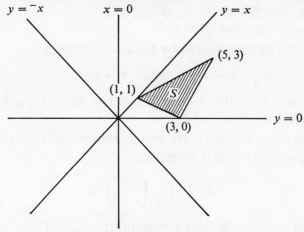

Fig. 5

2. The parts of Figure 6 show an object (shaded) and its image (unshaded) under a simple transformation. In each case:

(*a*) describe the transformation geometrically;

(*b*) write down the coordinates of three object points and their corresponding images;

(*c*) describe the transformation as a mapping of $\begin{pmatrix} x \\ y \end{pmatrix}$.

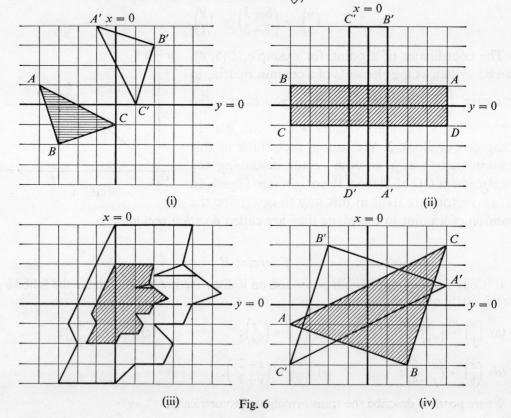

Fig. 6

44

5.1   Matrices to describe transformations

You have seen how simple transformations can be represented as mappings of the matrix $\begin{pmatrix} x \\ y \end{pmatrix}$ and we will now take a closer look at these mappings.

The translation (see Figure 3)

$$\mathbf{T}: \begin{pmatrix} x \\ y \end{pmatrix} \rightarrow \begin{pmatrix} x+5 \\ y+3 \end{pmatrix},$$

which changes the coordinates by increasing the x coordinate by 5 and the y coordinate by 3 can be written as

$$\begin{pmatrix} x \\ y \end{pmatrix} \rightarrow \begin{pmatrix} x \\ y \end{pmatrix} + \begin{pmatrix} 5 \\ 3 \end{pmatrix}.$$

In this form the numbers 5 and 3 which produce the transformation are separated from the matrix $\begin{pmatrix} x \\ y \end{pmatrix}$ which is the position vector of the object point.

In the case of reflections, rotations and enlargements this dependence of the coordinates of the image on the coordinates of the object is not quite so obvious.

However, a careful look at the following examples will help you to see a pattern emerging.

$$\begin{pmatrix} x \\ y \end{pmatrix} \rightarrow \begin{pmatrix} y \\ x \end{pmatrix} = \begin{pmatrix} 0.x + 1.y \\ 1.x + 0.y \end{pmatrix} = \begin{pmatrix} 0 & 1 \\ 1 & 0 \end{pmatrix} \begin{pmatrix} x \\ y \end{pmatrix},$$

$$\begin{pmatrix} x \\ y \end{pmatrix} \rightarrow \begin{pmatrix} x-y \\ x+y \end{pmatrix} = \begin{pmatrix} 1.x + {}^-1.y \\ 1.x + 1.y \end{pmatrix} = \begin{pmatrix} 1 & {}^-1 \\ 1 & 1 \end{pmatrix} \begin{pmatrix} x \\ y \end{pmatrix},$$

$$\begin{pmatrix} x \\ y \end{pmatrix} \rightarrow \begin{pmatrix} 3x \\ -4x+3y \end{pmatrix} = \begin{pmatrix} 3.x + 0.y \\ -4.x + 3.y \end{pmatrix} = \begin{pmatrix} 3 & 0 \\ -4 & 3 \end{pmatrix} \begin{pmatrix} x \\ y \end{pmatrix},$$

$$\begin{pmatrix} x \\ y \end{pmatrix} \rightarrow \begin{pmatrix} {}^-x \\ y \end{pmatrix} = \begin{pmatrix} {}^-1.x + 0.y \\ 0.x + 1.y \end{pmatrix} = \begin{pmatrix} {}^-1 & 0 \\ 0 & 1 \end{pmatrix} \begin{pmatrix} x \\ y \end{pmatrix}.$$

In each of these transformations the coordinates of the image points depend on x and y and this dependence is described by the matrix product on the right.

(*a*) Which 2×2 matrix would correspond to the transformation

$$\begin{pmatrix} x \\ y \end{pmatrix} \rightarrow \begin{pmatrix} 2x-3y \\ 5x+y \end{pmatrix} ?$$

The transformation

$$\begin{pmatrix} x \\ y \end{pmatrix} \rightarrow \begin{pmatrix} 7x+y \\ 2x-5y \end{pmatrix}$$

can be written as

$$\begin{pmatrix} x \\ y \end{pmatrix} \rightarrow \begin{pmatrix} 7 & 1 \\ 2 & -5 \end{pmatrix} \begin{pmatrix} x \\ y \end{pmatrix}$$

and this has the advantage that it separates out the numbers which determine the transformation from the position vector of the object point.

It is sometimes helpful to think of the matrix

$$\begin{pmatrix} 7 & 1 \\ 2 & -5 \end{pmatrix}$$

as a machine which converts

$$\begin{pmatrix} x \\ y \end{pmatrix} \quad \text{into} \quad \begin{pmatrix} 7x+y \\ 2x-5y \end{pmatrix}$$

(see Figure 7).

(b) If the matrices

$$\begin{pmatrix} 1 \\ 0 \end{pmatrix}, \quad \begin{pmatrix} 2 \\ 3 \end{pmatrix} \quad \text{and} \quad \begin{pmatrix} 1 \\ -1 \end{pmatrix}$$

are fed into the machine in Figure 7, what matrices will emerge?

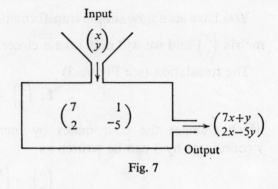

Fig. 7

Example 3

A transformation is defined by the matrix

$$\begin{pmatrix} 2 & -1 \\ 1 & 3 \end{pmatrix}.$$

Find the image $A'B'C'D'$ of the square $A(3, 4)$, $B(3, {}^-1)$, $C({}^-2, {}^-1)$, $D({}^-2, 4)$ under this transformation.

The transformation is

$$\begin{pmatrix} x \\ y \end{pmatrix} \rightarrow \begin{pmatrix} 2 & -1 \\ 1 & 3 \end{pmatrix} \begin{pmatrix} x \\ y \end{pmatrix},$$

hence the position vectors of A', B', C' and D' are given by:

$$A' \quad \begin{pmatrix} 2 & -1 \\ 1 & 3 \end{pmatrix}\begin{pmatrix} 3 \\ 4 \end{pmatrix} = \begin{pmatrix} 2.\ 3+{}^-1.\ 4 \\ 1.\ 3+\ 3.\ 4 \end{pmatrix} = \begin{pmatrix} 2 \\ 15 \end{pmatrix};$$

$$B' \quad \begin{pmatrix} 2 & -1 \\ 1 & 3 \end{pmatrix}\begin{pmatrix} 3 \\ -1 \end{pmatrix} = \begin{pmatrix} 2.\ 3+{}^-1.{}^-1 \\ 1.\ 3+\ 3.{}^-1 \end{pmatrix} = \begin{pmatrix} 7 \\ 0 \end{pmatrix};$$

$$C' \quad \begin{pmatrix} 2 & -1 \\ 1 & 3 \end{pmatrix}\begin{pmatrix} -2 \\ -1 \end{pmatrix} = \begin{pmatrix} 2.{}^-2+{}^-1.{}^-1 \\ 1.{}^-2+\ 3.{}^-1 \end{pmatrix} = \begin{pmatrix} -3 \\ -5 \end{pmatrix};$$

$$D' \quad \begin{pmatrix} 2 & -1 \\ 1 & 3 \end{pmatrix}\begin{pmatrix} -2 \\ 4 \end{pmatrix} = \begin{pmatrix} 2.{}^-2+{}^-1.\ 4 \\ 1.{}^-2+\ 3.\ 4 \end{pmatrix} = \begin{pmatrix} -8 \\ 10 \end{pmatrix}.$$

The geometrical effect of the transformation is shown in Figure 8.

When using a matrix to help us find image points it is usual to write down the position vectors of all the points under consideration in the form of a matrix as shown:

$$\begin{pmatrix} 2 & -1 \\ 1 & 3 \end{pmatrix} \begin{matrix} A & B & C & D \\ \begin{pmatrix} 3 & 3 & -2 & -2 \\ 4 & -1 & -1 & 4 \end{pmatrix} \end{matrix} = \begin{matrix} A' & B' & C' & D' \\ \begin{pmatrix} 2 & 7 & -3 & -8 \\ 15 & 0 & -5 & 10 \end{pmatrix} \end{matrix}.$$

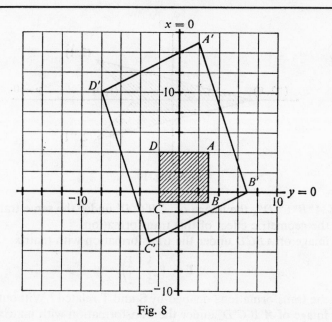

Fig. 8

Exercise F

1. (a) Find the image of the trapezium in Figure 9
under the transformations defined by the matrices:

$$A = \begin{pmatrix} 1 & 0 \\ 0 & -1 \end{pmatrix}; \qquad B = \begin{pmatrix} -1 & 0 \\ 0 & 1 \end{pmatrix};$$

$$C = \begin{pmatrix} -1 & 0 \\ 0 & -1 \end{pmatrix}; \qquad D = \begin{pmatrix} 0 & 1 \\ 1 & 0 \end{pmatrix};$$

$$E = \begin{pmatrix} 0 & -1 \\ 1 & 0 \end{pmatrix}; \qquad F = \begin{pmatrix} 0 & 1 \\ -1 & 0 \end{pmatrix};$$

$$G = \begin{pmatrix} 1 & 0 \\ 0 & 1 \end{pmatrix}; \qquad H = \begin{pmatrix} 0 & -1 \\ -1 & 0 \end{pmatrix}.$$

(b) What is the geometric effect of each of
these transformations?

(c) How many lines of symmetry has the figure
formed from all the images?

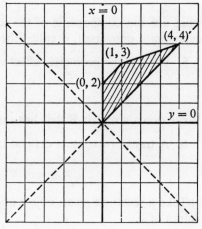

Fig. 9

2. (a) Find the image of the arrowhead (see Figure 10) under the transformation with
matrix

$$\begin{pmatrix} -2 & 0 \\ 0 & -2 \end{pmatrix}.$$

(b) Calculate the fraction $\dfrac{\text{area of image}}{\text{area of object}}.$

3. The square $A(0, 2)$, $B(-2, 0)$, $C(0, -2)$, $D(2, 0)$ is mapped by a transformation with
matrix

$$S = \begin{pmatrix} 1 & -1 \\ 1 & 1 \end{pmatrix}.$$

(a) Find the image $A'B'C'D'$.

47

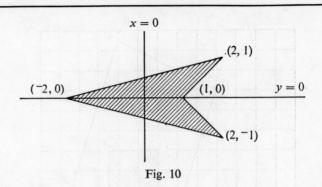

Fig. 10

(b) Now find $A*B*C*D*$, the image of $A'B'C'D'$ under the same transformation.

(c) Describe the geometric effect of this transformation.

(d) Find the image of $ABCD$ under the transformation with matrix

$$\mathbf{T} = \begin{pmatrix} \tfrac{1}{2} & \tfrac{1}{2} \\ -\tfrac{1}{2} & \tfrac{1}{2} \end{pmatrix}.$$

(e) How are the transformations defined by $\mathbf{S}$ and $\mathbf{T}$ related? Without any further calculation state the image of $A'B'C'D'$ under the transformation with matrix $\mathbf{T}$.

4. If
$$\mathbf{A}\begin{pmatrix} x \\ y \end{pmatrix} = \begin{pmatrix} x \\ y \end{pmatrix},$$

what are the components of the matrix $\mathbf{A}$? This matrix, which has the effect of mapping every point onto itself, is called the *identity matrix*.

5. What is the geometric effect of the transformation defined by

$$\mathbf{E} = \begin{pmatrix} 3 & 0 \\ 0 & 3 \end{pmatrix}?$$

Write down a matrix $\mathbf{F}$ that has the opposite effect. $\mathbf{F}$ is said to be the *inverse* of $\mathbf{E}$.

6. A transformation is defined by the matrix

$$\begin{pmatrix} 1 & k \\ 0 & 1 \end{pmatrix}.$$

Take a rectangle as an object and find out the nature of this transformation for different values of k.

Summary

Many simple geometrical transformations can be described using 2×2 matrices. They can be described in the form:

$$\begin{pmatrix} x \\ y \end{pmatrix} \to \begin{pmatrix} a & b \\ c & d \end{pmatrix} \begin{pmatrix} x \\ y \end{pmatrix}.$$

The matrix can be thought of as a machine which converts the position vector of an object point $\begin{pmatrix} x \\ y \end{pmatrix}$ into the position vector of the image point $\begin{pmatrix} ax+by \\ cx+dy \end{pmatrix}$.

48

4

RATES OF CHANGE

Times change and we change with them
JOHN OWEN, *Epigrams*

1. CONTOURS

You will remember reading about contours in Book 1 when we were discussing how to describe the position of a point in space using three coordinates. Figure 1 shows a contour map of a small region of countryside. How would you describe the physical features of the region?

If the line *AH* represents a straight road, describe the journey along it. Taking the road as $y = 0$ and a vertical line (out of the plane of the paper) through *A* as $x = 0$, write down the coordinates of *A, B, C, D, E, F, G* and *H*, and plot them on graph paper. Discuss whether you need to take the same scale on both lines. Will you join the points with straight lines or with a curve? The figure you obtain is called a *section*.

Where do you think the highest point of the road is? Discuss whether you can mark it on the contour map with any confidence. Which part of the road is steepest? How could you tell without drawing the section?

49

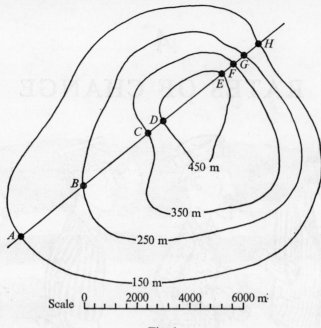

450 m

350 m

250 m

150 m

Scale 0   2000   4000   6000 m·

Fig. 1

2. GRADIENT OF A ROAD

Assume for the present that the slope of the road between *C* and *D* is steady. The road rises 100 m in about 800 m horizontally. We call this a *gradient* of 100 m in 800 m, or by simple proportion 1 m in 8 m. The gradient measures the steepness of the slope. Why is this the same gradient as 1 mm in 8 mm? As 1 cm in 8 cm? Since these are all the same we are quite safe in talking of a gradient of 1 in 8. Notice particularly that this means 1 unit *up* for 8 units along *horizontally*. (It is also possible to define the gradient in terms of 8 units along the road.) Since the road will not usually have exactly the same slope between any two points it is an *average* gradient over a section of the road. We shall see later how to deal with an actual gradient at a particular point.

There are other ways of describing a gradient.

On the Continent, it is usual to work out the gradient as a percentage. A gradient of 1 in 8 is equivalent to $12\frac{1}{2}$ in 100. The ratio $12\frac{1}{2}$ in 100 is then $12\frac{1}{2}\%$ as shown in the typical sign in Figure 2.

In mathematics, it is more convenient to have a gradient expressed as a fraction or, if this is awkward, as a decimal. The gradient above would be expressed as a gradient of $\frac{1}{8}$ or 0·125.

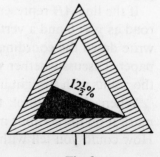

$12\frac{1}{2}\%$

Fig. 2

50

Exercise A

1. (a) From the contour map in Figure 1 express the average gradient between the points *B* and *C*: (i) in the form 1 in *n*, (ii) as a Continental gradient on a road sign, (iii) as a mathematical gradient.

(b) Write down the average mathematical gradient of the road between: (i) *A* and *B*, (ii) *F* and *G*, (iii) *A* and *D*. Discuss how we might distinguish uphill from downhill as we go from *A* to *H*.

(c) What is the average mathematical gradient between *A* and *H*? Discuss the meaning of this.

2. Convert the following gradients into mathematical gradients, writing your answers in decimal form:

(a) 1 in 5;   (b) 1 in 4;   (c) 1 in 100;   (d) 1 in 1000;

Could the gradient of a horizontal road be written in the form 1 in *n*?

3. Write the following percentage gradients in the form 1 in *n*: (a) 5%, (b) 25%, (c) 8%.

4. A hill has to have a 'steep hill' sign in a certain district if its gradient exceeds 1 in 10. Will any part of the road in Figure 3 be so marked? If so where? Discuss whether it would be possible to make a new road from *A* to *B* in the district shown avoiding any 'steep' hills.

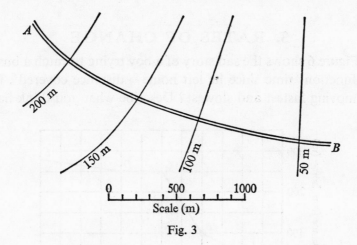

Scale (m)

Fig. 3

5. What gradient (mathematical) would describe a rise of 25 m in ½ kilometre?

6. Draw an accurate contour map, giving a scale and labelling the contours, containing: (a) a road of constant gradient 15% (but not necessarily straight) and (b) a road whose gradient varies from 0 to 15%.

7. Figure 4 shows a section of a hill. How steep is the hill? Would a car go up it? Does the diagram give a true impression?

8. Figure 5 shows the suggested design for a dangerous hill sign in this country. Compare it with the Continental sign in Figure 2. What would be the figures for a hill 'twice as steep' in each case? Which do you think is the more effective?

51

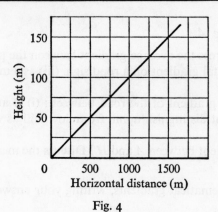

Fig. 4

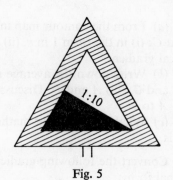

Fig. 5

9. A geographer defines the gradient between two points as

$$\frac{\text{vertical interval}}{\text{horizontal equivalent}}.$$

What do you think these words mean? What type of gradient is this? Why is it more convenient to use the horizontal distance rather than the distance along the road? Is there any disadvantage?

3. RATES OF CHANGE

The graph in Figure 6 shows the sad story of a boy trying to catch a bus. It shows the graph of the function 'time since he left home → distance covered'. Between what times was he moving fastest and slowest? Describe what you think happened.

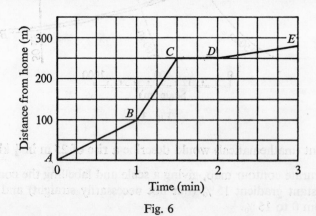

Fig. 6

In the section *BC* of the graph the boy runs 150 m in $\frac{1}{2}$ min. We say that he runs at a *rate* of 150 m per $\frac{1}{2}$ min. Is this the same rate as 150 cm per $\frac{1}{2}$ second? Or 150 km per $\frac{1}{2}$ h? It is obviously essential to include the units in a rate of change, since a rate of change compares two different quantities, in this case distance with time.

52

A convenient way of writing this rate of change (or speed) is to write 150 m/½ min or (simplifying by doubling top and bottom) 300 m/1 min. We can also write this as 300 m/min. What is his speed in centimetres per second (cm/s)? Write down the speed of the boy in metres per minute in the sections *AB*, *CD*, *DE* of the graph. Notice that the rate of change is the *gradient* of the line (with the distances measured from the scales and the units included).

Discuss what difference it would make to these figures if the graph in Figure 6 were plotted on a different scale.

Exercise B

1. Draw the graph of a boy who walked at 50 m/min for 45 s, then stopped for 30 s, then walked at half his previous speed for another 2 min. How far did he walk altogether? How far would he have walked altogether if he had walked at twice his previous speed when he restarted after his rest?

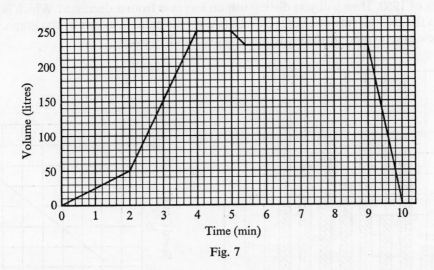

Fig. 7

2. Figure 7 shows a graph of the volume of water in a bath. Describe what you think was happening, giving rates in the proper units where appropriate.

3. Figure 8 shows the temperature out of doors in England on a certain day. Write down the average rate of change of temperature between noon and 2 p.m., 2 p.m. and 6 p.m., 6 p.m. and 8 p.m., and 8 p.m. and 10 p.m. What time of year do you think it was? Copy the graph and make up some suitable figures for the hours from 8 a.m. to noon. Discuss how we could indicate whether the rate of change means that it is becoming hotter, or colder.

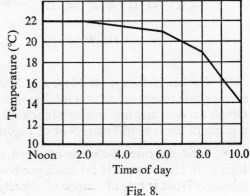

Fig. 8.

53

4. A boy cycles for $\frac{1}{2}$ h at 20 km/h, then covers a further 4 km at 30 km/h. He then waits 20 min and, after that, pedals home, doing the journey in 40 min. Graph the function 'time → distance travelled'. What was his average speed for the whole ride? If he had turned straight round without waiting, at what speed could he have returned so as to arrive at the same time? If the vertical scale were to denote distance from home, how would the graph differ from that drawn?

5. Using the same axes, draw the graphs which describe a 4 h journey made by a man called Arthur who walks at $3\frac{1}{2}$ km/h, and by a man called Benjamin who walks at 4 km/h but stops for 15 min rest after every hour of walking. Assuming that they leave town at the same time, who arrives first at the 4th, 8th and 12th kilometre-posts? Describe the sort of walking race at which each excels.

6. Figure 9 is a graph showing the total sums of money on deposit in London banks on the last day of June and December of the years shown.

Write down the average rates of change in £100 M. per month during the first and second half years of 1960. How will you distinguish an increase from a decrease? Which is the half year with the greatest rate of change? Comment on the pattern shown by the graph. Discuss how a new graph could be drawn to show the general trend.

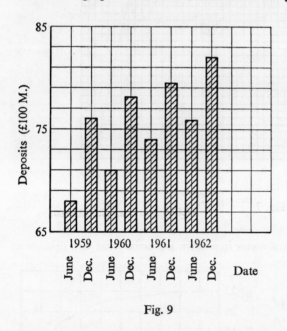

Fig. 9

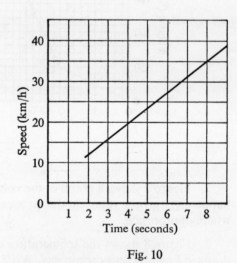

Fig. 10

7. On her birthday, 1st May, a girl had £1 in the bank. Her savings increased at an average rate of 20p per month for 3 months and then at 25p per month for the rest of year. Graph the data and find out how much she had saved by New Year's Day. Discuss whether a graph of the type of Figure 9 or of Figure 10 better illustrates these data.

8. Find the rate of change of speed of the car whose performance is represented in Figure 10. Give answer in (a) km/h per hour and (b) m/s per second. (The starting data are missing.) What is rate of change of velocity called?

9. Part of a temperature graph of a patient during recovery from an illness is shown in Figure 11. Write down the rate of decrease of temperature. How could this be given as a rate of *increase*? Would you expect such a graph to be a straight line?

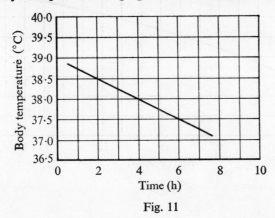

Fig. 11

10. Bacteria are multiplying in a culture tray. Originally there are about 2,000,000. The rate of increase is approximately constant for 10 h. Conditions are then varied and for the next 10 h the rate of increase is again constant and about twice the previous rate. At the end of 20 h there are about 11,000,000 bacteria. Sketch the graph of growth. Find the rates of increase in millions of bacteria per hour. Is this the way you would expect the number of bacteria to increase?

4. RATE OF CHANGE AT AN INSTANT

Figure 12 shows the mass of a baby boy at 3-monthly intervals during the first 18 months of his life. His mass did not increase in a series of jerks. It is natural therefore to join the points with a smooth curve, as in Figure 13, rather than with the straight-line segments of the previous graphs we have considered in this chapter.

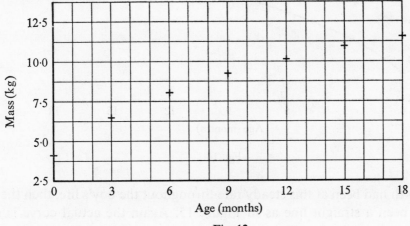

Fig. 12

55

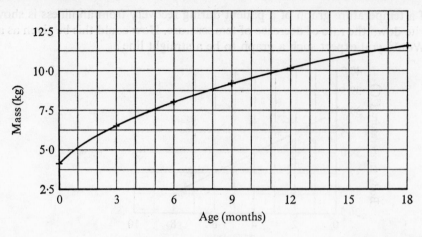

Fig. 13

Trace the figure in pencil, lightly. Draw the line that would represent the same gain in mass if it had occurred at a constant rate. Mark in red pencil the part of the curve when he was growing at more than this steady rate, and in blue pencil the part when he was growing at less. What was happening at the point where red and blue meet?

Consider how we could find the rate of growth at 6 months. If the growth continued from this time at the same steady rate, the graph would appear like the solid line in Figure 14. The actual graph has been continued dotted for comparison.

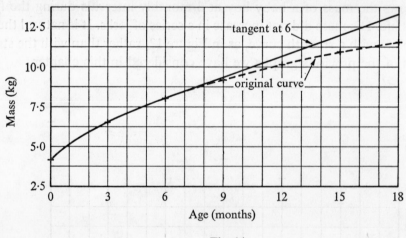

Fig. 14

If the growth had been at this steady rate throughout the boy's life, then the graph would have been a straight line as in Figure 15. Again the actual curve is shown dotted.

56

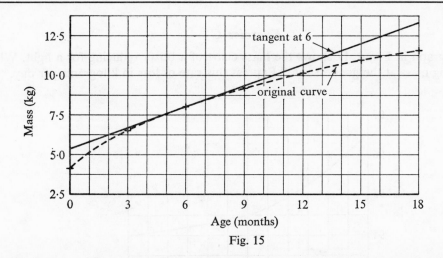

Fig. 15

We now see that the rate of growth at 6 months can be obtained by drawing a *straight line* with the same gradient as the curve at that point. We can then measure its gradient as in the last section. This line is said to *touch* the curve at that point. The Latin word for 'I touch' is '*tango*' and the line is called a *tangent*.

Example 1. The graph in Figure 16 shows the speed of a car drawing away from traffic lights. Find at what rate its speed is increasing after 5 seconds.

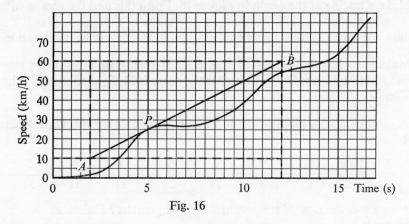

Fig. 16

The point on the graph at $t = 5$ is marked P. The tangent at P has been drawn. We find the gradient of this line by marking any two convenient points on the line, A and B, and measuring the increase in speed (about $60-10 = 50$ km/h) and the time that has elapsed ($12-2 = 10$ seconds).

Rate of increase of speed (acceleration) $= \dfrac{50 \text{ km/h}}{10 \text{ s}} = 5$ km/h per second (approx.).

Why were A and B convenient points? Would two other points have done instead? Recalculate the acceleration using two other points.

Exercise C

1. The graph in Figure 17 shows the mass chart of a boxer reducing for a fight. When was he losing mass at the greatest rate? Express this rate of loss in kilograms per day.

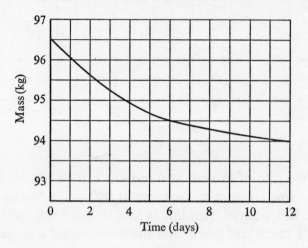

Fig. 17

2. Make a tracing of the graph in Figure 16. From this find the acceleration of the car at times 4 s and 6 s after starting. Account for the shape of the graph. Was it a rapid acceleration? Mark the point of most rapid acceleration and estimate the acceleration at that point.

3. Make a tracing of the graph in Figure 13. From this find the rate of growth of the boy at 3 months and 9 months. Discuss whether the curve is likely to continue in the same manner in the following months.

4. A saucepan is filled with sugar and water and heated slowly. The temperature readings are as follows:

Time (min)	0	1	2	3	4	5	6
Temperature (°C)	20	21	24	29	32	34	35

At what time was the rate of temperature change greatest? Estimate:
  (a) this rate;
  (b) the average rate for the first 3 min;
  (c) the rate of temperature change after 5 min.

5. Figure 18 shows the graph of the height of an oat seedling. Discuss the meaning of the zig-zag stretch of the base-line. Estimate its rate of increase of height in cm per day at 12 days and 18 days after planting. Use your answer to estimate the height after 30 days. What assumption do you make?

6. Figure 19 shows the sketch of the graph of the height of an oat seedling. Criticize it.

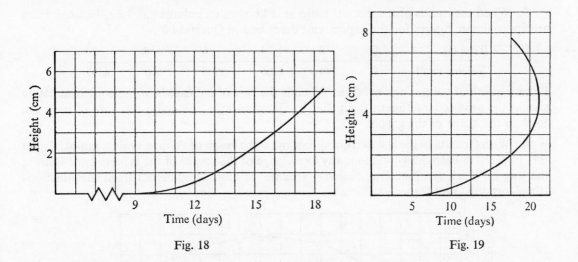

Fig. 18   Fig. 19

D 7.   The table below gives some data produced from an experiment on the cooling of a liquid. Plot the points representing the temperature at stated times and draw short line segments to represent the rates of cooling given. What do you find?

Time (min)	0	1	2	3	4	5	6
Temperature (° C)	60	50	42	36	32	29	28
Rate of cooling degC/min	10	9	8	7	6	5	4

Is it possible to draw a curve fitting these data? Can you ever be sure of the rates of change of a function given by a table of values? What assumption do we normally make?

D 8.   A boy blew up a spherical balloon. The following table shows the radius at various times.

Time (s)	0	2	4	6	8	10
Radius (cm)	0	4	7	9	10	10½

(a) Discuss how this data may have been collected.

(b) Plot the data and then draw your estimate of the function 'time → radius' (that is, radius up the page and time across the page). When was the rate of increase of radius greatest? Discuss why this occurs. Read the rate in centimetres per second.

(c) Draw up a new table of values showing the times when the radius had a given measurement (see below). Take any necessary readings from the graph.

Radius (cm)	0	2	4	6	8	10
Time (s)						

(d) Plot the readings taken from the graph (b) and graph the function 'radius → time' (time up the page and radius across the page.) At what point is the gradient of this graph smallest? Describe the geometrical connection between the two curves.

(e) Discuss the meaning of this gradient. How is it related to your answer to (b)?

(f) How could these data have been collected direct? Why are so many sets of experimental data *time-based*?

9. When the radius of a spherical balloon is known, its volume can be *calculated*. Here are approximate figures for the experiment described in Question 8

Time (s)	0	2	4	6	8	10
Volume (cm³)	0	240	1200	2700	3800	4500

Draw a graph of volume against time. When is the rate of increase in volume greatest? Why should the answer be different from that to Question 8(*b*)? Estimate this rate of increase. Explain the shape of the graph.

10. With the data of the last two questions, draw the graph of volume against radius. Could this graph have been drawn without any knowledge of the results of the experiment? Discuss the way in which the function 'radius → volume' is basically different from the functions 'time → radius' and 'time → volume'.

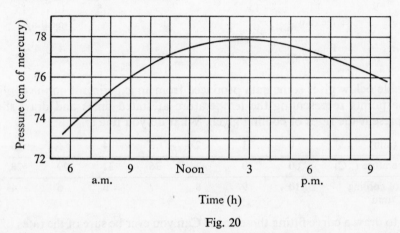

Fig. 20

11. (*a*) Figure 20 shows the barometric pressure taken from a recording machine. Write down the rate of change of pressure at 10.0 a.m. and at 6.0 p.m. What major difference is there between your answers? Discuss how we might indicate this. What was the gradient of the graph at 3.0 p.m.? What was the rate of change of the pressure? Why is this of interest?

(*b*) At 10.0 a.m. on the morning following, the rate of change of pressure was +0·6 cm of mercury per hour and the pressure stood at 75·2 cm. Estimate the pressure at 11.30 a.m. Discuss the problem of estimating the pressure during the afternoon.

Summary

Road gradient. 1 in *d*, that is, 1 unit *up*, for *d* units *horizontally* (see Figure 21).

Mathematical gradient, 1/*d*, or expressed as decimal; it is a pure *number*.

Average rate of change of (say) temperature over a certain interval of time is

$$\frac{\text{change in temperature (degC)}}{\text{change in time (min)}}.$$

When simplified it may be expressed in degrees Celsius per minute (degC/min).

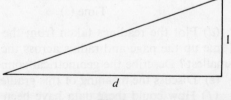

Fig. 21

60

A rate of change must have its units stated.

A rate of change is the mathematical gradient of a graph, the distances across and up the page being measured in the units of their respective scales.

Fig. 22

The gradient at a point of a curve is the gradient of a tangent drawn to touch the curve at that point (see Figure 22).

The rate of change at an instant is found by finding the rate of change represented by the tangent to the curve at that instant.

Figure 23 is the graph of the function '$q \to p$'. Figure 24 is the graph of the relation '$p \to q$'.

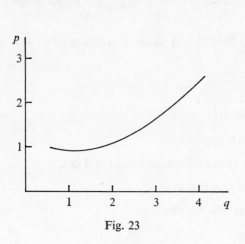

Fig. 23

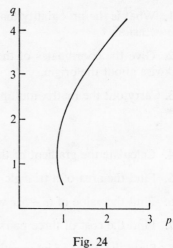

Fig. 24

REVISION EXERCISES

SLIDE RULE SESSION NO. 1

Calculate the following, giving all answers as accurately as you can.

1. $943 \div 0.026$.
2. 41×650.
3. 2.43×16.2.
4. $374 \div 12.7$.
5. $\dfrac{1.82 \times 0.64}{52.7}$.
6. $\dfrac{2.47}{21.4 \times 0.98}$.
7. $\dfrac{0.153 \times 7.62}{42.1 \times 89.1}$.
8. $\sqrt{(57.2)}$.
9. 3.95^2.
10. $\sqrt{(4.25)}$.

SLIDE RULE SESSION NO. 2

Calculate the following, giving all answers as accurately as you can.

1. $(0.0155)^2$.
2. 22.5×19.6.
3. $0.159 \div 0.0725$.
4. 1.64×12.6.
5. 705×0.0915.
6. $3.05 \div 695$.
7. $158.5 \div 0.124$.
8. $\dfrac{13.3 \times 495}{67.5 \times 0.722}$.
9. 43.5^2.
10. $\sqrt{(43.5)}$.

A

1. What is the probability that when a coin is tossed twice it will come down heads on both occasions?

2. Give the coordinates of the image of the point (2, 3) under a rotation of 270° anti-clockwise about the origin.

3. Carry out the matrix multiplication.

$$\begin{pmatrix} 1 & 2 \\ -3 & 0 \end{pmatrix} \begin{pmatrix} 4 & 5 \\ 6 & 7 \end{pmatrix}.$$

4. Calculate the gradient of the line joining (1, 6) to (3, 2).

5. Find the area of a triangle whose base is 7 cm and whose height is 4 cm.

6. Find the value of $(a-b)c$ when $a = {}^-3$, $b = 4$ and $c = {}^-2$.

7. Find the cost of three pairs of stockings at 28p for one pair.

8. State the point of intersection of the lines $x = 2$ and $y = 2x$.

9. Find the longest side of a right-angled triangle of which the other two sides are 5 cm and 12 cm.

10. Add 111_2 and 1011_2, giving the answer in binary form.

B

1. 'The die has just come down six twice in succession, so the probability that it will come down six again next time is less than $\frac{1}{6}$.' True or false?

62

2. One angle of an isosceles triangle is 124°. Find the others.

3. Write down the inverse of the function $x \to 3x$.

4. Calculate $\frac{5}{12} - \frac{6}{15}$, giving the answer as a fraction in its simplest terms.

5. Give the number-base of the correct addition $27 + 6 = 34$.

6. What ordered pair belongs to the set $\{(x, y): x + y = 3\} \cap \{(x, y): x = {}^{-}3\}$?

7. Calculate $0 \cdot 1 \times 0 \cdot 01$.

8. What regular solid has 6 faces, 12 edges and 8 vertices?

9. What is the image of the point $(5, 5)$ after reflection in the line $y = x$?

10. Calculate $15 \times 10 \times 5 \times 0$.

C

1. The earth's surface is divided up as follows: area of land, $1 \cdot 49 \times 10^8$ square kilometres; area of sea, $3 \cdot 62 \times 10^8$ square kilometres. If a returning space capsule comes down anywhere at random on the earth's surface, what is the probability that it will arrive in the sea?

2. A grocer stocks five kinds of washing powder. Figure 1 is a bar chart showing the result of a survey of the proportion of customers buying each variety. What is the probability that a customer for washing powder, chosen at random, buys Wosh?

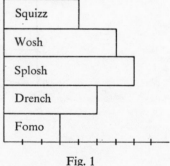

Fig. 1

3. The coordinates of the vertices of triangle T_1 are $(1, 0)$, $(3, 0)$ and $(3, 1)$. Rotation through 180° about $(1, 1)$ maps T_1 onto T_2, and similarly rotation through 180° about $(2, 2)$ maps T_2 onto T_3, whilst rotation through 180° about $(3, 3)$ maps T_3 onto T_4.

(a) Show on a diagram the positions of T_1, T_2, T_3 and T_4.

(b) Describe the single transformation which would map (i) T_1 onto T_3, (ii) T_1 onto T_4.

(c) Can any one of the triangles be mapped onto one of the others by means of a reflection? Justify your answers.

4. The vertices of a triangle are $O(0, 0)$, $A(4, 0)$, $B(0, 4)$. P is a point whose images in the three sides of the triangle OAB are Q, R and S. Find the position of P if triangle QRS is the image of triangle OAB under a reflection in the line $x + y = 2$.

5. Calculate the following matrix products where possible:

(a) $(1 \quad 2)\begin{pmatrix} 1 \\ -2 \end{pmatrix}$;

(b) $(1 \quad 2)\begin{pmatrix} 1 & 3 \\ -2 & 4 \end{pmatrix}$;

(c) $(1 \quad 2 \quad 0)\begin{pmatrix} 1 & 3 \\ -2 & 4 \end{pmatrix}$;

(d) $\begin{pmatrix} 1 & 3 & 0 \\ 2 & -4 & 6 \end{pmatrix}\begin{pmatrix} -5 \\ 1 \\ 2 \end{pmatrix}$;

(e) $\begin{pmatrix} 0 & 1 \\ 0 & 6 \end{pmatrix}\begin{pmatrix} 1 & -3 \\ 0 & 0 \end{pmatrix}$;

(f) $\begin{pmatrix} 0 & 1 \\ 0 & 6 \end{pmatrix}(1 \quad 2 \quad 3)$.

6. Packets of Wosh are sold in giant, large and standard sizes; these packets contain 900 g, 720 g and 480 g respectively, and their costs to the shopkeeper are 12p, 10p and 8p respectively.

(a) Express these facts as column matrices, one for mass and one for cost.

(b) If a shopkeeper ordered 20 giant, 30 large and 10 standard packets, write down the

63

mass of Wosh ordered as the product of two matrices, then work it out. Convert your answer to kilograms.

(c) In a similar way, find the total cost of the order in £'s.

7. Calculate the gradients of the lines joining:

(a) (1, 2) and (4, 5); (b) (1, 2) and (-2, 5); (c) (1, 2) and (-2, -1);

(d) (4, 5) and (-2, -1); (e) (6, 5) and (23, 5).

8. Figure 2 illustrates the progress of a motor car starting from rest. Estimate its greatest acceleration in metres per second per second.

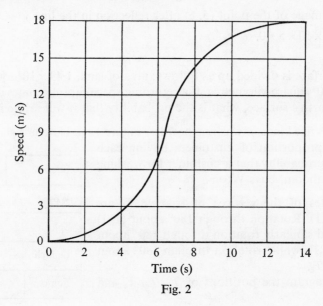

Fig. 2

D

1. A boy has a bag full of fruit drops, of three different flavours. There are 17 orange flavoured, 12 lemon flavoured and 15 lime flavoured ones in the bag. What is the probability that one taken out at random will be orange flavoured? If the boy takes out three drops (orange, lime, lime respectively), what is the probability that the next one will be orange?

2. (In this question assume it is equally likely that a child born will be a son or a daughter.)

(a) Point out the error in the following argument: 'If you have a family of two children you can have two sons *or* a son and a daughter *or* two daughters; that is to say, there are three distinct possibilities, all equally likely. So the probability of two children being both sons is $\frac{1}{3}$.'

(b) Calculate the probability that in a family of three children *at least* one child will be a son.

3. C_1 is a circle of radius 1 unit with its centre at the origin. The translation $\binom{2}{0}$ maps C_1 onto C_2; a rotation through 120° about the origin maps C_2 onto C_3; and reflection in the line $y = 0$ maps C_3 onto C_4. The figure consisting of the four circles so far obtained is now reflected in the line $x = 0$. With a scale of 1 cm to 1 unit draw a figure showing the original circle and all the images. Describe its symmetry.

4. **R** denotes a rotation through 80° about (0, 0).
(*a*) Describe the transformations **R²**, **R⁻¹**, **R⁴**.
(*b*) If **U** denotes a rotation through 40° about (0, 0), find two integers x such that $\mathbf{R}^x = \mathbf{U}$.

5. (i) Give examples of:

(*a*) a row matrix; (*b*) a column matrix; (*c*) a square matrix;
(*d*) a 2 × 3 matrix; (*e*) a 3 × 2 matrix.

(ii) **A** is a 3 × 2 matrix, **B** is a 3 × 5 matrix, **C** is a 2 × 3 matrix. Why is it impossible to work out the product **ABC**? Which product of these three matrices *can* be worked out? State the order of the product matrix which results.

6. A transformation is defined by the matrix $\begin{pmatrix} 2 & -1 \\ 1 & 2 \end{pmatrix}$. Find the image, $P'Q'R'S'$, under this transformation of the square $PQRS$ whose vertices are (2, ⁻1), (2, 3), (⁻2, 3), (⁻2, ⁻1). Draw a diagram showing the square and its image. How would you describe the transformation?

7. A car accelerates from rest, and readings are taken of its speeds at various times:

Time (s)	0	1	2	3	4	5	6	7	8	9	10
Speed (km/h)	0	9	23	47	64	73	79	84	87	89	90

Plot these readings on a graph (take time across the page) and so find:
(*a*) the speed at time 3·5 s;
(*b*) the time when the speed is 62 km/h;
(*c*) the acceleration at time 3 s.

8. Draw lines from the following information:
(*a*) gradient 0 and passing through (2, 3);
(*b*) gradient 2 and passing through (2, 3);
(*c*) gradient ⁻2 and passing through (⁻2, ⁻3).

E

1. Construct a topological map corresponding to this direct route matrix:

$$\text{From}\begin{matrix} & \overbrace{\begin{matrix} & A & B & C & D & E \end{matrix}}^{\text{To}} \\ \begin{matrix} A \\ B \\ C \\ D \\ E \end{matrix} & \begin{pmatrix} 0 & 1 & 1 & 1 & 1 \\ 1 & 0 & 1 & 0 & 1 \\ 1 & 1 & 0 & 1 & 0 \\ 1 & 0 & 1 & 0 & 1 \\ 1 & 1 & 0 & 1 & 0 \end{pmatrix} \end{matrix}.$$

In what ways is a topological map not a true representation of (say) a network of roads?

2. A group of people were questioned about the Sunday newspapers they read. 19 people favoured the *Sunday Mail*, 32 the *Scandalmonger*, 20 the *Highbrow Weekly* and 49 the *Sunday Supplement*. Illustrate this information on a pie chart.

3. Draw a triangle with its vertices at (1, ⁻1), (1, 2) and (⁻1, 2). Give the coordinates of the vertices of the triangle onto which it is mapped by an enlargement with scale factor 2 and centre (0, 1).

4. The operation $*$ means 'take the first number, square it, then divide by the second'; for example, $3 * 4 = 9 \div 4 = 2\frac{1}{4}$. Work out:

(a) $2 * 4$;   (b) $4 * 2$;   (c) $(1 * 2) * 4$;   (d) $1 * (2 * 4)$.

Is the operation $*$ commutative? Is it associative? Explain your answers.

5. Refer to Figure 3.

(a) Express **BD** in two different ways, and so write down **c** in terms of **a** and **b**.

(b) If $AE = 2AD$, comment on the shape of the quadrilateral $ABCE$.

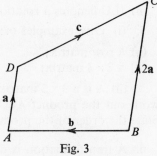

Fig. 3

6. Write the following numbers in standard form, correct to 3 s.f.:   (a) 22;   (b) 2897;   (c) 678,963;   (d) 0·6;   (e) 0·0004567.

7. Every day I buy one ChuChu bar and a bar of Brown's Chocolate. A year ago they cost 5p and 10p each, but since then their prices have risen by 20% and 40% respectively. What is the percentage rise in my total daily outlay on these two items?

8. A regular pentagon is drawn with its vertices on a circle whose radius is 4 cm. Calculate the perimeter of the pentagon. If the radius of the circle were doubled, by what factor would (a) the perimeter, (b) the area of the pentagon be increased?

F

1. Carry out the following duodecimal calculations. (@ stands for 'ten' and $*$ stands for 'eleven'.)   (a) $1@7 + **3$;   (b) $794@ - 487*$;   (c) $23* \times 1@3$;   (d) $69 \div 3$.

2. All the members of a form play cricket or tennis; 18 play both; 21 play cricket; 23 play tennis. Draw a Venn diagram to illustrate this information, and so find the number in the form.

3. Give the answers to the following in their lowest terms:

(a) $\frac{2}{3} + \frac{3}{4} - \frac{7}{8}$;   (b) $\frac{3}{5} \times \frac{10}{11} \times \frac{22}{9}$;   (c) $\frac{3}{8} \div \frac{9}{16}$;   (d) $(\frac{1}{8} + \frac{1}{4}) - (\frac{3}{16} - \frac{1}{24})$.

4. A regular polyhedron has 12 edges and 6 vertices. Using Euler's relation $F + V = E + 2$, find its number of faces. What is this polyhedron called? Draw a net which could be used for constructing it.

5. D is a point on the side BC of the triangle ABC, and $\angle ABD = 72°$, whilst
$$\angle ACB = \angle BAD = 36°.$$
Sketch the figure and find all the other angles. Given that the lengths of AB and BD are x and y respectively, express the length of AC in terms of x and y.

6. What can be said about x in the following cases?

(a) $2^x = 32$;   (b) $\frac{1}{2}(x-2) = \frac{1}{4}(x+1)$;   (c) $\frac{1}{x} = \frac{5}{8}$;

(d) $\sqrt{x} = 1·6$;   (e) $3(4x+8) = 6(2x+4)$.

7. (0, 4) and (4, 0) are two of the vertices of a square. In how many possible ways can the square be completed? Give the coordinates of its other two vertices in each case.

8. An accurate drawing of a field is made, on a scale of 1 cm to 15 m. What is the scale factor for the drawing? If the area of the field is 7500 m², what would be the area of the drawing, in square centimetres?

5

THE CIRCLE

Do not disturb my circles.†
ARCHIMEDES

1. WHAT IS A CIRCLE?

Look at Figure 1. The human eye is quite good at recognizing circles, whether seen 'straight on' as in (a), or from an angle as in (b). Were you deceived by (c)? The background should make it clear that this is an elliptical light-fitting—the angle from which the photograph has been taken was chosen to make it appear circular.

Make a tracing of the essential parts of (a) and (c) and use your compasses to see whether the outlines are circles or not. Discuss the method you employ. Why does a pair of compasses produce a circle?

Your answer to the last question will have led you to something like a definition of a circle. The point of your compasses is fixed, and the pencil is held at a fixed distance from the point.

† The story is that Archimedes spoke these words to a Roman soldier who, during the siege of Syracuse, 212 B.C., burst into his study to find him at work on a geometrical problem. The soldier, unable to obtain any replies to his questions, killed Archimedes.

(a)   (b)   (c)

Fig. 1

Definition

A circle is the set of all points in a plane at a fixed distance from a fixed point. Why do we say 'in a plane'?

You will already know various technical words relating to a circle. Figure 2 will remind you of them.

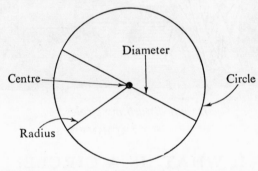

Fig. 2

Strictly the word *radius* (plural, *radii*) means a line from the centre to a point of the circle. But we can say 'this circle has a radius of one metre', meaning that its radii all have *length* one metre. There is no confusion in practice. This also applies to the word *diameter*.

Measure the diameter of the circle in Figure 2. What is the connection between its diameter and its radius?

Our definition of a circle should have made it clear that the physical model of a circle is a carefully bent thin wire, *not* a circular disc (although the edge of a disc is a circle). An *arc* is any part of a circle. By common usage, 'the area of a circle' means the area of the region bounded by it, but we shall more often refer to the area of a disc.

2. THE SYMMETRY OF THE CIRCLE

Draw a circle of radius 5 cm and cut out the disc it bounds. Fold the disc in half: open it and fold it in half again, but in a different way. Repeat this as many times as you can. What do you notice? Has a circle a line of symmetry? How many? Has it rotational symmetry? If so, discuss its order. Has it point symmetry?

Exercise A

1. The rim of a saucer is a circle. Name three further articles which include circles, stating clearly the relevant portions.

2. If a circle rolls along a straight line, what is the locus (path) of its centre? If a square rolls along a straight line, what is the locus of its centre? Why are wheels circular?

3. Is it possible to draw another closed curve with the properties you noticed in the first part of Question 2? If so, draw it.

4. Is there any closed curve, other than a circle, which has a centre such that all lines through it are lines of symmetry?
   If so, draw or describe it.

5. Roll a 10p piece along a ruler and draw the locus of the point on its edge nearest to the Lion's crown. Is the locus circular?

6. Draw a circle and cut it out. Mark any two points on the circle and fold one point over onto the other (the crease will be along the mediator of the line segment joining them). What do you find?

7. Suppose you found a large ring of stones, say 100 m across. Discuss how you might find out whether they form an accurate circle. (No aerial photography is allowed!)

8. Take a 10p piece and a 1p piece. Place them so that they touch, and draw round them. Mark a point P on the edge of the 10p piece and a point H on the edge of the 1p piece so that the distance PH is as large as possible. What do you find about P, H and the point at which the coins touch? Explain your findings.

9. Draw two points A and B, making them 5 cm apart. Can you draw circles of radius 2 cm, $2\frac{1}{2}$ cm, 3 cm, 5 cm and 10 cm to pass through both A and B?
   Is there (a) a smallest, (b) a largest, circle which will pass through both A and B? What can you say about the centres of all such circles?

10. Draw two lines, AB and AC, so that $\angle BAC = 47°$ and $AB = AC = 5$ cm. Measure BC. Draw a pair of congruent circles, centres B and C, to cut each other. Write down an ordering satisfied by the radius. Draw the line through the points where they cut. What relation does it have to $\angle BAC$?

11. Draw a triangle ABC with $AB = 6\cdot4$ cm, $BC = 5\cdot4$ cm and $CA = 5\cdot6$ cm. Draw the mediators of AB and BC. If they cut at O, what can you say about O in relation to A, B and C? What will happen if you draw a circle with centre O and radius OA?

69

12. Cut out of thin card a scalene triangle, that is one having no two sides equal. Find the three mediators of its sides by folding. Use what you learned in Question 11 to draw a circle into which the triangle will fit exactly.

13. Mark a point A on a sheet of paper. Place a ruler so that one edge passes through A, and draw a line along the *other* edge. Repeat many times. Describe what you find.

14. Draw a straight line. Draw a circle of radius 3 cm with its centre on this line, and repeat many times. Discuss what you find. What previous question does this throw light on?

15. Draw on a sheet of paper two lines, OA and OB, at right-angles to each other. Cut a triangle PQR out of card. Move the triangle to various positions on the paper, keeping P on OA and Q on OB. Trace the locus of R. Test it to see whether it is circular. Does it make any difference if triangle PQR is (*a*) isosceles, (*b*) equilateral?

3. THE CIRCUMFERENCE OF A CIRCLE

Discuss how you would measure the distance round the circles in: (*a*) a new penny, (*b*) a bicycle wheel, (*c*) a cocoa tin, (*d*) a traffic roundabout, (*e*) a pencil. Take care to specify exactly what you will be measuring. This distance, or length, is called the *circumference* of the circle.

Discuss whether it is easier to measure the radius or the diameter of circular objects.

In the light of your discussion use the most appropriate method to measure the circumference and to measure (or work out from the diameter) the radius of as many common objects as you can. Draw up a list as follows:

Name of object and precise description of part measured	Circumference	Radius	Circumference / Radius

Complete the fourth column by dividing the circumference by the radius giving your answers as accurately as you think proper. Will the accuracy be the same for all the objects? Tick the measurements of which you are most confident. Graph your findings, taking radius across and circumference up the page. What do you notice? Discuss whether or not it is a good idea to find the average of all the entries made by your class in their fourth columns.

You will find that in each case the fraction works out at about 6, probably slightly greater. Your graph should therefore be a straight line (why?). We can express this result in an approximate formula. If we let C and r stand for the number of units of length in circumference and radius respectively, then

$$C/r = 6 \quad \text{or} \quad C = 6r \text{ (approximately)}.$$

Exercise B

(Use the approximate formula C = 6r throughout.)

1. Find the approximate circumference of:
(a) a plate, radius 11 cm
(b) the big wheel at a fair, radius 8 m;
(c) a circular layout of model railway track, radius 1 m;
(d) the circle traced out by a conker whirled on a 70 cm string.

2. Measure the circumference of your neck and calculate its approximate radius.

3. Find out the actual dimensions of a '65 centimetre bicycle wheel'. How far forward in metres does the cycle travel with one revolution of its wheels?

4. Find the approximate radius of:
(a) a steering wheel 125 cm in circumference;
(b) the trunk of a tree of 5 m girth;
(c) the circular wall of a city which is 4 kilometres round.

5. My hat size is 17·5. Assuming this to refer to a length measured in centimetres, find out whether it is likely to be radius, diameter or circumference. Check with your own hat size.

6. Rope is usually graded by its circumference. Calculate the approximate *diameter* of (a) a 5 cm rope, (b) a 15 cm rope. What size rope would you expect to use for a clothes line?

7. Figure 3 shows a running track. The ends are semicircles of radius 50 m. How long are the straights if one lap is 500 m?

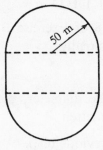
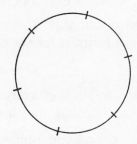

Fig. 3　　　　　　　　　　　　　　　　Fig. 4

8. Draw a circle of radius 5 cm and mark six points on it 5 cm apart (as in Figure 4). Join the six points to form a regular hexagon. Is the perimeter of this a good approximation to the circumference of the circle? Draw a second regular hexagon with its sides parallel to those of the first, and just enclosing the circle. How many points of this hexagon lie on the circle? Is the perimeter of this hexagon as good an approximation as the other to the circumference of the circle? Calculate or measure the two perimeters involved and write down an ordering which relates them to the circumference of the circle. Does this support the formula $C = 6r$? If not, what might be a better formula?

Repeat the above on another circle of the same radius taking 12 points instead of 6 points. Do the regular 12-sided figures give you a better or a worse estimate of the circumference?

Discuss what would happen if the number of points were increased to 100, 1000, etc. Is there a largest number of points we could take? We say that, if we could go to the *limit*, then the perimeter of the regular polygon involved would be equal to the circumference of the circle. Why does the last sentence contain the word 'if'? Can you now justify describing a circle as 'the limit' of a regular polygon?

9. The mean radius of the earth is about 6400 kilometres. Calculate how far it is round the equator.

10. In gauge 'O' model railways it is possible to get either 30 cm or 60 cm radius curved track. Where are the centres of the circles formed by the actual rails? Do the rails have the same radius? Discuss what we mean by the 'length' of an oval track made from a complete circle of 60 cm radius and four straights each 30 cm long. How much shorter is a similar layout in 30 cm radius track?

D 11. Figure 5 shows a sketch of a wire model of a sphere. It is to be made from circles of wire, some of radius 60 cm and some of radius 45 cm. Find the total length of wire required. Would you use the formula $C = 6r$ if you were buying the wire to make it?

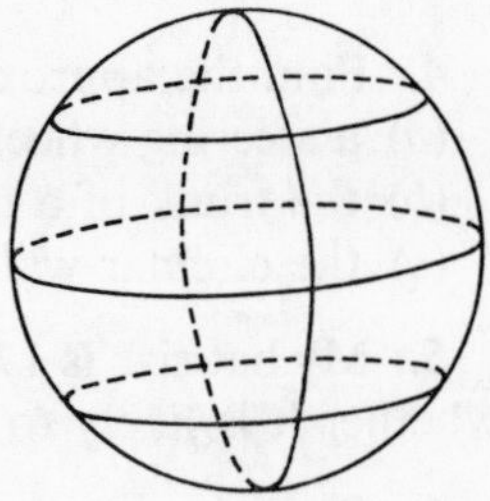

Fig. 5

D 12. Figure 3 shows the inner boundary of the inner lane of a running track. There are three lanes, each 1 m wide. They are marked by lines parallel to those shown. If three competitors start and finish level, and run along the inner boundaries of their lanes, find out how far each has run. How is this compensated for in practice?

4. THE NUMBER CALLED π

Your measurements and your answer to Question 8 of Exercise B will have convinced you that the formula for the circumference is really:

$$C = \text{6-and-a-bit} \times r.$$

If d denotes the number of units of length in the diameter, then $d = 2r$. The circumference formula could, therefore, equally be written

$$C = \text{3-and-a-bit} \times d \quad \text{(half the previous bit!)}.$$

Let us look at this 3-and-a-bit more closely.

The Babylonians and the ancient Jews thought that the bit did not matter. They used 3 as the multiplier. It is interesting to look this up in the Bible. Read the First Book of Kings, Chapter VII, Verse 23.

The ancient Egyptians, as we can see by the Rhind Papyrus, used the fraction $(\frac{16}{9})^2$ as the multiplier. This works out at about 3·16.

The ancient Greeks worked very hard to find more accurate versions of this important number. Archimedes gave various ones, among them $3\frac{1}{7}$ and $3\frac{10}{71}$. In the end he said that the true number lay between them, that is, between 3·1429 and 3·1408.

The Chinese were also aware of $3\frac{1}{7}$. This is quite a good approximation and is often used today. Tsu Chung Chieh (about A.D. 430) gave the number as 355/113 or 3·14159.

Modern mathematicians using electronic computers can work out the same number to many thousands of decimal places. This number, however, is still an approximation. They have proved that none of the fractional values are exact; indeed, it is impossible to find an exact fraction for this number (remember that this was also the case with $\sqrt{2}$). To 20 decimal places we obtain

$$3·14159\ 26535\ 89793\ 23846.$$

It is no wonder that it is convenient to have a special name (pi) and a special symbol (π) for so troublesome a number! π is the Greek letter *p*. You will see later why it is better to use the special letter to denote 3-and-a-bit, rather than 6-and-a-bit.

We can now write the circumference formula as

$$C = 2\pi r.$$

We shall take the value of π to be 3,

or   3·1,

or   3·14, or possibly $3\frac{1}{7}$,

or   3·142,

or   3·1416

according to the accuracy of the data and the required accuracy of the answer. Remember that the value of π will *always* be an approximation.

Is there a special mark for π on your slide rule?

Exercise C

1. Use your slide rule to calculate the circumferences of circles with the following radii:

   (*a*) 6·1 cm;   (*b*) 29·4 cm;   (*c*) 18 m;   (*d*) 0·045 cm.

2. Calculate the circumferences of circles with the following radii:

   (*a*) 14 m;   (*b*) 3500 m;   (*c*) 2·1 km;   (*d*) 0·7 mm.

In this question $3\frac{1}{7}$ is an easier approximation to use for the value of π than 3·14. Why is this so?

3. A 500 metre length running track is circular. Its radius is roughly twice the length of a cricket pitch (approx. 20 m). True or false? State what value of π you will use and why.

4. Use a slide rule to find the radii of circles with the following circumferences:

   (*a*) 88 m;   (*b*) $4\frac{1}{2}$ cm;   (*c*) 5100 m;   (*d*) 25·7 cm.

Sketch a slide rule setting that enables you to read the answers to (*b*), (*c*), and (*d*) in one setting.

5. The radius of a wheel is 1·032 cm (to the nearest thousandth of a centimetre). Take 3·142 as your approximation to π and use long multiplication to find the circumference of the wheel. To what accuracy will you give your answer?

In the following questions decide for yourself which value to select for π. Make it clear in your answer which is your choice and why.

6. The minute hand of Big Ben is 3·3 m long. How far does the tip move in an hour?

7. Cotton is wound on a cotton reel of radius 1 cm. There are said to be 1000 turns and the length is given as 54 m. Is this reasonable?

8. A tricycle has wheels whose *diameter* including the tyres is 42 cm. What is their circumference? How far, in metres, does a wheel go forward in 80 revolutions? What is the forward speed, in m/s, of the tricycle when the wheels are rotating at 80 revolutions per minute?

9. The radius of the cylinder on the winch at the top of a well is 10 cm. How many times must the handle be turned to draw up a bucket of water through 4·8 m?

10. A flywheel is rotating at 450 revolutions per minute. If it is 1 m in *diameter*, how fast would Frank the fly (son of Fred), sitting on the edge, be travelling in metres per second? Could Frank possibly sit on such a flywheel?

11. Taking the radius of the earth to be 6400 kilometres and the time for a rotation to be 24 h, find, in km/h, the speed of rotation about the earth's axis of a man standing on the equator. Is a man in London travelling at the same speed?

5. THE AREA BOUNDED BY A CIRCLE

Figure 6(*a*) shows a disc of radius $1\frac{1}{2}$ cm. What is its circumference? The region it bounds has been divided into four equal parts, one of which is split into two halves. These parts have been re-assembled in Figure 6(*b*).

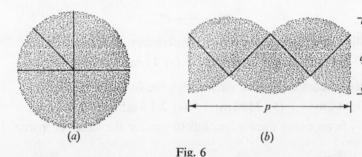

(*a*)   (*b*)

Fig. 6

Describe the shape of (*b*) as clearly as you can. Discuss the distances p and q. What light does (*b*) throw on the area of the disc?

Figure 7(*a*) shows a congruent disc divided into eight equal parts, one of which is again split into two halves. The parts have again been re-assembled and the result is shown in Figure 7(*b*).

74

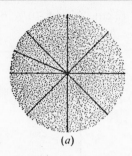

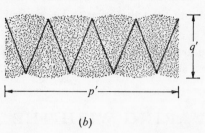

(a)   (b)

Fig. 7

Estimate p' and q'. Use your answers to make a better estimate of the area of the disc. Sketch the shape of the re-assembled figure if the disc were divided into 16 equal parts.

If a disc of radius r units were split into a very large number of equal parts, what would be the dimensions of the figure into which it could be re-assembled? What would be its area?

You will be certain, by now, that the area of a disc of radius r units is given by the formula

$$A = \pi r^2,$$

where A is the area in square units. (Why is there a multiplier 2 in the formula for the circumference but not in that for the area?)

This formula can be proved to be exact for any disc.

Exercise D

1. Taking the value of π to be 3, calculate the areas enclosed by the circles whose radii are:

          (a) 4 cm;   (b) 100 m;   (c) 20 m.

Be careful to include the units in your answers.

2. A circle encloses an area of about 75 cm². Taking the value of π to be 3, what will be the square of its radius? In what units? What will be the actual radius, approximately, and in what units?

3. Taking the value of π to be 3, estimate the radii of circles which enclose areas of:

          (a) 300 km²;   (b) 12 m²;   (c) 150 cm².

4. A brake disc has a *diameter* of 8 cm. What is its radius? What is its approximate area?

5. A circular plaque has to be gilded. Its radius is 15 cm; and the workman, who knows how much gold leaf is needed per square centimetre wants to order the gold for the job. Calculate the area for him. What is a suitable approximation to take for π?

6. A circular cattle enclosure has to enclose about 120 m². What should its radius be? Justify the accuracy you use.

7. Taking the value of π to be $\frac{22}{7}$, find the area of a circular plate of radius 14 cm.

8. A radar screen is circular and has a *diameter* of 42 cm. About 10% of its area is ineffective. Taking the value of π to be $\frac{22}{7}$, find its effective area.

9. Find the area of the sports ground shown in Figure 8. Use a suitable approximate value of π.

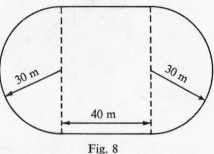

Fig. 8

6. SQUARING WITH THE SLIDE RULE

We discovered how to find squares and square roots from the slide rule in Book 2 and we shall now go into this in more detail.

One difficulty we shall meet when using the slide rule is that often it will provide only the digits of the answer, and the decimal point will have to be found by approximating.

Example 1

(a) Calculate 45.3^2.
Approximating, $45.3^2 \approx 50^2 = 2500$.
Slide rule digits are 205.
Hence, $45.3^2 = 2050$, to slide rule accuracy.
(b) Calculate 0.216^2.
Approximating, $0.216^2 \approx 0.2^2 = 00.4$.
Slide rule digits are 467.
Hence $0.216^2 = 0.0467$, to slide rule accuracy.

Exercise E

Use your slide rule to calculate Questions 1–20.

1. 34^2.
2. 19^2.
3. 5.4^2.
4. 186^2.
5. 860^2.
6. 26.5^2.
7. 5.15^2.
8. 1230^2.
9. 0.52^2.
10. 0.91^2.
11. 0.22^2.
12. 0.084^2.
13. 0.0031^2.
14. 0.0032^2.
15. 105^2.
16. 0.105^2.
17. 8090^2.
18. 0.602^2.
19. 0.62^2.
20. 0.00077^2.

21. Use your slide rule to calculate the areas of squares of sides:

(a) 3.45 cm;   (b) 615 m;   (c) 86.5 cm.

22. Use your slide rule to calculate the area of a circle of radius 1.5 cm. It is possible to obtain the answer after only one movement of the slide. Sketch the slide setting that enables you to do this.

23. Read off, with the setting sketched in Question 22, the areas of circles of radii:

(a) 2.45 cm;   (b) 1.62 cm;   (c) π cm.

24. Use a single setting to read off the areas of circles of radii:
    (a) 6·48 cm; (b) 9·25 cm; (c) 8·03 cm.

25. Calculate the areas of circles with the following radii:
    (a) 24·8 cm; (b) 152 m; (c) 0·45 cm.

7. SQUARE ROOTS

What is the relation between the function 'square' and the function 'take the (positive) square root'? Express each in functional notation.

What are the squares of 3, 4, 30, 40, 300, 400?

What can you say about the number of digits in the squares of numbers with: (a) one, (b) two, (c) three, (d) n digits?

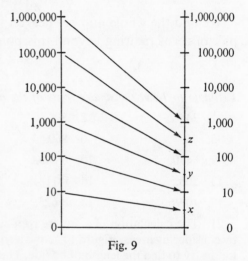

Figure 9 shows a mapping from the square root function. The number scales are logarithmic (like those on your slide rule) to save space. What are the numbers x, y, z approximately? (You will need to look at your slide rule.) What can you say about the number of digits to the left of the decimal point, in the square roots of numbers with: (a) one, (b) two, (c) three, (d) four, (e) $2n$, (f) $2n+1$ digits?

Can you give *more* information than just the number of digits?

It will be clear by now that, where there is an even number of digits, each digit in a square root corresponds to a pair of digits in the number itself. A convenient way, therefore, to find the number of digits in the square root of a number is to pair off its digits. 'Pairing off' can also be used where there is an odd number of digits, but the square root must have one digit extra for the odd digit.

Fig. 9

Example 2

Make estimates (1 s.f.) of (a) $\sqrt{4800}$; (b) $\sqrt{5{,}150{,}000}$.

Pairing off to the left, from the decimal point

(a)
$$\sqrt{48}\;|\;00$$
$$\approx 7\;|\;0 \;\text{'}$$

(b)
$$\sqrt{5}\;|\;15\;|\;00\;|\;00$$
$$\approx 2\;|\;0\;\;|\;0\;\;|\;0 \;\;\cdot$$

To make an estimate correct to one significant figure it is enough to find the whole number nearest to the square root of the left-hand pair of digits or single digit and to put a nought under each other pair.

A similar discussion of the roots of numbers less than 1 will convince you that it is still true that each digit of the root corresponds to a pair of digits in the number itself. In this case it is necessary to pair off to the right from the decimal point.

Example 3

Estimate, correct to 1 s.f., (*a*) $\sqrt{0\cdot048}$, (*b*) $\sqrt{0\cdot0000515}$.
Pairing off from the decimal point:

(*a*) $\qquad\qquad\qquad \sqrt{0\cdot}\,|\,04\,|\,8$
$\qquad\qquad\quad = \;0\cdot\,|\,2\,|\qquad$ (approximately),

(*b*) $\qquad\qquad\quad = \sqrt{0\cdot}\,|\,00\,|\,00\,|\,51\,|\,5$
$\qquad\qquad\qquad 0\cdot\,|\,0\,|\,0\,|\,7\,|\qquad$ (approximately).

We find the whole number nearest to the square root of the first pair that is not a pair of zeros (pairing beyond this point is unnecessary).

Exercise F

Estimate to 1 s.f. the square roots of the numbers in Questions 1–20.

1. 34.	2. 3·4.	3. 0·034.	4. 34,000.
5. 86.	6. 860.	7. 0·086.	8. 0·86.
9. 6450.	10. 0·645.	11. 645,000.	12. 0·00645.
13. 505.	14. 0·118.	15. 24·5.	16. 0·000204.
17. 10·96.	18. 3·625.	19. 250·27.	20. 0·0003.

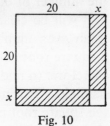

Fig. 10

21. The calculation of a square root such as $\sqrt{580}$ can also be done by considering areas. Figure 10 shows a square of area 580 square units. Let us try to find the length of its side. The answer is plainly between 20 and 30, so a square of side 20 units has also been drawn. Write down the total area of the shaded rectangles in terms of x. Since the bottom right-hand square is small in comparison, this area is roughly $580-20^2$, or 180 square units. Show that the greatest natural number less than x is 4. What does this give you as an estimate of $\sqrt{580}$?

22. Taking 37 as an estimate of $\sqrt{1400}$, draw a figure similar to Figure 10. Calculate x to 1 significant figure and hence give a closer estimate of $\sqrt{1400}$. How would you get an even closer estimate?

23. Use the method of the two previous questions to obtain $\sqrt{2000}$ to three significant figures.

8. SQUARE ROOTS USING THE SLIDE RULE

Sketch the flow diagram for finding the square root of a number from your slide rule. When you use your rule to calculate $\sqrt{34,500}$ you will have to notice that the decimal point is after the fifth digit and decide whether to work from 3·45 or from 34·5 on the A-scale. Make a rough estimate of $\sqrt{345\cdot00}$. Does this help you?

Example 4

Using a slide rule, calculate (*a*) $\sqrt{920}$, (*b*) $\sqrt{0\cdot0092}$.

(*a*) Pairing off from the decimal point to the left

$$\frac{\sqrt{9}\ |\ 20}{\approx\ 3\ |\ 0.}$$

Looking below 9·2 on the A-scale one finds 3·03 on the D-scale. Looking below 92 on the A-scale one finds 9·6 on the D-scale. From the approximation it is plainly the former that is needed.

The slide rule figure needed is therefore 303, so $\sqrt{920} = 30\cdot3$ (to slide rule accuracy).

(*b*) Pairing off from the decimal point to the right

$$\frac{\sqrt{0\cdot}\ |\ 00\ |\ 92}{\approx\ 0\cdot\ |\ 0\ \ |\ 9.}$$

The slide rule figure needed is therefore 96, so $\sqrt{0\cdot0092} \approx 0\cdot096$.

Exercise G

Use your slide rule to calculate the square roots of the numbers in Questions 1–19.

1. 275.	2. 27·5.	3. 0·0275.	4. 0·0000275.
5. 4040.	6. 4·04.	7. 8,920,000.	8. 89,200.
9. 0·00684.	10. 1085.	11. 0·0382.	12. 0·00208.
13. 56,155.	14. 27·185.	15. 300·5.	16. 23·4².
17. $\frac{5}{33}$.	18. $9\frac{2}{7}$.	19. $(3\cdot48 \times 10^{12})$.	

20. Find the radii of circles whose areas are:

(*a*) 4050 cm²;   (*b*) 12000 m²;   (*c*) 2·85 m².

21. Find:

(*a*) the side of a square of area 345 m²;

(*b*) the *diameter* of a circle of area 345 m².

22. The end face of a casting is to be square, with four circles of radius 1·5 cm cut from it (see Figure 11). If the shaded area is to be 40 cm², find the length of the side of the square.

23. A farmer needs some hurdles, each 2m long, to enclose a circular area of about 55 m². How many will he need?

Fig. 11

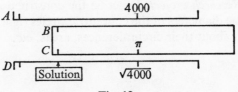

Fig. 12

24. A boy was asked to calculate the radius of a circle enclosing an area of 4000 m². His slide rule setting is shown in Figure 12. Could he get the right answer from it?

25. How long a piece of string would you need to enclose an area of 1 m²? Try to guess the answer, and then check your answer by calculating it.

D 26. Draw the triangle whose sides are 1·95 cm, 2·60 cm and 3·25 cm, as shown in Figure 13. By considering squares on its sides, show that it is right-angled. Why will you not use a slide rule? Express the areas of the semi-circles drawn on its sides in terms of π. What do you find? Did you need to work them out?

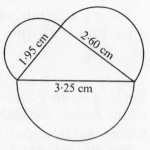

D 27. The triangle in Figure 14 is congruent to that in Figure 13. Find the connection between the areas of the quadrants (quarters) of circles on its sides and those of the semi-circles on the sides of the previous triangle. Make a statement concerning the areas of the quadrants shown.

Fig. 13

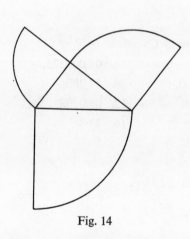

Fig. 14

Fig. 15

D 28. Water is flowing into a tank through two pipes of internal diameters 1·95 cm and 2·60 cm respectively. It is proposed to remove these and substitute a single pipe of diameter 3·25 cm. Pressure and so on being equal, will the flow be increased, decreased or neither? (Look at your answer to Questions 26 or 27.)

D 29. *Research project*. Describe the construction of the pattern of circles in Figure 15. Measure the diameters of the concentric circles (ignoring the central blob). Find out as much as you can about their circumferences, areas, etc.

9. SECTORS AND SEGMENTS

Figure 16 shows two familiar objects cut in different ways. The two-dimensional regions outlined in black are approximately the shapes of *sectors*, (*a*) and *segments*, (*b*).

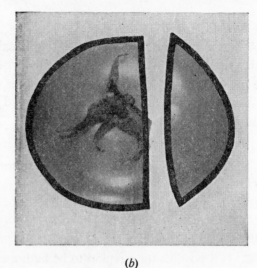

(a)   (b)

Fig. 16

Sector of a circle

This is a region bounded by part of the circle and two radii. Note that there are two sectors corresponding to any two radii. The larger is called the *major* sector and the smaller the *minor* sector. The simplest way of defining the size of a sector is to give its radius and the angle between the radii. Find the angles of the two sectors in Figure 16. What relation is there between these angles?

Example 5

Find the perimeter of a sector of angle 200° cut from a circle of radius 3 cm (see Figure 17).

The perimeter consists of the arc (the curved line) and the two radii.

200° corresponds to $\frac{200}{360}$ ths of a complete turn.

The length of arc, therefore, is

$$\frac{200}{360} \times \text{circumference}$$
$$= \frac{5}{9} \times 2\pi \times 3 \text{ cm}$$
$$= \frac{10}{3}\pi \text{ cm} = 10\cdot47 \text{ cm} \quad (\text{taking } \pi \text{ to be } 3\cdot142).$$

The perimeter, then, is $(10\cdot47 + 2 \times 3)$ cm $= 16\cdot5$ cm (to 3 s.f.).

Fig. 17

Example 6

Find the area of a 35° sector of a circle of radius 5 cm.

The area of the sector is $\frac{35}{360}$ ths of the area enclosed by the circle.

$$= \frac{35}{360} \times \pi \times 5^2 \text{ cm}^2$$
$$= 7\cdot64 \text{ cm}^2 \quad (\text{by slide rule})$$
$$= 7\cdot6 \text{ cm}^2 \quad (\text{to 2 s.f.}).$$

Segment of a circle

A line joining two points of a circle is called a *chord*. A chord divides the region inside the circle into two segments, the larger is called the *major* segment, the smaller the *minor* segment.

What special name do we give to a chord which divides a circle into two congruent segments?

<h3 align="center">Exercise H</h3>

1. State which of the following are sectors, and which are segments of approximate circles:

(*a*) the 'half moon' of a finger nail;   (*b*) a fan;
(*c*) the region of a circular clockface between the hands at 4.15;
(*d*) the inside of a letter D;   (*e*) the end of a railway tunnel.

2. Is it possible for a region to be both a sector and a segment at the same time?

3. Find the perimeter of an 81° sector cut off from a circle of radius 7 cm. Take the value of π to be $\frac{22}{7}$.

4. Taking a circle of radius 12 cm and the value of π to be 3, copy and complete the following table:

Angle between radii	Length of arc	Area of sector
15°		
30°		
45°		
60°		

Comment on the relation between the sets of figures in the three columns. What has this got to do with a pie chart?

5. Find the areas of sectors cut from a circle of radius 13 cm by radii at angles of:

(*a*) 31°;   (*b*) 124°;   (*c*) 236°.

6. A box for Brie cheese is made in the shape of a 30° sector from a circle of radius 20 cm. What is the area of its top? The box is 2 cm deep. Find the volume of the box.

7. Taking the value of π to be 3, find the angle between two radii which cut off an arc of length 9 cm from a circle of radius 6 cm.

8. Taking the value of π to be 3·14, find the angle of a sector of a circle of radius 1 m whose curved boundary is of length 1 m

9. Figure 18 shows a circular cone made from paper. If it were cut along the straight line *OB*, would it fold out flat? What shape is the net of a circular cone? The distance *OB* is called its *slant* height. How would you find its true height?

Fig. 18

10. Draw and cut out the nets for several cones of slant height 5 cm. Take various angles for the sectors involved. Make them up into cones. What is the effect of increasing the angle?

Discuss how you would calculate the angle if you wished the radius of the base circle to be 3 cm. Are there any limits to the radius of the base circle?

D 11. A cone has a slant height of *l* cm, and a base radius of *r* cm. Find the circumference of the base and the angle of the sector which forms its net. Find also the area of curved surface of the cone.

12. Figure 19 shows a circle with centre *O* and radius 10 cm. It is divided into two segments by the line *AB* of length 12 cm. Use trigonometrical tables to find $\angle AOD$ and hence $\angle AOB$. By subtracting the area of a triangle from the area of a sector, find the area of the minor segment cut off by *AB*.

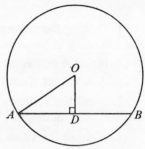

13. Figure 19 represents the cross-section of a railway tunnel, *AB* being the ground. The length of *AB* is 10 m, and the length of *OA* is 6 m. Calculate:

(*a*) the height of the tunnel;   (*b*) $\angle AOB$;
(*c*) the area of the end of the tunnel;
(*d*) the volume of the tunnel, if its length is 200 m.

Fig. 19

10. THE CYLINDER

Take a rectangle of paper, measuring 15 cm by 10 cm, as shown in Figure 20. Bend it so that *AB* lies on *DC*, and so that the ends are circles. The object formed is called a *circular cylinder*. If you bend it so that the ends are ellipses (or ovals) it is called an *elliptical cylinder*, and other shapes are also possible. You must bend the paper carefully so that the ends are exactly the same shape and size. What is the approximate radius of the end-circles in your model?

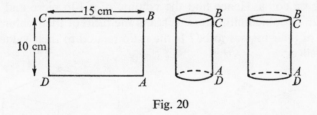

Fig. 20

Now make a second cylinder with height 10 cm and base radius 4 cm approximately. What shape and size of paper will you need for its net?

In general terms, if the radius of the base is *r* units, and the height is *h* units, then we shall require a piece of paper measuring $2\pi r$ units by *h* units. We have the formula for the curved surface area *A*, in square units:

$$A = 2\pi rh.$$

The area of the base is πr^2 square units. Think of these as the small squares of mm graph paper. If each of these is the base of a wooden match of height *h* units, then they will form a solid of volume $\pi r^2 h$ cubic units. The smaller the square units chosen to cover the base, the more nearly will the bundle of matches form a circular cylinder. It is therefore reasonable to express the volume V, in cubic units, by the formula

$$V = \pi r^2 h.$$

Exercise I

1. Taking the value of π to be 3, find the area of the curved surfaces of the cylinders with the following dimensions:

(a) radius 4 m, height 3 m;   (b) radius 3 m, height 4 m.

Did you expect them to be equal? Say why.

2. Find the volumes of the cylinders in Question 1. Did you expect them to be equal? Explain your findings.

3. Taking the value of π to be 3·14, use your slide rule to find the area of the curved surface and the volume of a cylinder of height 2·45 cm and base radius 0·55 cm.

4. The volume of a cylinder is 80 cm³ and the area of its base is 16 cm². Find its height and the radius of its base, to slide rule accuracy.

5. The area of the curved surface of a cylinder is 18 m². Taking the value of π to be 3, make a statement about its height and base radius. Give two possible sets of dimensions. How many possible sets are there in all?

6. 120 g of seaside rock has a volume of about 200 cm³. If the radius of the cylindrical rock is 1·5 cm, about how long must the stick be?

7. A down pipe on the side of a house has a radius of 4·5 cm and a length of 4 m. You have a tin of paint that will cover 2 m². Is this enough to paint the pipe? If it is more than enough, will you have enough left over to paint another pipe of the same size? If not, what fraction of one would you expect to be able to paint?

8. Measure the diameters of a 10p piece and a 5p piece, and the height of a pile of, say, 10 of each of these coins. Hence find the volume of a 10p piece and of a 5p piece, as accurately as you can, in cubic millimetres. What is the ratio of their volumes? What would you expect the ratio of their masses to be? Is the ratio related to their values? Find out how banks 'count' their silver.

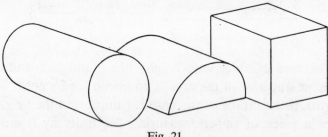

Fig. 21

D 9. Figure 21 shows three of the bricks in a child's building set: a cylinder, a half-cylinder and a cube.

They all have a volume of 1 cm³ and are 1 cm long. Find their other dimensions. Which do you think has the largest, and which the smallest, surface area?

Calculate the areas and check your guess.

D 10. In the third century, Pappus discovered a simple formula for the volume of the solid formed by rotating (amongst other figures) a circle through 360° about a line in its plane. The solid shown in Figure 22 has the shape of a motor car inner tube. The shaded circle is the 'generating' circle. Where is the axis of rotation? Describe the locus of the centre of the circle. The volume is the product of the area of the generating circle and the length of the locus of its centre. Write down a formula to express this, giving suitable letters to the lengths that have to be known. Calculate the volume of the inner tube in Figure 22, given that the diametric distances are $AD = 24$ cm and $AB = 7$ cm.

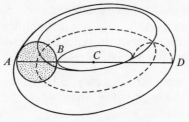

Fig. 22

D 11. Describe the solid formed by rotating the rectangle with vertices A (3, ⁻10), B (4, ⁻10), C (4, 10) and D (3, 10) about the line $x = 0$. Write down the coordinates of the centre of the rectangle $ABCD$. Use Pappus's Theorem to find the volume of the solid formed.

Exercise J

Miscellaneous

1. Taking the value of π to be 3, 3·14 or $\frac{22}{7}$ as seems appropriate, calculate the circumference of a circle of radius:

(a) 4 m;   (b) 7·0 cm;   (c) 5·24 cm.

2. Choosing the value of π as in Question 1, calculate the area enclosed by a circle of radius: (a) 0·83 cm;   (b) 21 m;   (c) 1 km.

3. Choosing the value of π as before, find the radius of a circle of circumference:

(a) 462 m;   (b) 1350 m.

4. Use your slide rule to find the radius of a circle of area:

(a) 40 cm²;   (b) 845 m².

5. Taking the value of π as $\frac{22}{7}$, find the length of arc cut off:
(a) from a circle of radius 35 cm by two radii at 60°;
(b) from a circle of radius 210 cm by two radii at 135°;
(c) from a circle of radius 1·4 m by two radii at 300°.

6. Taking the value of π from you slide rule, find the area of a sector:
(a) of 48° from a circle of radius 4·55 cm;
(b) of 240° from a circle of radius 2·03 cm.

7. Use your slide rule to find the angle of a sector:
(a) of area 10 m² from a circle of radius 3·5 m;
(b) of area 10 m² from a circle of radius 1·85 m.

D 8. Express $\frac{22}{7}$ as a decimal correct to 4 decimal places. To four decimal places $\pi = 3.1416$. To how many places is $\frac{22}{7}$ a correct approximation to π? If you worked out the area enclosed by a circle of radius 10 cm to 4 significant figures taking $\pi = \frac{22}{7}$, estimate the size of your error. Express this as a percentage of the better approximation.

D 9. The distance round the equator is 40070 kilometres, and the distance round the earth via north and south poles is 40008 kilometres. In Section 4 (on p. 73) you were told the value of π to 20 places: use as many as you need (but not more than is necessary) to calculate the diameter of the equator correct to the nearest kilometre. Assuming that the distance round the earth through the poles is equal to the circumference of a circle with diameter equal to the mean of the equatorial diameter and the distance through the earth between the north and south poles, calculate the distance between the poles correct to the nearest kilometre. Express the difference as an approximate percentage of the equatorial diameter.

10. The front wheel of a penny-farthing bicycle has three times the radius of the back wheel. How many times does the back wheel rotate while the front wheel is turning twice? (You do not need to use the value of π.)

11. The diameter of a 10p piece is 28 mm. Ten 10p pieces are melted down and made into a new monster coin of the same thickness. What will be its diameter? (You do not need to use the value of π.)

12. Two circles have radii of 2 m and 3 m respectively. Write down expressions for (a) their circumferences and (b) their areas, but do not work them out. Write down the ratio of their circumferences and the ratio of their areas. A third circle has a radius of 5 m. Write down the ratios of (a) its circumference and (b) its area to those of the 2 m circle.

13. Two radii of a circle of radius 18 cm make an angle of 135°. What is the ratio of the areas of the two sectors? Is any of the information superfluous?

14. A cyclist is travelling at 8 m/s. His bicycle wheels have a diameter of 65 cm. What is their circumference in metres? Find the approximate number of revolutions per minute made by the wheels.

15. The material for a wigwam is cut in the form of a 210° sector of a circle radius 3 m. What area of material is used? What is the height of the wigwam?

16. Water is flowing through a cylindrical pipe of radius $1\frac{1}{2}$ cm at the rate of roughly 1 m³ every 4 min. At what speed is the water moving in the pipe in cm/s?

17. 1 litre (1000 cm³) of water is used to fill a cylindrical jug of radius 5 cm and height 8 cm; the remainder is poured into a measuring cylinder of cross-sectional area 10 cm². How far up will it come?

18. A circle of radius 10 cm is drawn completely inside one of radius 20 cm on graph paper with a $\frac{1}{5}$ cm grid. Estimate the ratio of the number of grid points inside the smaller circle to the number between the two circles.

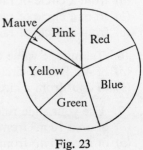

19. Figure 23 shows a pie chart representing the favourite colours of 30 children at a party. Measure the angles of the appropriate sectors, and find the number of children who liked (a) the most, (b) the least popular colour.

Fig. 23

Summary

A circle is the set of all points in a plane at a fixed distance (the radius) from a fixed point (the centre). Any subset of adjacent points of this set is called 'an *arc* of the circle'. A *chord* is a straight line joining two points of a circle.

Circumference of a circle (radius *r*) $C = 2\pi r$.

Area enclosed by circle $A = \pi r^2$.

Squares are found by slide rule by reading from scale D to scale A.

Square roots are found by reading from scale A to scale D.

In both cases the position of the decimal point must be found by estimation. In the case of square roots care has also to be taken to choose between 72 and 7·2 on the A scale when calculating (say) $\sqrt{720}$. The simplest method is to pair off the digits from the decimal point.

Sector: region bounded by two radii and an arc (top view of a slice of round cake).

Segment: region bounded by a chord and an arc (side view of slice of tomato).

Area of sector is $\dfrac{\theta}{360} \times$ area enclosed by circle ($\theta°$ is the angle of the sector).

Area of curved surface of *cylinder* (height *h*), $A = 2\pi rh$.

Volume of cylinder
$$V = \pi r^2 h.$$

6
NETWORKS

O what a tangled web we weave!
WALTER SCOTT, *Marmion*

1. ROUTE MATRICES

In the chapter on topology in Book 2 we saw how the 'routes' on a network can be represented by a matrix.

The matrix

$$\begin{array}{c} \quad\quad\quad\quad \text{to} \\ \quad\quad A\;\; B\;\; C \\ \begin{array}{c} \\ \text{from} \end{array} \begin{array}{c} A \\ B \\ C \end{array} \begin{pmatrix} 0 & 1 & 0 \\ 1 & 0 & 2 \\ 0 & 2 & 0 \end{pmatrix} \end{array}$$

represents the network in Figure 1.

An entry of 1 or 2 in the matrix means that there are one or two routes between two points, or nodes. An entry of 0 means that there is no route between two points.

Fig. 1

The routes are shown as curved lines in the figure, since we are not concerned with the shortest route from *A* to *B*, say, but with the fact that there *is* a route from *A* to *B*.

There is, of course, no objection to drawing the routes as straight lines, but in cases where there are two routes, as, for example, from B to C, one will have to be curved.

A network can be *directed*. For example, in Figure 2 there is a route from A to B but not from B to A and so on.

The matrix is

$$\begin{array}{c} \\ \\ \text{from} \end{array} \begin{array}{c} \\ A \\ B \\ C \end{array} \begin{array}{c} \quad\;\; to \\ A\;\; B\;\; C \\ \begin{pmatrix} 0 & 1 & 0 \\ 0 & 0 & 2 \\ 0 & 1 & 0 \end{pmatrix}. \end{array}$$

Why does the leading diagonal, that is, the one from top left to bottom right, contain only 0s in both cases?

What symmetrical feature does the first matrix have that the second does not have? Why is this?

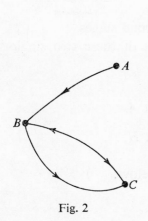

Fig. 2

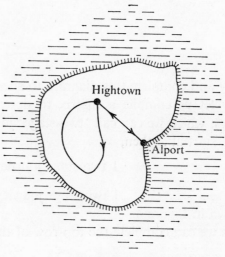

Fig. 3

(*a*) On an island there are two towns, Alport and Hightown. The island bus company runs a single bus which operates on two routes:

(i) from Alport to Hightown in either direction;

(ii) a 'circular' route from Hightown through some small villages and back to Hightown.

The route matrix, S, to describe these journeys, is

$$\begin{array}{c} \\ A \\ H \end{array} \begin{array}{c} A\;\; H \\ \begin{pmatrix} 0 & 1 \\ 1 & 1 \end{pmatrix}. \end{array}$$

Why does the leading diagonal of this matrix contain a number other than 0? Under what circumstances would this number have been a 2?

What is the position after the bus has completed two single-stage journeys? By a single-stage journey we mean either $A \to H$, or $H \to A$, or $H \to H$.

Suppose the bus starts at A, then it must first go to H, that is, $A \to H$.

For a second journey it could either go back to A or make the circular journey from H back to H. In Figure 4, $A \to H$ and $H \to A$ have been drawn as separate arcs.

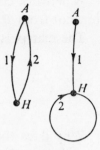

That is,

1st stage   2nd stage

$A \longrightarrow H \begin{array}{c} \nearrow A \\ \searrow H \end{array}$

Fig. 4

Now suppose the bus starts at Hightown.

For the first journey it can go either to Alport or back to Hightown, that is,

1st stage

$H \begin{array}{c} \nearrow A \\ \searrow H \end{array}$

Copy and complete this diagram to show possible second stages.

Now let us compile a matrix to describe the result of these two single-stage journeys, which we can call 'two-stage' journeys.

If we start at A then,

1 two-stage journey will finish at A

and   1 two-stage journey will finish at H,

as shown in Figure 4.

Thus we can complete the top row of the matrix as below:

$$\begin{array}{c} \\ A \\ H \end{array} \begin{array}{c} A\ H \\ \begin{pmatrix} 1 & 1 \\ & \end{pmatrix} \end{array}.$$

You should find that the complete matrix is:

$$\begin{array}{c} \\ \\ \text{from} \end{array} \begin{array}{c} \\ \\ A \\ H \end{array} \begin{array}{c} \text{to} \\ A\ H \\ \begin{pmatrix} 1 & 1 \\ 1 & 2 \end{pmatrix} \end{array}.$$

(*b*) Take the first matrix for 'one-stage' journeys and multiply it by itself; that is,

$$\begin{pmatrix} 0 & 1 \\ 1 & 1 \end{pmatrix} \begin{pmatrix} 0 & 1 \\ 1 & 1 \end{pmatrix}.$$

What do you notice?

If we let S denote the matrix

$$\begin{pmatrix} 0 & 1 \\ 1 & 1 \end{pmatrix} \quad \text{then we can write} \quad S^2 = \begin{pmatrix} 1 & 1 \\ 1 & 2 \end{pmatrix}.$$

Can you see why the two-stage matrix in (a) above is equal to S^2? Consider two-stage journeys starting and finishing at H. These are

$$H \rightarrow A \rightarrow H$$

and

$$H \rightarrow H \rightarrow H.$$

The 2 in S^2 indicates these two possibilities and is found by multiplying the numbers in the second row by those in the second column.

$$\begin{pmatrix} 1 & 1 \end{pmatrix} \quad \begin{pmatrix} 1 \\ 1 \end{pmatrix}$$

$$\begin{pmatrix} \text{Number of routes} \\ H \rightarrow A \end{pmatrix} \times \begin{pmatrix} \text{Number of routes} \\ A \rightarrow H \end{pmatrix} + \begin{pmatrix} \text{Number of routes} \\ H \rightarrow H \end{pmatrix} \times \begin{pmatrix} \text{Number of routes} \\ H \rightarrow H \end{pmatrix}$$

$$\begin{pmatrix} 1 & \times & 1 \end{pmatrix} \quad + \quad \begin{pmatrix} 1 & \times & 1 \end{pmatrix}$$

$$= 2.$$

(c) Calculate S^3 and find out what information it gives.

Summary

If a directed network is represented by a route matrix S which shows all possible *single*-stage journeys, then S^2 will show all possible *two*-stage journeys.

In Exercise A 3×3 and larger matrices are involved. These, as you will remember from Chapter 3, are combined in the same way as 2×2 matrices, for example,

$$\begin{pmatrix} \cdot & \cdot & \cdot \\ 1 & 0 & 1 \\ \cdot & \cdot & \cdot \end{pmatrix} \begin{pmatrix} \cdot & \cdot & 0 \\ \cdot & \cdot & 1 \\ \cdot & \cdot & 1 \end{pmatrix} = \begin{pmatrix} \cdot & \cdot & \cdot \\ \cdot & \cdot & 1 \\ \cdot & \cdot & \cdot \end{pmatrix},$$

since $(1 \times 0) + (0 \times 1) + (1 \times 1) = 1.$

The 2nd row of the first matrix and the 3rd column of the second are combined to give the number in the 2nd row and 3rd column of the product matrix.

Exercise A

1. Compile a route matrix for the network in Figure 5. By multiplying the matrix by itself, find the matrix which describes the two-stage journeys. List these by tracing them in the diagram, for example, $A \rightarrow C \rightarrow B$ and so on.

2. Repeat Question 1 for the network in Figure 6.

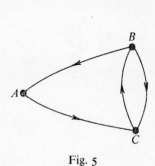

Fig. 5

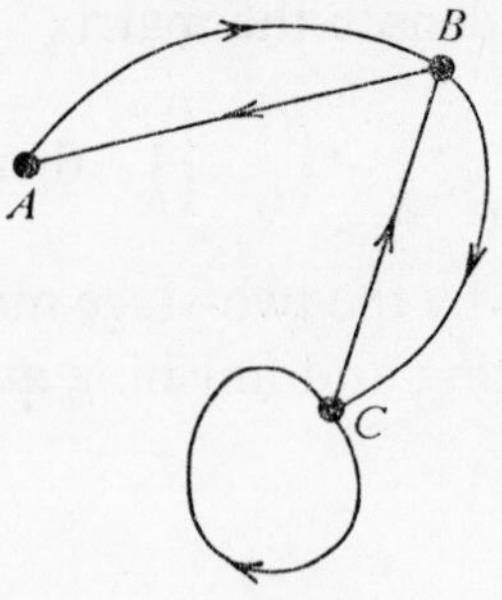

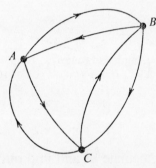

Fig. 6

3. Write down the route matrix S for the network in Figure 7. Find S^2 and explain why the first columns of S and S^2 contain only 0s.

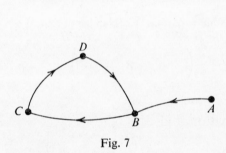

Fig. 7

Fig. 8

4. Compile a matrix S to describe the route system in Figure 8. Find S^2 and S^4. How many four-stage routes are there:
   (a) starting and finishing at the same point;
   (b) starting and finishing at different points?

5. Compute the matrices S^3 and S^4 for the matrix

$$S = \begin{pmatrix} 0 & 1 \\ 1 & 1 \end{pmatrix} \quad \text{in Section } 1\,(a).$$

Do you see a well-known sequence emerging in the numbers that occur in these matrices? Can you guess what S^5, S^6 and S^7 are?

6. If a matrix S describes a network in which there is no more than one route between any two points and no route from a point to itself (for example, the network in Figure 7 but not those in Figures 5, 6 and 8), explain why the leading diagonal of S^2 contains only 0s. Under what circumstances would this also be true for S^3?

2. DOMINANCE MATRICES

We can apply the ideas in Section 1 in an interesting, though not too serious manner to the results of games.

(*a*) Suppose four boys Alan, Brian, Charles and David play each other at table tennis. If Alan beats Brian then we represent the game like this:

Figure 9 shows a network indicating the results of all the matches.

The matrix, **T**

$$
\begin{array}{c}
 \\
A \\ B \\ C \\ D
\end{array}
\begin{array}{cccc}
A & B & C & D \\
\end{array}
\begin{pmatrix}
0 & 1 & 0 & 1 \\
0 & 0 & 1 & 1 \\
1 & 0 & 0 & 0 \\
0 & 0 & 1 & 0
\end{pmatrix},
$$

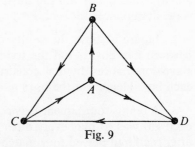

Fig. 9

describes this network.

If we add the numbers in any particular row, what does it tell us?

If we add the numbers in any particular column, what does it tell us?

Both Alan and Brian won 2 games and lost 1.

Can you say whether Alan or Brian is the better player?

Can you say whether Charles or David is the better player?

Now Alan beat Brian, and Brian beat Charles. We say that Alan has 'two-stage dominance' over Charles. Has Alan two-stage dominance over Charles in any other way? Finding the possible two-stage dominances is similar to finding two-stage journeys when dealing with route matrices.

Now

$$
\mathbf{T^2} =
\begin{pmatrix}
0 & 1 & 0 & 1 \\
0 & 0 & 1 & 1 \\
1 & 0 & 0 & 0 \\
0 & 0 & 1 & 0
\end{pmatrix}
\begin{pmatrix}
0 & 1 & 0 & 1 \\
0 & 0 & 1 & 1 \\
1 & 0 & 0 & 0 \\
0 & 0 & 1 & 0
\end{pmatrix}
$$

$$
=
\begin{pmatrix}
0 & 0 & 2 & 1 \\
1 & 0 & 1 & 0 \\
0 & 1 & 0 & 1 \\
1 & 0 & 0 & 0
\end{pmatrix}.
$$

This gives the matrix for two-stage dominances:

$$
\begin{array}{c}
 \\
A \\ B \\ C \\ D
\end{array}
\begin{array}{cccc}
A & B & C & D \\
\end{array}
\begin{pmatrix}
0 & 0 & 2 & 1 \\
1 & 0 & 1 & 0 \\
0 & 1 & 0 & 1 \\
1 & 0 & 0 & 0
\end{pmatrix}.
$$

By totalling the 1st row and then the 2nd row we see that Alan has 3 'two-stage dominances' over other players, whereas Brian has only 2.

Alan has, then, a total of 5 'one- and two-stage dominances' and Brian has 4.

On this basis Alan could claim to be the better player. Who could claim to be the better of Charles and David?

Exercise B

1. The four boys Alan, Brian, Charles and David played each other at snooker. Alan won all his matches, David won none. Brian beat Charles and David.

Draw a network to describe these results. Compile a matrix and square it. Find the total of one- and two-stage dominances for each boy.

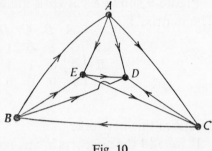

2. Figure 10 shows the results of ten matches played between five boys. Find the totals of one- and two-stage dominances, by first constructing a matrix, for each boy. Hence put the boys in an order of merit.

Fig. 10

3. A tennis tournament between six girls, in which each girl was to play every other girl, was rained off after each had played four matches.

> Anne beat Catherine;
> Betty beat Anne, Freda and Catherine;
> Catherine beat Freda and Daphne;
> Daphne beat Anne and Edna;
> Edna beat Anne, Betty and Freda;
> Freda beat Daphne.

Compile matrices showing one- and two-stage dominances and hence put the girls in order of merit.

4. If a dominance matrix T has a row or column of 0s, explain the meaning of this.

Show that T^2 will also have a corresponding row or column of 0s and explain this in terms of matches played.

5. Consider whether or not it would be helpful in Questions 1, 2 and 3 to consider three-stage dominances.

6. If a person has three-stage dominance over himself, then in the network there will be a triangular arrangement of arcs such as BE, EC and CB in Figure 10. In this example, B, E and C each have three-stage dominances over themselves.

Are there any other such triangular arrangements of paths in Figure 10?

Find, by examining different cases, the maximum number of triangular paths of this kind in tournaments involving (*a*) four players, (*b*) five players, in which each person plays every other person once, and no draws occur.

7. (*a*) An international football match is soon to take place between England and Brazil. During the previous months each country has had matches with some of four other countries which have also had some matches with each other.

The results were as follows:

> Brazil beat Germany and Mexico;
> England beat Luxembourg and Sweden;
> Germany and Mexico both beat Sweden;
> Luxembourg beat Germany.

Draw a network to represent these results and compile a matrix to describe the network.

By finding one-, two- and three-stage dominances forecast the result of the England–Brazil match. Consider the question of giving different emphasis to the various dominances.

(b) If, shortly before the England–Brazil match, Luxembourg played Sweden and won, discuss, by constructing new matrices for one-, two- and three-stage dominances, whether or not you would alter your forecast.

8. One difficulty so far has been that we have had no means of including draws in the calculations. This can be overcome in the following manner.

If A beats B, this can be shown by a double arrow (see Figure 11 (a)) and an entry 2 in the matrix in row A and column B.

If A draws with C, this can be shown by arrows in either direction (see Figure 11 (b)) and entries of 1 in the matrix in   (a) row A, column C,

and   (b) row C, column A.

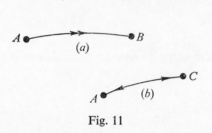

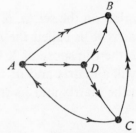

Fig. 11   Fig. 12

Alan, Brian, Charles and David all played each other in a chess tournament and the results are indicated in Figure 12.

Compile a matrix for this network and square it. Who should be awarded the prize?

3. RELATIONS AND MATRICES

The networks we have been using so far are similar to the diagrams drawn for relations in Book 2.

We can use matrices to represent and investigate relations.

(a) Figure 13 shows the relation

'is a parent of'

on a set of four members of a family {a, b, c, d}.

We can represent this relation by means of a matrix, **R**, in the following manner:

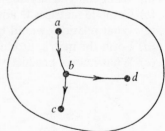

Fig. 13

$$\begin{array}{c} \\ a \\ b \\ c \\ d \end{array} \begin{array}{cccc} a & b & c & d \\ \begin{pmatrix} 0 & 1 & 0 & 0 \\ 0 & 0 & 1 & 1 \\ 0 & 0 & 0 & 0 \\ 0 & 0 & 0 & 0 \end{pmatrix} \end{array}.$$

The 1 in the first row indicates that a is a parent of b. Why is there not a 1 opposite b in the first column? Find the matrix $\mathbf{R}^2$. What relation does it represent? How does this link up with the idea of two-stage routes? What relation would $\mathbf{R}^3$ represent? Find it and explain why it has all zero entries.

(b) Suppose we form another matrix by interchanging the rows and columns of $\mathbf{R}$, that is, what was formerly the first row will now be the first column and so on.

We denote this matrix by $\mathbf{R}'$, that is,

$$
\begin{array}{c}
\begin{array}{cccc} a & b & c & d \end{array} \\
\begin{array}{c} a \\ b \\ c \\ d \end{array}
\begin{pmatrix}
0 & 0 & 0 & 0 \\
1 & 0 & 0 & 0 \\
0 & 1 & 0 & 0 \\
0 & 1 & 0 & 0
\end{pmatrix}.
\end{array}
$$

What relation on the set $\{a, b, c, d\}$ does this matrix represent?

The matrix $\mathbf{R}'$ is called the *transpose* of $\mathbf{R}$.

What is the transpose of $\mathbf{R}'$?

When will a matrix and its transpose be the same? Give an example of a relation for which the matrix and its transpose are the same.

Summary

A matrix may be used to represent a relation. If a is related to b, then a 1 is put in the position determined by row a and column b. Otherwise the entry is 0.

The transpose of a matrix is formed by interchanging rows and columns.

If a matrix represents a particular relation, then its transpose represents the inverse relation.

Exercise C

1. Figure 14(a) shows the relation D, 'is the daughter of', on a set of five people and Figure 14(b) shows the relation S, 'is the sister of', on the same set.
   (a) What can you say about the sex of the members of the set?
   (b) Compile matrices $\mathbf{D}$ and $\mathbf{S}$ to represent these relations.
   (c) What relations would be represented by $\mathbf{D}'$ and $\mathbf{S}'$?
   (d) Form the matrix product $\mathbf{DS}$. What relation does it represent?
   (e) What matrix product would give a matrix representing the relation 'is an aunt of'?

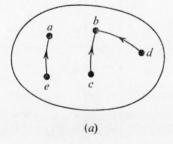

(a)

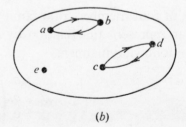

(b)

Fig. 14

2. Figure 15 shows the relation 'is on the left of' for three people sitting round a table. Compile a matrix **R** to represent this relation. Find **R²**. What relation does it represent?

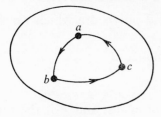

Fig. 15

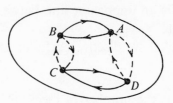

Fig. 16

3. The full arcs in Figure 16 represent the relation 'is the image after reflection in $y = 0$ of' and the dotted arcs the relation 'is the image after reflection in $x = 0$ of' on the set of four points $\{A, B, C, D\}$ of an (x, y) graph. Compile matrices **Y** and **X** to represent these relations. Work out the matrix products **XY** and **YX**, and explain why they are the same.

What relation does the resulting matrix represent?

4. Figure 17 shows the relation 'is perpendicular to' on the set of three lines $\{l, m. n\}$ where the lines lie in a plane. Compile a matrix **R** to describe this relation. Why does **R** = **R′**? Find **R²**. Discuss what relation it could be said to represent and explain the meaning of the various entries that occur in it.

5. Make up an example of your own in which the relation 'is the brother-in-law of' appears as the combination of two other relations.

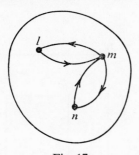

Fig. 17

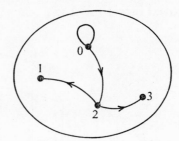

Fig. 18

6. Figure 18 shows the relation 'is twice' on the set $\{0, 1, 2, 3\}$ for clock arithmetic. Compile a matrix **D** to describe this relation. Draw another figure to show the relation 'is three times' on the same set, and compile a matrix **T** to describe this relation. Work out the products **DT** and **TD** and comment on your results.

7. If a matrix **R** represents the following relations on a set of numbers, what relation is represented by (i) **R²**, (ii) **R′** in each case:

    (a) 'is twice';   (b) 'is a factor of';   (c) 'is the square of'?

4. NETWORKS AND POLYHEDRA

There is an important link between networks and polyhedra which we shall now investigate.

In Book 1 we discovered Euler's relation for polyhedra

$$F+V = E+2,$$

where F is the number of faces, E is the number of edges, and V is the number of vertices.

In Book 2 we found a similar relation connecting the number of nodes (N), arcs (A) and regions (R) of a network, namely,

$$R+N = A+2.$$

4.1 Schlegel diagrams

In order to see the connection between these two relations we perform a topological transformation on a polyhedron which enables us to see all the faces at once. One face of the polyhedron is removed and the rest stretched outwards so as to be visible.

Figure 19 shows the principle applied to a cube. In Figure 19(a) the face $W'X'Y'Z'$ has been removed; in Figure 19(b) the stretching is taking place and it is complete in Figure 19(c). The infinite region surrounding the network in Figure 19(c) corresponds to the removed face $W'X'Y'Z'$.

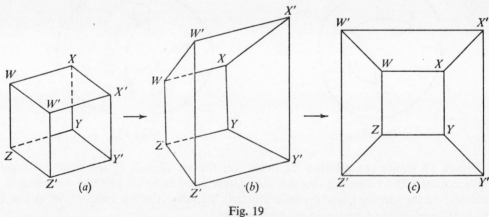

Fig. 19

Similarly Figure 20 shows the principle applied to a regular octahedron. It is first viewed from directly above one of its triangular faces.

These Schlegel diagrams, as they are called, demonstrate that faces, edges and vertices of polyhedra are equivalent to regions, arcs and nodes of networks.

98

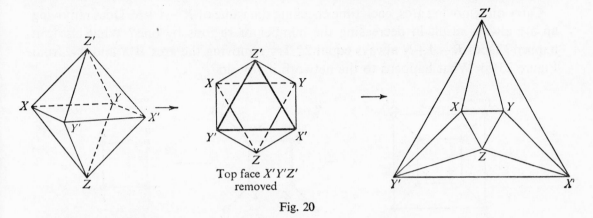

Fig. 20

4.2   Euler's relation

We can now try to show why this relation always holds.

We first rewrite the relation in the form

$$R - A + N = 2.$$

In the Schlegel diagram for the cube (see Figure 21), the face $W'X'Y'Z'$ of the cube has been removed and corresponds to the region surrounding the network. The number of vertices and edges is the same for the cube and the Schlegel diagram. Thus we have,

Faces or regions	6
Edges or arcs	12
Vertices or nodes	8

and

$$F - E + V = 2,$$

$$R - A + N = 2.$$

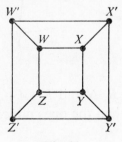

Fig. 21

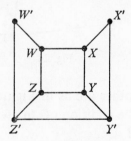

Fig. 22

(a) Suppose we remove the arc $W'X'$, as in Figure 22. We have *one* arc less. Is the number of regions altered? Is the number of nodes altered? Is $R - A + N$ still equal to 2? Remove another arc. What happens? Figure 23(b) shows all the outer arcs removed. (W', X', Y', Z' are now 1-nodes.)

Carry on removing arcs, each time checking the value of $R-A+N$. Does removing an arc always result in decreasing the number of regions by one? What else can happen? Does $R-A+N$ always equal 2? Try removing the arcs WX and YZ from Figure 23(b). What happens to the network if you do?

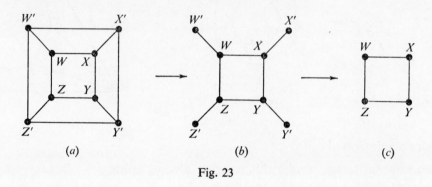

(a)   (b)   (c)

Fig. 23

Eventually we could reduce the network to the single arc WX with nodes W and X. For this simplest of networks

$$R = 1, \quad A = 1 \quad \text{and} \quad N = 2$$

giving $$R-A+N = 2.$$

Clearly we could reduce any network in this way to a single arc.

(b) Suppose we look at the problem the other way round by building up a network, starting with a single arc, XY. Adding a second arc, as in Figure 24, A increases by one. What happens to R, N and $R-A+N$? (Note again that Z is a vertex, or 1-node.)

Fig. 24   Fig. 25

Add another arc as in Figure 25. What happens to R, N and $R-A+N$?

Could the addition of an arc have any effect other than the ones noticed in these two cases?

(c) Find $R-A+N$ for each of the networks in Figure 26. (Figure 26(b) consists of both the triangles.)

Why did you not get 2 for Figure 26(b)? What would you have to add to the figure in order to make $R-A+N$ equal to 2? Figure 26(a) is a *connected* network. Figure 26(b) is not *connected*.

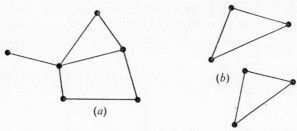

Fig. 26

Summary

Euler's relation for a polyhedron can be considered as equivalent to Euler's relation for a plane network. This is seen by drawing the Schlegel diagram, the region surrounding the diagram corresponding to one face of the polyhedron.

We have
$$F - E + V = 2,$$

or
$$R - A + N = 2.$$

The removal or addition of an arc, in such a way that the network remains connected, does not alter the value of $R - A + N$. In this way we have established that Euler's relation holds for all networks.

It is important that the network is *connected* that is, there is a continuous path, from any one vertex to another.

Exercise D

1. Find R, A, N and $R - A + N$ for the networks in Figure 27.

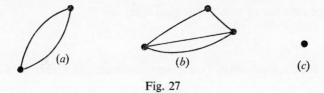

Fig. 27

2. A vertex or 2-node can be inserted at any point on a network (see Figure 28).

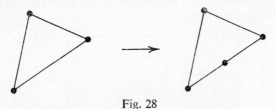

Fig. 28

Why does $R - A + N$ remain unaltered?

3. Draw the Schlegel diagram for a tetrahedron. Can you start with a triangle and build up the network for a tetrahedron by adding nodes? If not what else needs to be done?

4. For the purposes of proving Euler's relation for a polyhedron, why have we to use a Schlegel diagram and not a net? For example, why (a) rather than (b) in Figure 29?

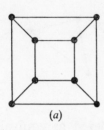

(a)

(b)

Fig. 29

5. Draw four examples of connected networks such that all the vertices are 3-nodes, that is, exactly 3 arcs meet at each vertex. Figure 30 shows an example.

Make a table showing the values of R, A and N for each of the four networks. Add an extra column showing values of $R-2$. Can you spot relations connecting (a) R and A, (b) R and N?

6. The 3-node network in Figure 30 has 8 3-nodes. We could say that its *node-sum* is 24. Can you explain why the node sum is also twice the number of arcs? Would this be true for any network?

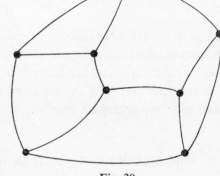

Fig. 30

7. The network in Figure 30 has 2 regions with 3 arcs, 2 regions with 4 arcs, and 2 regions with 5 arcs (one of these is the outside region).

If a is the average number of arcs per region then

$$a = \frac{(2 \times 3) + (2 \times 4) + (2 \times 5)}{6} = 4.$$

Find a for each of the four networks you have constructed in Question 5 and check that

$$3N = 2A = aR$$

in each case. Can you explain why this result is true for all 3-node networks?

8. Using a (as found in Question 7) and R for each of the four networks in Question 5, copy and complete the following table.

R				
$\dfrac{12}{R}$				
a				

Can you spot a relation connecting a and $12/R$?

D9. (a) Why must a 3-node network have at least one region with less than six arcs?
(b) Can you draw a network of hexagons (with curved edges) on a sphere?

102

5. COLOURING POLYHEDRA

When dealing with the colouring of regions in Book 2, we met the 'four-colour theorem', that is, 'no more than four colours are necessary in order to colour a map in such a way that no two regions sharing a common boundary are the same colour'.

This has never been proved, though no one has yet drawn a map requiring five colours. However, it has been proved that a map requiring five colours is bound to have at least 32 regions.

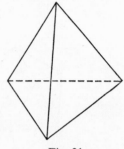

Fig. 31

(*a*) Consider colouring a tetrahedron in such a way that no two faces with an edge in common are the same colour. Can any two faces be the same colour? How many colours will be needed? If four colours were used, how many different tetrahedra of the same shape could be coloured so that you could distinguish each one from the others? If the tetrahedra were regular, would your answer to the previous question be different? If so, what would be the number in this case?

In the following exercise we shall make use of the Schlegel diagrams mentioned in the last section.

An alternative method to colouring regions, although less attractive, is to number them. No two regions with the same number must have an arc in common. Do not forget to colour or number the outside region corresponding to the removed face.

Exercise E

1. Six colours could be used to colour a cube. What is the least number of colours that could be used if adjacent faces have to be different colours? Could you colour two cubes, using the same colours, in this way so that they can be distinguished from each other.

Sketch an arrangement of colours, using as few as possible, on a Schlegel diagram.

2. Draw two different Schlegel diagrams for a square-based pyramid:
(*a*) by first removing the square base;
(*b*) by first removing a triangular face.
What is the minimum number of colours required for this solid?

3. Draw a Schlegel diagram for a triangular prism and show, by colouring it, that four colours are necessary for this solid.

4. Draw a Schlegel diagram for the regular octahedron (see Figure 20) and hence show that only two colours are necessary to colour an octahedron.

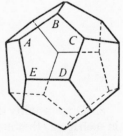

Fig. 32

5. Figure 32 shows a regular dodecahedron with the face *ABCDE* removed. Draw a Schlegel diagram for this solid. On this diagram devise a colouring plan using only four colours.

Make a model of a dodecahedron and colour it according to your plan. Compare your model with a neighbour who has used the same four colours and try to decide whether your arrangements of colours are the same or not.

6.

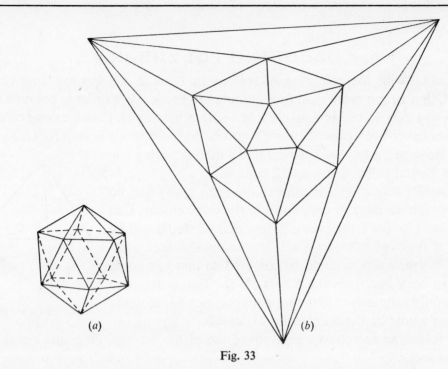

(a)   (b)

Fig. 33

Figure 33 shows a regular icosahedron and the corresponding Schlegel diagram. There are very many different ways of colouring an icosahedron with three colours. Sketch a few of them.

7. Draw three regions on a plane as in Figure 34 such that each borders on the other two. Can you add a fourth region such that it borders on the three already drawn but is not a part of any of them? If not, draw another diagram containing 3 regions such that each borders on the other two, and again try to add a fourth region bordering on the three.

If you succeed, try to add a fifth region bordering on each of the four already drawn.

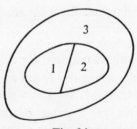

Fig. 34

8. Draw a fairly complicated network and put a small coloured ring around each node in such a way that no two adjacent nodes (that is, ones joined by an arc) are the same colour. Try to use as few colours as possible. Alternatively the nodes can be numbered in such a way that no two adjacent nodes have the same number.

6. INCIDENCE MATRICES

We shall now investigate another way of compiling matrices to describe networks;
a way which has important applications in electrical circuit theory.

The matrix **R**,

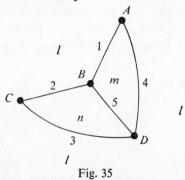

Fig. 35

$$\text{nodes}\;\; \begin{array}{c} A \\ B \\ C \\ D \end{array} \overset{\overset{\text{arcs}}{1\;\;2\;\;3\;\;4\;\;5}}{\begin{pmatrix} 1 & 0 & 0 & 1 & 0 \\ 1 & 1 & 0 & 0 & 1 \\ 0 & 1 & 1 & 0 & 0 \\ 0 & 0 & 1 & 1 & 1 \end{pmatrix}},$$

describes the network in Figure 35 in the following
way: the 1 in the first row and first column indicates
that node A is 'incident' on arc 1; A is also on arc 4
but not on arcs 2, 3 or 5.

(*a*) We can also have incidence matrices which show the relationship between arcs
and regions and between nodes and regions.

Copy and complete these two incidence matrices, for the network in Figure 35.

$$\text{arcs}\;\; \begin{array}{c} 1 \\ 2 \\ 3 \\ 4 \\ 5 \end{array} \overset{\overset{\text{regions}}{l\;\;m\;\;n}}{\begin{pmatrix} & & 0 \\ & & 1 \\ & & 1 \\ & & 0 \\ & & 1 \end{pmatrix}}$$

S

$$\text{nodes}\;\; \begin{array}{c} A \\ B \\ C \\ D \end{array} \overset{\overset{\text{regions}}{l\;\;m\;\;n}}{\begin{pmatrix} & & \\ & & \\ 1 & 0 & 1 \\ & & \end{pmatrix}}.$$

T

Some entries are shown to help you. For example,

in **S**, region n has arcs 2, 3 and 5 on its boundary;

in **T**, node C is on the boundary of regions l and n.

(*b*) Now work out the matrix product **RS**. The result of combining, for example,
the second row of **R** with the third column of **S** is shown below.

$$\text{2nd row}\; \begin{pmatrix} 1 & 1 & 0 & 0 & 1 \\ \cdot & \cdot & \cdot & \cdot & \cdot \\ \cdot & \cdot & \cdot & \cdot & \cdot \end{pmatrix} \begin{pmatrix} \cdot & \cdot & 0 \\ \cdot & \cdot & 1 \\ \cdot & \cdot & 1 \\ \cdot & \cdot & 0 \\ \cdot & \cdot & 1 \end{pmatrix} = \text{2nd row}\; \begin{pmatrix} \cdot & \cdot & \cdot \\ \cdot & \cdot & 2 \\ \cdot & \cdot & \cdot \end{pmatrix},$$

R   **S**   **RS**

3rd column   3rd column

$$(1 \times 0)+(1 \times 1)+(0 \times 1)+(0 \times 0)+(1 \times 1) = 2.$$

Carefully compare the matrix you obtain with the matrix **T** in (*a*). What do you notice?

Try to explain why the multiplication produces the result you have observed.

Would it be correct to say **RS** = 2**T**?

(*c*) When dealing with route matrices we multiplied a matrix by itself. However, in this case the matrix **R** in (*a*) above has four rows and five columns, that is, it is a 4×5 matrix. Why is it then not possible to find $\mathbf{R}^2$? We can get over this difficulty by forming the transpose **R′** of **R** by interchanging rows and columns. That is, **R′** is

$$
\begin{array}{c}
 \\
1 \\
2 \\
3 \\
4 \\
5
\end{array}
\begin{array}{cccc}
A & B & C & D \\
\end{array}
\left(
\begin{array}{cccc}
1 & 1 & 0 & 0 \\
0 & 1 & 1 & 0 \\
0 & 0 & 1 & 1 \\
1 & 0 & 0 & 1 \\
0 & 1 & 0 & 1
\end{array}
\right).
$$

R′ is a 5×4 matrix and is compatible for multiplication with **R**.

Find the matrix **RR′**.

(*d*) Now compile a route matrix **M** for the network in Figure 35.

For example,

$$
\begin{array}{c}
A \\
B \\
C \\
D
\end{array}
\begin{array}{cccc}
A & B & C & D
\end{array}
\left(

\right).
$$

Compare this matrix with **RR′**. What features do they have in common? Why does **RR′** produce these features? Explain the significance of the numbers on the leading diagonal of **M**.

Summary

For a given network, three incidence matrices can be compiled. If **R**, **S** and **T** stand for

$$
\mathbf{R} \quad
\begin{array}{c}
\text{arcs} \\
\text{nodes}
\end{array}
\left(

\right)
\qquad
\mathbf{S} \quad
\begin{array}{c}
\text{regions} \\
\text{arcs}
\end{array}
\left(

\right)
\qquad
\mathbf{T} \quad
\begin{array}{c}
\text{regions} \\
\text{nodes}
\end{array}
\left(

\right)
$$

and if the route matrix **M** is

$$
\begin{array}{c}
\text{nodes} \\
\text{nodes}
\end{array}
\left(

\right),
$$

then (*a*) **RS** = 2**T**,

(*b*) **RR′** differs from **M** only in the leading diagonal.

106

Exercise F

1. Draw networks described by the following incidence matrices:

(a)   arcs   (b)   arcs

nodes $\begin{pmatrix} 1 & 1 \\ 1 & 1 \end{pmatrix}$;   nodes $\begin{pmatrix} 1 & 0 & 0 & 1 & 1 \\ 1 & 1 & 1 & 1 & 0 \\ 0 & 1 & 1 & 0 & 1 \end{pmatrix}$;

(c)   regions   (d)   regions

arcs $\begin{pmatrix} 1 & 1 \\ 1 & 1 \\ 1 & 1 \end{pmatrix}$;   nodes $\begin{pmatrix} 1 & 1 & 1 & 0 \\ 1 & 1 & 1 & 1 \\ 0 & 1 & 0 & 1 \end{pmatrix}$.

2. Find **R**, **S** and **T** for the network in Figure 36 and verify that **RS** = 2**T**.

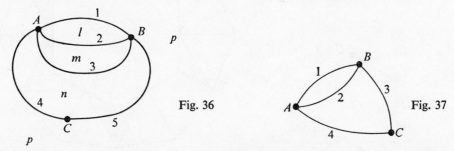

Fig. 36   Fig. 37

3. (a) Find the product **R'R** for the network in Figure 35. Is it the same as **RR'**?

(b) Compile a matrix to describe the network as follows:

$$
\begin{array}{c}
\text{arcs} \\
\begin{array}{cccccc}
 & 1 & 2 & 3 & 4 & 5 \\
\end{array} \\
\text{arcs} \begin{array}{c} 1 \\ 2 \\ 3 \\ 4 \\ 5 \end{array}
\begin{pmatrix}
 & & & & \\
 & & & & \\
 & 1 & & & \\
 & & & & \\
 & & & &
\end{pmatrix}.
\end{array}
$$

The '1' shown indicates that arcs 3 and 2 have *one* node in common.
Compare this matrix with **R'R**.

4. Repeat Question 3 for the network in Figure 37. What is the meaning of the numbers on the leading diagonal of **R'R**?

5. (a) Find **TT'** for the network in Figure 35.

(b) Compile a matrix as follows:

$$
\begin{array}{c}
\text{nodes} \\
\begin{array}{ccccc}
 & A & B & C & D \\
\end{array} \\
\text{nodes} \begin{array}{c} A \\ B \\ C \\ D \end{array}
\begin{pmatrix}
2 & & & \\
 & & & \\
 & & & \\
 & & &
\end{pmatrix}.
\end{array}
$$

An entry in this matrix means that two nodes are on the boundary of the same region, for example, *A* and *B* are both on the boundary of regions *l* and *m*. What features does this matrix have in common with (i) **TT'**, (ii) **RR'**?

107   8-2

6. Find S'S and T'T for the network in Figure 35.

(*a*) Explain the meaning of the common leading diagonal.

(*b*) Explain the meaning of the other numbers in each matrix.

7. (*a*) Find **R**, **RR'** and the route matrix **M** for the network in Figure 38. Check that if the numbers in the leading diagonal of **RR'** are replaced by 0s then we get **M**.

(*b*) Find out whether **RS = 2T** for this network. Discuss how you might overcome any difficulties that arise.

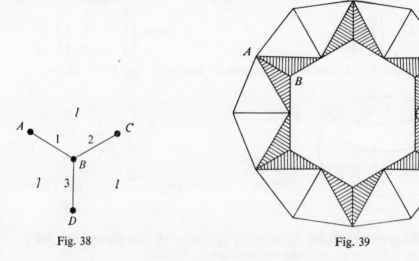

Fig. 38   Fig. 39

Exercise G

Miscellaneous

1. How many colours are needed if the rotatable ring of 12 tetrahedra in Figure 39 is to be painted so that adjacent faces are of a different colour?

2. A Hamiltonian path (named after the famous Irish mathematician, Sir William Hamilton who proposed this problem in 1859) is a continuous path along the edges of a polyhedron or network which passes through each vertex once only and returns to the starting point. (It is not necessary to traverse all the arcs.) On Schlegel diagrams indicate, by arrows, Hamiltonian paths for: (*a*) a cube; (*b*) an octahedron; (*c*) a dodecahedron. Can you draw a network containing no 1-nodes on which a Hamiltonian path cannot be found?

3. Take a long rectangular strip of paper (see Figure 40). Join the ends together by giving one end a half-turn twist, so that *A* is joined to *A'* and *B* to *B'*. The result is called a Moebius band. This is a curious object as it has only one edge and only one side! We could also make other loops or bands by giving more than one twist before joining the ends together.

Fig. 40

Make loops as indicated in the following table and cut them as instructed. $\frac{1}{2}$ means cut along the centre line, $\frac{1}{3}$ means cut along a line one-third of the width from an edge all the way round.

Copy and complete the table.

Number of twists	Number		Cut	Result of cut	
	Edges	Sides		Number of loops	Other observations
1			$\frac{1}{2}$		
1			$\frac{1}{3}$		
2			$\frac{1}{2}$		
2			$\frac{1}{3}$		
3			$\frac{1}{2}$		
3			$\frac{1}{3}$		

4. Figure 41 represents a road network (not to scale) with the numbers indicating distances in kilometres.

Find the shortest route from A to B.

A salesman lives at A. He has to visit all the towns (nodes) at least once and return to A. Find the shortest distance in which he can do this.

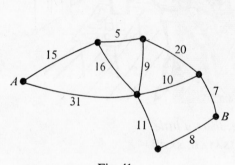

Fig. 41

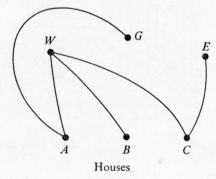

Houses

Fig. 42

5. There is a famous topological problem about supplying water, gas and electricity to three houses. It is required that no pipes or wires must cross each other.

Figure 42 shows the situation with some of the joins made. Let us suppose we can complete the network. Why would it be a 3-node network? There would be 6 nodes and 9 arcs. Use Euler's relation to determine the number of regions. Explain why no region could be bounded by only 3 arcs. In Question 8 of Exercise D we found the relation

$$a = 6 - 12/R.$$

Using the value of R you have found, determine a. To what conclusion does this lead you?

7

THREE-DIMENSIONAL GEOMETRY

Line upon line—here a little, there a little.

ISAIAH, XXVIII

1. POINTS, LINES AND PLANES

A *point* marks a particular position, and therefore has no size. (Why not?) As it has neither length nor breadth nor thickness, we say that it has no dimensions.

A *line*, which is a set of points, is understood

(*a*) to be 'straight', and

(*b*) to extend indefinitely in both directions: it does not have 'ends'.

A line is unbounded

A ray is bounded at one end

A segment is bounded at both ends

Fig. 1

Strictly speaking the term *line segment* should be used for part of a line with two definite ends, and the term *half-line* (or *ray*) for part of a line with one definite end and extending without limit in one direction. However, the word 'line' is sometimes loosely used in referring to a segment or half-line.

As a line has length but no breadth or thickness we say it is one-dimensional.

110

With any point of the line as origin, *one* coordinate will specify the position of any other point of the line.

A *plane* (again a set of points) is understood

(*a*) to be 'flat', and

(*b*) to extend indefinitely in all directions.

The terms *half-plane* and *region* can be used to refer to some part of a plane. A half-plane is bounded by one straight line whereas a region is bounded by any number of lines or curves. A region may be bounded all the way round, but it does not have to be.

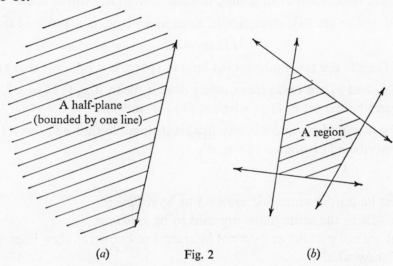

A half-plane
(bounded by one line)

A region

(*a*)   Fig. 2   (*b*)

A plane has length and breadth but no thickness. For this reason, and because two coordinates are needed to specify the position of a point with respect to any origin (fixed point) on the plane, it is said to be two-dimensional.

For discussion

1. Can you draw a point on paper with a pencil?

2. Can you draw a line?

3. 'A circle is one-dimensional'. True or false?

4. 'A plane is a set of lines.' True or false?

5. How many dimensions has the surface of a sphere?

6. Give the number of members in each of the following sets. In some cases there may be more than one answer; give them all:

(*a*) {lines containing *A*} if *A* is any point;

(*b*) {lines containing both *A* and *B*} if *A* and *B* are any two different points;

(*c*) {lines containing all of *A*, *B*, and *C*} if *A*, *B* and *C* are any three different points;

(*d*) {planes containing *A*} if *A* is any point;

(*e*) {planes containing *A* and *B*} if *A* and *B* are any two different points;

(*f*) {planes containing *A*, *B* and *C*} if *A*, *B* and *C* are any three different points;

(*g*) {planes containing *A*, *B*, *C* and *D*} if *A*, *B*, *C* and *D* are any four different points;

(*h*) {planes containing *l*} if *l* is any line;

(*i*) {planes containing *l* and *m*} if *l* and *m* are any two parallel lines;

(*j*) {planes containing *l* and *m*} if *l* and *m* are any two intersecting lines;

(*k*) {planes containing *l* and *m*} if *l* and *m* are two non-parallel non-intersecting lines.

7. If a plane contains part of a line, does it contain the whole line?

8. (*a*) If *l* and *m* are two non-parallel lines in a plane, is it possible that

$$l \cap m = \emptyset?$$

(*b*) If *l* and *m* are two non-parallel lines in space, is it possible that $l \cap m = \emptyset$?

9. (*a*) If π_1 and π_2 are two planes, what does it mean if $\pi_1 \cap \pi_2 = \emptyset$?

(*b*) Describe the set $\pi_1 \cap \pi_2$ when $\pi_1 \cap \pi_2 \neq \emptyset$.

10. (*a*) If π is any plane and *l* is any line, is it possible that $\pi \cap l = \emptyset$?

(*b*) Describe $\pi \cap l$ when $\pi \cap l \neq \emptyset$.

Definitions

Points that lie on the same line are said to be *collinear*.

Points that lie in the same plane are said to be *coplanar*.

Lines that are not parallel and do not intersect are known as *skew* lines. (Hence the expression 'skew-whiff'.)

You will find the answers to many of the questions you have just been discussing in the table below. The third column of the table should help you to relate these new ideas to everyday experience.

Elements	Number of planes containing elements of first column	Examples
One point	∞	Adjustable car mirror (pivoted at a single point)
Two points	∞	Door on two hinges
Three collinear points	∞	Door on three hinges
Three non-collinear points	1	Three-legged stool on floor (will not wobble)
Four non-collinear points	0 or 1	Four-legged stool (may wobble, may not)
One line	∞	Door (line of hinges)
One line, one point not on the line	1	Door and door-stop; lid of grand piano supported at a single point
Two parallel lines	1	Railway lines
Two intersecting lines	1	Bottom edges of open Christmas card (forming V shape); scissors
Two skew lines	0	Power line crossing over telephone line

Note that '∞' denotes 'an infinity'. This is not any particular number. It means that, however many elements (points, lines, planes) are considered, more could be added.

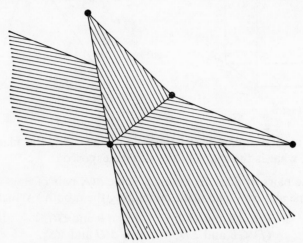

Fig. 3. Three non-collinear points determine a plane;
but four points are *not* necessarily coplanar.

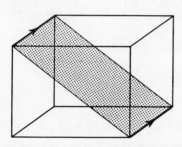

Fig. 4. Two parallel lines determine a plane.

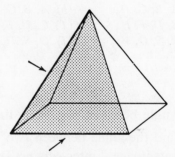

Fig. 5. Two intersecting lines determine a plane.

Figures 3, 4 and 5 illustrate some of the facts tabulated above. Note carefully that two lines in space must be *either* parallel *or* intersecting *or* skew, and that, whereas a pair of parallel or intersecting lines determines a plane, a pair of skew lines does not.

Exercise A

Framework models of a cube and square-based pyramid are required. The questions refer to the cube and pyramid lettered as in Figures 6 and 7. In Figure 7, V is vertically above the mid-point O of the square base ABCD.

1. For a *solid* cube, do you come out at any other vertex if you saw through *FH* and come out at *D*? (Assume that the saw makes a plane cut.)

2. Describe the smaller of the two solids you obtain if you saw through *EG* and come out at *B*. What special shape is triangle *EGB*?

113

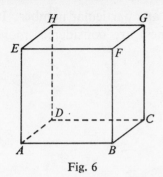

Fig. 6

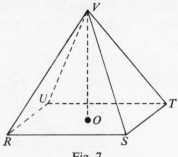

Fig. 7

3. If the top of a solid square-based pyramid is sawn off, the plane of the cut being parallel to the base, what is the shape of the surface exposed?

4. Which of these pairs of lines determine a plane? (A pair of lines is said to determine a plane if there is one and only one plane containing them both.) Which pairs are skew?

(a) *AB* and *CD*;	(b) *AB* and *HG*;	(c) *AB* and *GC*;	(d) *EB* and *HC*;
(e) *GF* and *DC*;	(f) *GB* and *ED*;	(g) *VU* and *VS*;	(h) *VS* and *RS*;
(i) *VU* and *TS*;	(j) *RT* and *VO*.		

5. Which of these sets of four points determine a plane?

(a) *A, B, C, D*;	(b) *A, B, G, H*;	(c) *A, B, G, C*;	(d) *D, E, F, G*;
(e) *B, D, F, H*;	(f) *C, D, F, H*;	(g) *R, S, T, U*;	(h) *R, S, T, V*;
(i) *R, S, O, V*;	(j) *O, S, U, V*.		

2. ANGLES

2.1 Angle between two skew lines in space

To find the angle between two skew lines l and m, translate one of them, l say, so that its image l' intersects m. Then the angle between l and m is defined to be the angle between l' and m.

For example, the angle between *AB* and *CG* (in Figure 8) is 90°. (Imagine *AB* to be translated until it coincides with *DC*; and note that, since the figure represents a cube, $\angle DCG = 90°$.)

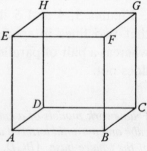

Fig. 8

What is the angle between *FH* and *AD*? Does it make any difference which of the two lines you translate; that is, if, in the definition, we had translated m so that m' intersected l, would the angle between m' and l equal that between m and l'?

What is the angle between *AB* and *FG*? What happens when you translate *AB* so that it meets *DC*? What can you say about the angle between these two lines? What can you say about the set of lines {*AB, DC, EF, HG*}?

114

2.2   Angle between line and a plane

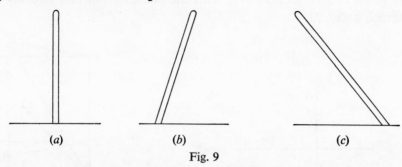

(a)   (b)   (c)

Fig. 9

Each of the three drawings in Figure 9 represents a thin pole stuck into the ground. See if you agree with these statements:

1.   Figure 9(a) shows an upright pole.
2.   Figure 9(b) shows a pole making an angle of about 72° with the ground.
3.   Figure 9(c) shows a pole making an angle of about 50° with the ground.

If you think these statements *are* true, perhaps you have been deceived. The drawings could all be of the same pole. The apparent angle between pole and ground depends on where you look from. So if we want only one answer to the question 'What is the angle between pole and ground?', we shall have to decide which of the many possible angles we really mean.

Suppose that the sun is shining from directly above the pole in question. Then the shadow of the pole is called its *projection* onto the plane of the ground, and we agree that the angle between the pole and its projection is to be called *the* angle between the pole and the ground. If the pole were allowed to fall, this is the angle through which it would turn.

What would be the projection onto the ground of a vertical pole? What can you say about any angle between the ground and such a pole?

Definitions

The angle between a line and a plane is the angle between the line and its projection onto the plane.

A line is perpendicular to a plane if the projection of the line onto the plane is a single point.

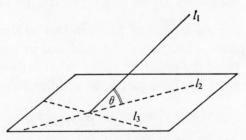

Fig. 10. Angle between line and plane.

In Figure 10, l_2 is the projection of l_1 onto the plane and so the angle between l_1 and the plane is the angle marked θ. How does θ compare in size with the angle between l_1 and l_3, where l_3 is *any* other line of the plane passing through the point of intersection of l_1 with the plane?

115

In Figure 11, l_4 is perpendicular to the plane. l_5 is *any* line of the plane passing through the point of intersection of l_4 with the plane. What can you say about the angle between l_4 and l_5?

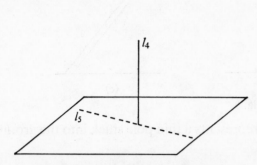

Fig. 11. Line perpendicular to plane.

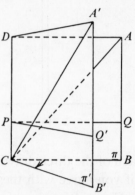

Fig. 12

Figure 12 illustrates a Christmas card which has been opened out so that it will stand up. If the card was closed to begin with, the plane π' had to be turned through a certain angle until it occupied the position shown. (Name the axis of rotation.) This angle, through which π' was turned, is defined to be *the* angle between π and π'. It is equal to $\angle BCB'$.

Is $\angle BCB'$ the same as $\angle ADA'$? Is it the same as $\angle ACA'$? What angles do BC and $B'C$ make with CD? Name an angle to which $\angle BDB'$ is equal.

P is any point between C and D. How does $\angle BPB'$ compare in size with $\angle BCB'$? If QP and $Q'P$ are both perpendicular to CD, how does $\angle QPQ'$ compare in size with $\angle BCB'$?

Definition

The angle between two planes is defined to be the angle between any pair of lines, one in each plane, which meet on and are at right-angles to the line of intersection of the planes. (Look at the printed lines on a partly opened exercise book.)

Fold a piece of paper in two so that it stands up like a Christmas card. Unfold, draw a line across the fold and at right-angles to it, and stand the paper up again. What is the connection between what you have just done and the definition above?

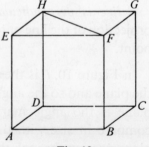

Fig. 13

Exercise B

Questions 1–6 refer to the cube shown in Figure 13.

1. What are the angles in degrees between:

    (a) AB and BE;   (b) DC and BE;   (c) FC and EA;

    (d) FG and AD;   (e) FG and DH?

2. How many lines of the cubical framework are perpendicular to *AD*?

3. Name eight lines which make an angle of 45° with *AC*.

4. Name the projection of:

(*a*) *FD* onto *ABCD*;   (*b*) *FD* onto *BCGF*;   (*c*) *EC* onto *CDHG*;
(*d*) *AC* onto *EFGH*;   (*e*) *EA* onto *ABCD*.

5. The angle between *FD* and the plane *BCGF* is ∠*DFC*.
State the angles between:

(*a*) *FD* and *EAHD*;   (*b*) *BH* and *EADH*;   (*c*) *FC* and *ABCD*.

Give in degrees the angles between:

(*d*) *GC* and *ABCD*;   (*e*) *GH* and *ABCD*.

6. By calling any new point required *X*, state the projection of

(*a*) *EF* onto *ACGE*;   (*b*) *AF* onto *AEGC*.

7. Referring to the square-based pyramid illustrated in Figure 14, where *VO* is perpendicular to the base:

(*a*) state the projection of

(i) *RV* onto *RSTU*;   (ii) *RV* onto *VSU*;

(*b*) state the line of intersection of the planes *RTV* and *USV*;
(*c*) state in degrees the angle between the planes *RSTU* and *RTV*;
(*d*) state in letters the angle between the planes *RSTU* and *RSV*.

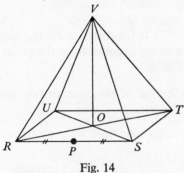

Fig. 14

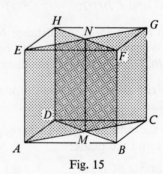

Fig. 15

Questions 8–10 refer to the cube shown in Figure 15.

8. State the lines of intersection of the planes:

(*a*) *ABCD* and *BCGF*;   (*b*) *ABCD* and *BCHE*;   (*c*) *ABCD* and *BDHF*;
(*d*) *BDHF* and *ACGE*;   (*e*) *ADHE* and *EFGH*.

9. Give in each case the angle in degrees between the pairs of planes in Question 8.

10. Would it be true to say that the angle between the planes:

(*a*) *ADGF* and *EFGH* is ∠*AFE*;   (*b*) *EGB* and *EFGH* is ∠*BNF*;
(*c*) *ABGH* and *ABCD* is ∠*GBD*;   (*d*) *CDEF* and *ABGH* is 90°;
(*e*) *ABCD* and *ACGE* is 45°?

117

11. (Refer to Figure 16.) Name an angle in each case which defines the angle between the following pairs of planes:

(a) *ABCD* and *ABGH*;   (b) *ABGH* and *CDHG*;   (c) *BDHF* and *ADHE*;
(d) *ADGF* and *EFGH*;   (e) *ADGF* and *BCGF*.

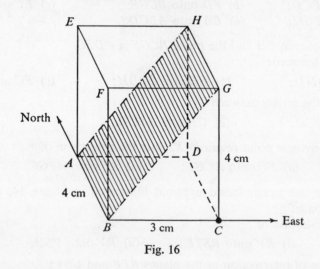

Fig. 16

12. (Refer to Figure 16.) Name in each case the angle between the line and the plane:

(a) *BG* and *ABCD*;   (b) *DF* and *ABCD*;   (c) *FG* and *ABGH*;
(d) *AG* and *CDHG*;   (e) *BH* and *ABFE*.

13. In Figure 15, is the distance *NM* the same as *NB*? Is the distance *FB* the same as *FM* or *FD*? What do you think would be sensible to take as *the* distance from the point *N* to the plane *ABCD*? What about *the* distance from *F* to *ABCD*?

14. Write down what you think should be the definition of *the* distance between a point and a plane.

15. If the cube in Figure 15 has edges of length 4 cm, give the distance in each case between the point and the plane:

(a) *F* and *ABCD*;   (b) *N* and *ABCD*;   (c) *F* and *CDHG*;
(d) *N* and *CDHG*;   (e) *E* and *BDHF*.

Exercise C

Miscellaneous

1. *ABCDV* is a pyramid. *ABCD*, an 8 cm square, is its base; and *V* is 6 cm vertically above *A*.
(a) Draw an oblique projection of the pyramid.
(b) Calculate the lengths of the line segments: (i) *BV*; (ii) *CV*; (iii) *DV*.
(c) Construct a model of the pyramid from straws.
(d) Calculate the angles between: (i) *BV* and the base; (ii) *CV* and the base; (iii) *BV* and *CV*.

2. In Figure 16 $ABCDEFGH$ is a cuboid with $ABCD$ horizontal, in which $AB = 4$ cm, $BC = 3$ cm, $CG = 4$ cm.

(a) Calculate the lengths of the segments: (i) BG, (ii) AC, (iii) AG.

(b) Calculate the angles between:

> (i)   the planes $AHGB$ and $ABCD$;
> (ii) the line AG and the plane $ABCD$;
> (iii) the skew lines EH and CD;
> (iv) the skew lines AH and FG;
> (v)   the skew lines AH and CD.

(c) What is the bearing of C from A?

3. Place a sheet of thin drawing paper over Figure 17. Copy the fifteen points (which you should be able to see through the paper)—but not the letters. Then, using a ruler, join each A to the two As on either side of it, each A to the nearest B, and each B to the two Cs on either side of it. What is the name of the solid you have drawn?

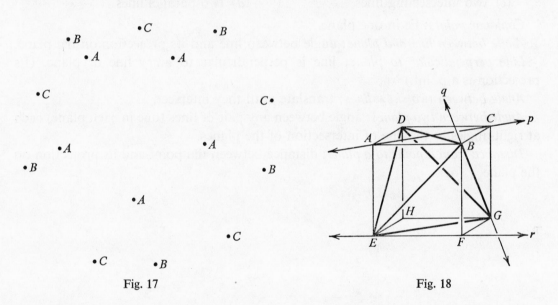

Fig. 17   Fig. 18

4. Figure 18 shows a tetrahedron in a cube of side 6 cm. Draw (or construct from straws) a large figure.

(a) Why are all the edges of the tetrahedron the same length?

(b) How close are the skew lines DB and EG at their nearest points?

(c) Name a line t which is perpendicular to both p and r.

(d) What angle does t make with q?

5. If P is the set of planes determined by the lines l and m, what can you say about l and m if

      (a) $n(P) = 0$;   (b) $n(P) = 1$;   (c) $n(P) > 1$?

6. The reflection in the plane π of the line p is p'. If p is identical to p', what are the two possible conclusions?

119

7. Complete these statements:

(*a*) If two planes are perpendicular to the same line, they are..................

(*b*) If a line is parallel to one plane and perpendicular to another, the two planes are ....

(*c*) If two planes do not intersect, they are...............

(*d*) If two lines do not intersect, they are either .... or ....

(*e*) The number of planes which pass through three collinear points is ....

Summary

Line: straight, infinitely long, determined by two points or two intersecting planes.

Skew lines: not intersecting, not parallel.

Collinear points: lie on one line.

Plane: infinite, determined by

(*a*) three points, (*b*) one line, one external point,

(*c*) two intersecting lines, (*d*) two parallel lines.

Coplanar points: lie in one plane.

Angle between line and plane: angle between line and its projection on the plane.

Line perpendicular to plane: line is perpendicular to *every* line of plane. (Its projection is a point.)

Angle between two skew lines: translate until they intersect.

Angle between two planes: angle between any pair of lines (one in each plane) each at right-angles to the line of intersection of the planes.

Distance from a point to a plane: distance between the point and its projection on the plane.

8

LINEAR PROGRAMMING

The advance and perfecting of mathematics are closely jointed to the prosperity of the nation.
NAPOLEON

In industry and commerce decisions have to be made which depend on many conditions. Intuition cannot always be relied upon and new techniques, many of them involving the use of computers, have been developed to aid decision making. In this chapter we shall study one of these techniques—linear programming—by looking at several simple problems and seeing how their solutions can be obtained by drawing graphs.

1. GRAPHING SOLUTION SETS

In many games of chance (for example, Monopoly) two dice are thrown and the numbers showing uppermost are added together. This total is then used to indicate how far a counter shall move on a board.

While playing a game of Monopoly, Adrian found himself wanting a total of at least 8 to avoid the penalty attached to landing on his opponent's property.

(*a*) There are several ways in which two dice could land to show a total of 8 or more. List them as a set of ordered pairs of numbers.

The set of all the possible answers which would satisfy Adrian is called the *solution set* of the problem.

The ways in which two dice (they are assumed to be red and blue for easy identification) can land can be conveniently represented at lattice points on a graph as in Figure 1.

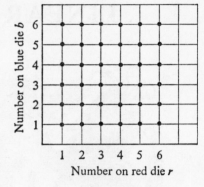

Fig. 1

(*b*) Make a copy of Figure 1 and put a small circle around each point which represents a member of Adrian's solution set.

If we let *r* stand for the number on the red die and *b* stand for the number on the blue die, then it is always true that

$$1 \leqslant r \quad \text{and} \quad 1 \leqslant b.$$

(The symbol '$\leqslant$' means 'less than or equal to'.)

(*c*) What other ordering is always satisfied by *r* and by *b*?

The total for the two dice is given by '$r+b$' and it is always true that

$$2 \leqslant r+b \leqslant 12.$$

(*d*) What ordering must hold if $r+b$ is to satisfy Adrian's condition?

(*e*) When it came to Betty's turn to move, she wanted a total greater than 5 and less than 9.

Give Betty's solution set as a set of ordered pairs.

This solution set could be defined as

$$B = \{(r, b): 5 < r+b < 9\},$$

where it is understood that *r* and *b* can only take the values 1, 2, 3, 4, 5 and 6.

Graphically this can be represented as in Figure 2(*a*) or 2(*b*).

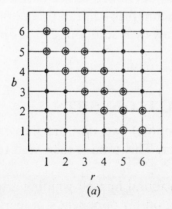

(*a*)

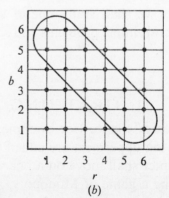

(*b*)

Fig. 2

122

(*f*) Make a copy of Figure 2(*b*) and on it draw a boundary around the set

$$C = \{(r, b): r = b\}.$$

(*g*) List the members of the set $B \cap C$ and describe this set in your own words.

Exercise A

1. Make a copy of Figure 1.

(*a*) Draw a small circle around each member of the set

$$P = \{(r, b): r < b\}.$$

b) Draw a small square around each member of the set

$$Q = \{(r, b): r+b > 7\}.$$

(*c*) Describe in your own words the sets P, Q and $P \cap Q$.

(*d*) How many members has $P \cap Q$?

2. A box contains 4 blue beads and 7 red beads. Each blue bead counts 2 points while each red bead counts $^-1$ point. A game is played in which each player in turn takes some beads from the box without looking, works out his points total, and then returns the beads to the box. The player scoring the highest total wins.

(*a*) Plot points (b, r) on a graph to represent the possible ways in which a person can take some beads from the box. ('*b*' is the number of blue beads taken and '*r*' the number of red beads taken.)

(*b*) Draw a ring around each dot on your graph representing a turn which produces a positive total of points. (For example (3 blue, 4 red), which gives a total of 2 points.)

(*c*) Draw a square around each dot representing a turn in which 7 beads are removed from the box.

What fraction of these gives a positive total?

(*d*) Draw a triangle around each dot representing a turn in which 2 beads are taken.

3. In some parts of the country 'mixed' hockey is popular. To ensure that a team does not contain too many men or women, each team has to fulfil the following conditions:

$$m+w = 11 \quad \text{and} \quad 5 \leqslant m \leqslant 8,$$

where m and w are the numbers of men and women in a team respectively.

(*a*) Find the set of ordered pairs (m, w) corresponding to the possible composition of a team, and plot them as points on a graph.

(*b*) What is: (i) the maximum, (ii) the minimum number of women in a team?

(*c*) Write down an ordering satisfied by w, similar to the one given for m above.

4. A housewife decides to buy a mixture of coal and coke. Her fuel bunker has a volume of 0·6 m³, while 50 kg bags of coal and coke have approximate volumes of 0·06 m³ and 0·09 m³ respectively.

(*a*) How many bags of coal would fill the bunker?

(*b*) If she buys 4 bags of coke, how many bags of coal could she buy?

(*Note*: the bunker does not have to be filled.)

(*c*) If x is the number of bags of coal bought, and y the number of bags of coke bought, plot the set of possible ordered pairs (x, y) as points on a graph.

(*d*) What is the volume of x bags of coal and y bags of coke? Write down an ordering satisfied by x and y based on volume.

(*e*) (i) Put a boundary on your graph around the points for which $y = 2x$.

(ii) What is the maximum mass of fuel which can be put into the bunker if this additional condition is to be satisfied?

5. A father with a family of 6 children decided to give them each either a book or a record for Christmas.

(*a*) If he buys *r* records and *b* books, plot on a graph the points (*r*, *b*) representing the ways in which the presents could be bought.

(*b*) What is the equation connecting *r* and *b*?

(*c*) The father's choice is limited by the fact that he wishes to spend at most £10 while the books and records he is interested in cost £2 and £1·25 each respectively. Put a circle around those points you have already plotted which represent ways fulfilling this further condition.

(*d*) If in addition he decides to buy at least 2 books, what alternatives are left open to him?

6. A car ferry has room for up to 12 cars. A bus (or lorry) takes up the space of 3 cars. If *c* is the number of cars and *b* the number of buses taken on one crossing, then

$$c \geqslant 0, \quad b \geqslant 0 \quad \text{and} \quad c + 3b \leqslant 12. \quad \text{(Why?)}$$

(*a*) Graph the points (*c*, *b*) satisfying these orderings.

(*b*) The tolls for a car and a bus are 10p and 15p respectively, while the running expenses of the ferry are 75p a crossing. On your graph draw in the line $10c + 15b = 75$ and hence put a small circle around each point on your graph which represents a profitable crossing.

(*c*) Assuming the ferry makes a profit, what is (i) the largest, (ii) the smallest number of vehicles it can take on a crossing?

(*d*) What is the greatest profit which can be made when (i) one bus and some cars, (ii) two buses and some cars are carried?

2. GRAPHING EQUATIONS AND ORDERINGS

In the first section you saw how to represent solution sets by points on a graph, and you might well have wondered what would happen if the number of members of a solution set became large. Many of the conditions which a problem has to satisfy can often be expressed in terms of equations and orderings which we learned to represent graphically in Book 1. Graphical representation often makes it possible for us to obtain a solution to a problem without much computation.

Consider the following example.

Example 1

If I go to a fair with 66p in my pocket, and the only attractions which interest me are the Dodgem Cars (which cost 5p a ride) and the Rockets (which cost 8p a ride), how many rides can I have?

There are, of course, many different answers to this question, and these can be found easily without using algebra. I can, for instance, just have 13 rides on the Dodgems; or 2 rides on each and take 40p home.

Working in this way I can draw a graph to represent my possible rides just as in Section 1 (see Figure 3).

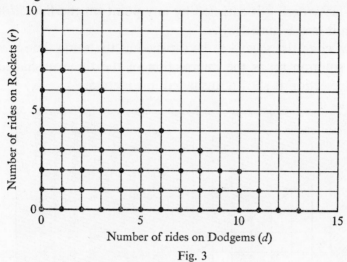

Fig. 3

If I have d rides on the Dodgems and r rides on the Rockets, then I spend $5d+8r$ pence and, as I only started with 66 pence,

$$5d+8r \leqslant 66.$$

Also, since negative rides have no meaning,

$$d \geqslant 0 \quad \text{and} \quad r \geqslant 0.$$

Consider each of these three orderings separately.

$d \geqslant 0$. This says that d can be zero or any number greater than zero. Graphically this means any point on the line $d = 0$ or any point to the right of it satisfies the ordering. In this chapter we shall denote this by shading out the area we are *not* interested in, as in Figure 4(a).

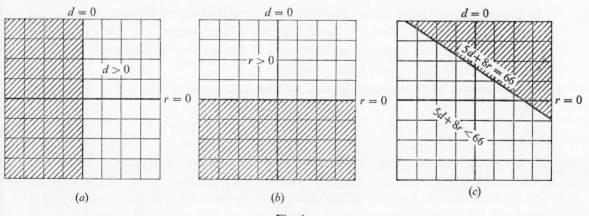

Fig. 4

$r \geqslant 0$. This ordering is satisfied by any point on the line $r = 0$ or above it (see Figure 4(b)).

$5d+8r \leqslant 66$. This ordering is satisfied by any point on the line $5d+8r = 66$ or any point beneath it (see Figure 4(c)).

Now these three conditions have to be satisfied at the same time and the region representing this solution set is the intersection of the three unshaded regions in Figure 4. This intersection is shown unshaded in Figure 5.

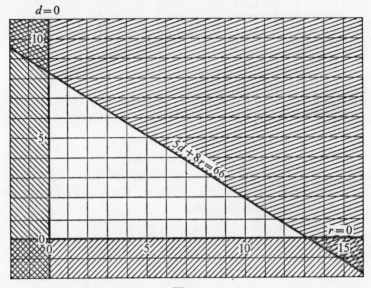

Fig. 5

You will see that the unshaded region in Figure 5 is the same as the region covered by dots in Figure 3. By representing the orderings on a graph in this way, we have a method for finding the boundary of the solution set without having to check each individual member.

In all the problems we have considered so far the solution set has consisted of ordered pairs of *integers*, but this need not always be the case. On other occasions answers involving fractions may be allowed but this will usually be clear from the question.

The following worked example will remind you how to graph equations and inequalities.

Example 2

Draw the graph of the equation $2x+3y = 12$ and hence represent the region $2x+3y < 12$.

You should realize that equations like this with only an x-term, a y-term and a constant (no term like $3x^2$ or xy or $5/x$) give straight-line graphs. To plot the graph first substitute some values of x (any value will do) and work out the corresponding values for y to obtain the coordinates of some points on the line. Two points are sufficient to determine a line, of course, but you would be well advised to work out a third as a check.

In this example, when
$$x = 0,$$
$$3y = 12$$
and so
$$y = 4.$$
Hence (0, 4) is one point on the line.

Similarly (3, 2) and (6, 0) are other points on the line.

The line can now be drawn as in Figure 6.

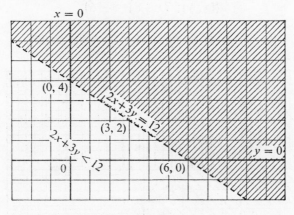

Fig. 6

The line divides the plane into two regions called *half-planes*. One of these (the shaded region in Figure 6) represents the ordering

$$2x + 3y > 12,$$

while the other (unshaded in Figure 6) represents the ordering

$$2x + 3y < 12.$$

To find which ordering the half-plane represents we select one particular point and see whether or not its coordinates belong to the solution set

$$\{(x, y): 2x + 3y < 12\}.$$

Substituting $x = 0$ and $y = 0$ in $2x + 3y < 12$ gives $0 < 12$ which is correct, so (0, 0) belongs to the solution set and we shade the half-plane not containing (0, 0). You will notice that in Figure 6 the line $2x + 3y = 12$ is drawn dotted. This has been done to show that this line does not belong to the region we are considering. We shall always follow this convention, that is, when illustrating an ordering such as $5d + 8r \leqslant 66$ (see Example 1 and Figure 5) the line $5d + 8r = 66$ is drawn unbroken

127

but had the ordering been $5d+8r < 66$ then the line $5d+8r = 66$ would have been drawn dotted. Following this convention will help you to solve difficult examples more easily.

Example 3

Represent on a graph the solution set of the three orderings $x < 6$, $y < 4$, $7x+8y > 56$.

We are looking for the intersection of the three regions

$$\{(x, y): x < 6\},$$

$$\{(x, y): y < 4\},$$

and $\{(x, y): 7x+8y > 56\},$

that is, the region

$$\{(x, y): x < 6, \quad y < 4, \quad 7x+8y > 56\}.$$

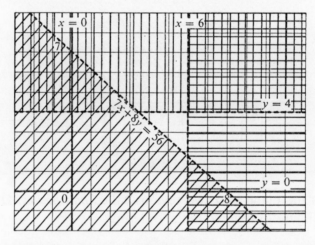

Fig. 7

First draw in the lines $x = 6$ and $y = 4$ (dotted) and shade the regions $x > 6$ and $y > 4$ leaving the regions we are interested in unshaded. The line $7x+8y = 56$ is drawn by first finding some points on it. Two particularly easy points to calculate are the ones where the line crosses $x = 0$ and $y = 0$. The points are $(0, 7)$ and $(8, 0)$. Notice that, following our convention, this line is drawn dotted.

Substituting $(0, 0)$ in the ordering $7x+8y > 56$ gives $0 > 56$ which is false, so the point $(0, 0)$ does *not* belong to the solution set and we shade out the half-plane containing $(0, 0)$.

The completed graph is shown in Figure 7.

Exercise B

1. On a single sheet of graph paper and using the same axes draw the lines representing the following equations. Indicate clearly which is which. (Show values of x from $^-4$ to 5 and of y from $^-4$ to 4.)

(*a*) $x = 2$;   (*b*) $y = ^-2$;   (*c*) $y = 2x$;
(*d*) $x+y = 3$;   (*e*) $3x-y = ^-7$;   (*f*) $5x-4y = 6$.

Refer to the graph you have drawn in Question 1 when answering Questions 2–5.

2. Draw separate freehand graphs on a small scale, to show the regions representing the following orderings. (Shade the parts of the plane containing points whose coordinates do not satisfy the orderings.)

(*a*) $x > 2$;   (*b*) $y < ^-2$;   (*c*) $y > 2x$;
(*d*) $x+y > 3$;   (*e*) $3x-y > ^-7$;   (*f*) $5x-4y < 6$.

3. Give the coordinates of the single member of each of the following sets:

(*a*) $\{(x, y): x+y = 3, \quad y = 2x\}$;   (*b*) $\{(x, y): 5x-4y = 6, \quad x+y = 3\}$;
(*c*) $\{(x, y): 3x-y = ^-7, \quad x+y = 3\}$;   (*d*) $\{(x, y): 5x-4y = 6, \quad y = 2x\}$;
(*e*) $\{(x, y): y = ^-2, \quad 3x-y = ^-7\}$.

4. On small freehand graphs show (by shading as in Question 2) the regions:

(*a*) $\{(x, y): x > 2, \quad y > ^-2\}$;   (*b*) $\{(x, y): x+y < 3, \quad x > 2\}$;
(*c*) $\{(x, y): 5x-4y < 6, \quad x+y < 3, \quad x > 0\}$;
(*d*) $\{(x, y): x+y > 3, \quad y < 2x, \quad x < 2\}$.

5. In the graph you drew to answer Question 1 there should be a triangle with vertices at the points $(^-3, ^-2)$, $(^-1, 4)$ and $(5, ^-2)$. Write down the three orderings for which the triangle and the points of the region bounded by it form the solution set.

6. (*a*) Draw a graph to show the region of points whose coordinates satisfy all five of the following orderings:

$$x > 0; \quad y > 0; \quad 2x+y > 4; \quad x+3y > 9; \quad x+y < 6.$$

(*b*) Put a dot on your graph for each member of the set

$$\{(x, y): x > 0, \quad y > 0, \quad 2x+y > 4, \quad x+3y > 9, \quad x+y < 6\},$$

which has whole number coordinates.

7. John went shopping with 20p in his pocket to buy fireworks.
(*a*) If he buys b bangers at 2p each and r rockets at 3p each, why must $2b+3r \leqslant 20$;
(*b*) Represent this ordering on a graph along with the orderings

$$b \geqslant 0 \quad \text{and} \quad r \geqslant 0.$$

(*c*) John wished to buy as many bangers as possible but his parents insisted that he must buy at least one rocket for every two bangers. This can be expressed as $2r \geqslant b$. Shade your graph to show this additional condition.
(*d*) Put a dot on your graph for each point representing a member of John's solution set.
(*e*) What is the largest number of: (i) bangers, (ii) fireworks which John can buy? Does he spend all his money?

129

8. A post office has to transport 900 parcels using lorries, which can take 150 at a time, and vans which can take 60.

(*a*) If *l* lorries and *v* vans are used, write down an ordering which must be satisfied.

(*b*) The costs of each journey are £5 by lorry and £4 by van and the total cost must be less than £44. Write down another ordering which must be satisfied by *l* and *v*.

(*c*) Represent these orderings on a graph and dot in the members of the solution set.

(*d*) What is:

  (i) the largest number of vehicles which could be used,

  (ii) the arrangement which keeps the cost to a minimum,

  (iii) the most costly arrangement?

3. LINEAR PROGRAMMING

We are now in a position to look at some problems which, although artificial, give some idea of the kind of situations where the techniques of linear programming (linear because all the conditions involve straight lines) are applicable.

Linear programming deals with problems in which a large number of simple conditions have to be satisfied at the same time. By drawing graphs we can first find a polygonal region containing the points which represent possible solutions. When the solution set is found it is the manager's or production engineer's task to decide which solution to take. This is usually done by trying to make, say, the profit as large as possible, or the time taken for the process as short as possible.

The following example illustrates the method.

Example 4

A haulage contractor has 7 six-tonne lorries, 4 ten-tonne lorries and 9 drivers available. He has contracted to move a minimum of 360 tonnes of coal from a pit-head to a power station daily. The six-tonne lorries can make 8 journeys a day and the ten-tonne lorries can make 6 journeys a day.

How should the contractor organize the use of his lorries to:

(*a*) carry the maximum tonnage each day;

(*b*) use the smallest number of drivers;

(*c*) run the lorries at minimum cost if a six-tonne lorry costs £5 a day and a ten-tonne lorry costs £8 a day?

Suppose the contractor uses

$$x \text{ six-tonne lorries} \quad \text{and} \quad y \text{ ten-tonne lorries.}$$

Then because of the limitation on the number of lorries and drivers available:

$$x \leqslant 7,$$
$$y \leqslant 4,$$

and
$$x+y \leqslant 9.$$

130

Working on a daily basis, a six-tonne lorry can carry as much as 48 tonnes a day, while a ten-tonne lorry can carry as much as 60 tonnes a day. Thus, to fulfil the contract of a minimum of 360 tonnes a day

$$48x + 60y \leqslant 360.$$

(This condition can be simplified by dividing by 12 to give $4x + 5y \geqslant 30$.)

Now that we have the conditions expressed as algebraic orderings they can be graphed to find the solution set. We remember that $x \geqslant 0$, $y \geqslant 0$ and that only points with whole number coordinates represent possible solutions (see Figure 8).

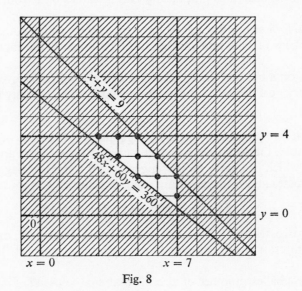

Fig. 8

From the graph it is clear that the points

(3, 4),   (4, 4),   (4, 3),   (5, 4),   (5, 3),   (5, 2),   (6, 3),   (6, 2),   (7, 2),   (7, 1)

all represent possible solutions.

It now remains to see which of these solutions best suits the contractor's policy.

(a) To find how to carry the maximum tonnage we can try each of the possible solutions in turn. (In practice not every solution has to be tried.) Using 5 six-tonne trucks and 4 ten-tonne trucks gives a maximum tonnage of 480 tonnes but this requires all the drivers.

(b) The smallest number of drivers which could be used is 7 and the required tonnage can be hauled whether the lorries are used (5, 2), (4, 3) or (3, 4). The cost, however, will not be the same in each case.

(c) The cost of using (x, y) lorries is £$(5x + 8y)$ and this is smallest when

$$(x, y) = (5, 2)$$

giving a cost of £41.

Exercise C

In this exercise the numbers will all be positive or zero.

1. A factory makes cricket bats and tennis rackets. A cricket bat takes 1 h of machine time and 3 h of craftsman's time, while a tennis racket takes 2 h of machine time and 1 h of craftsman's time. In a day the factory has available no more than 28 h of machine time and 24 h of craftsman's time.

(a) If the factory makes x bats and y rackets on a particular day, write down two orderings satisfied by x and y based on: (i) machine time, (ii) craftsman's time.

(b) Represent these orderings graphically taking values of x from 0 to 28 and of y from 0 to 24.

(c) What is the largest number of: (i) bats, (ii) rackets which could be made in a day?

(d) What numbers of bats and rackets must be made if the factory is to work at full capacity?

(e) The profits on a bat and on a racket are £1 and 50p respectively. Find the maximum profit to the factory on a day when it produces: (i) only bats, (ii) only rackets, and (iii) works at full capacity.

2. In an airlift it is required to transport 600 people and 45 tonnes of baggage. Two kinds of aircraft are available; the Albatross which can carry 50 passengers and 6 tonnes of baggage, and the Buzzard which can carry 80 passengers and 3 tonnes of baggage.

(a) If a Albatrosses and b Buzzards are used, explain why

$$5a + 8b \geqslant 60 \quad \text{and} \quad 2a + b \geqslant 15.$$

(b) Only 8 Albatrosses and 7 Buzzards are available. Represent, on a graph, the possible arrangements of aircraft which can supply the necessary transport. Dot in the members of the solution set.

(c) What is the smallest number of aircraft that can be used?

3. A factory manager has to decide how many of each of two types of machine to install. The facts about them are as follows:

	Factory floor space (m²)	Labour needed per machine (men)	Output per week (units)
Machine X	5000	9	300
Machine Y	6000	4	200

The factory has 45000 m² of floor space and only 54 skilled workers are available to work the machines.

(a) If he buys x of machine X and y of machine Y, write down two orderings satisfied by x and y based on (i) floor space and (ii) labour.

(b) Represent the possible solutions open to the manager graphically. Dot in each member of the solution set clearly.

(c) How many machines of each type will he buy to: (i) achieve maximum output, (ii) give work to all the skilled workers?

(d) If he satisfies (c)(ii), by how much will the factory's output be below the maximum possible?

4. A market gardener intends to split a 18 hectare field between lettuces and potatoes. The relevant details are as follows:

	Lettuces	Potatoes
Cost per hectare including labour (pounds)	5	3
Labour per hectare (man days)	3	I
Only £60 and 30 man days are available		

(a) If he plants l hectare of lettuces and p acres of potatoes, then

$$l+p \leqslant 18.$$

Write down two other orderings that must be satisfied by l and p.

(b) Represent these three orderings graphically.

(c) Calculate his profit, on the basis of £12 per hectare for lettuces and £8 per hectare for potatoes, for the solutions represented by each vertex (other than $(0, 0)$) of the polygon bounding the solution set. Which solution gives the greatest profit?

5. A manager of a theatre which holds 600 seats sells them at two prices: 15p and 25p. To cover his expenses he has to take at least £60 at the box office for each house.

(a) If he sells x seats at 15p and y seats at 25p, write down orderings based on: (i) the capacity of the theatre and (ii) the seats that have to be sold to make a profit.

(b) It is the manager's policy to have at least 200 seats available at the cheaper price. Express this as an ordering involving y, and represent all the orderings you have found graphically.

(c) (i) What profit would be made if the theatre were filled by holders of 15p tickets?

   (ii) What is the smallest number of seats that can be sold without sustaining a loss?

   (iii) What is the maximum profit that can be made on one house?

6. An architect estimates that the annual cost of heating a building is £1·50 for every square metre of window and 50p for every square metre of wall or roof. A local bye-law states that the area of the windows must be at least $\frac{1}{8}$th as much as the area of the walls and roof. What is the largest surface area a building can have if its annual heating cost is not to exceed £300?

[Hint: let x be the number of square metres of window and y the number of square metres walls and roof.]

Most practical problems in linear programming involve more than two quantities so that graphical solution becomes impossible. The following problem is intended to be done by the intelligent use of 'trial and error'.

†D7. An engineering manufacturer has a limited capacity for welding, for machining, for storing finished products and also a limited sales force. If six products can be made, each of which uses different proportions of these limited resources, the manager will have to decide what amounts of each product to make in order to achieve as large a profit as possible. The relevant information is contained in the table at the top of page 134.

(a) Let a, b, c, d, e, f be the daily numbers of each product manufactured and write down 4 orderings which these must satisfy.

† Reproduced from *Discovery*, September 1963.

Product	Man hours welding	Man hours machining	Man hours selling	Cubic metres storing	Profit
A	5	3	2	0·6	£4
B	3	6	5	0·2	£3
C	8	1	3	0·4	£5
D	2	2	4	0·1	£3
E	6	5	1	0·3	£4
F	6	0	4	0·6	£6
Approx. total daily capacity	120	70	80	10	

(b) Find sets of numbers (a, b, c, d, e, f) which satisfy these orderings and try to make the profit

$$£(4a + 3b + 5c + 3d + 4e + 6f)$$

as large as possible.

REVISION EXERCISES

SLIDE RULE SESSION NO. 3

Give all answers as accurately as you can.

1. $23 \times 67 \cdot 8$.
2. $1 \cdot 91 \times 9 \cdot 8$.
3. $2 \cdot 12 \div 1 \cdot 56$.
4. $230 \div 16 \cdot 2$.

5. $\sqrt{39 \cdot 5}$.
6. $\sqrt{395}$.
7. $1 \cdot 67^2$.
8. $16 \cdot 7^2$.

9. $\dfrac{1 \cdot 23 \times 2 \cdot 31}{3 \cdot 12}$.
10. $\dfrac{34 \cdot 5}{45 \cdot 3 \times 5 \cdot 34}$.

SLIDE RULE SESSION NO. 4

Give all answers as accurately as you can.

1. 19×37.
2. $0 \cdot 045 \times 77$.
3. $19 \div 37$.
4. $77 \div 0 \cdot 045$.

5. $19 \times \sqrt{61 \cdot 5}$.
6. $\sqrt{(220 \cdot 5 \times 8)}$.
7. $0 \cdot 0468^2$.
8. $\pi \times 8 \cdot 4^2$.

9. $1 \cdot 23 \times 2 \cdot 34 \times 345$.
10. $\dfrac{541 \times 7 \cdot 67}{23}$.

G

1. $ABCD$ is a quadrilateral and $\angle A = \angle B = 2\angle C = 6\angle D$. What is the angle at A?

2. The direct-route matrix

$$\begin{array}{c} & \text{to} \\ & \begin{array}{ccc} A & B & C \end{array} \\ \begin{array}{c} \\ \text{from} \ \ B \\ C \end{array} \begin{array}{c} A \\ \\ \ \end{array} \left(\begin{array}{ccc} 0 & 2 & 1 \\ 1 & 0 & 1 \\ 0 & 1 & 0 \end{array} \right) \end{array}$$

represents a network of roads. Without drawing the network say if it is possible, in any way at all, to reach A from C. If so, describe the route.

3. Is it possible for a plane to contain a pair of skew lines?

4. Is the point $(3, 4)$ inside the region $x+y \leqslant 7$?

5. If it is Monday today, what is the probability that it is Tuesday tomorrow?

6. Give the image of the point $(3, {}^-4)$ under a reflection in the line $x+y = 0$.

7. Give the result of squaring the matrix in Question 2.

8. Is it possible for a motor-car to be accelerating yet to have no velocity?

9. Calculate 6×7 in base eight.

10. Calculate the cost of 35 litres of petrol at 7p per litre.

135

H

1. Are a square and a triangle topologically equivalent?

2. Find the mean of 16, 15, 67, 45, 23, 14.

3. Find the mean of 906, 905, 957, 935, 913, 904 by using the result of Question 2.

4. O is $(0, 0)$, P is $(5, 0)$, Q is $(0, 4)$, P' is $(0, 5)$ and triangles OPQ, $OP'Q'$ are oppositely congruent. Give the coordinates of Q'.

5. Give the image of the point $(^-2, 3)$ under the translation $\begin{pmatrix} -3 \\ -4 \end{pmatrix}$.

6. Express 0·000368 in standard form, to 2 s.f.

7. Express the ratio 25p to £5 in the form $1:n$.

8. Write $^-2(2x^2-3)$ without brackets.

9. Find x if $3^x = 81$.

10. If $A \cap B = A \cap C$, must $B = C$?

I

1. If possible, draw the figures described, indicating any lengths or angles that have to be calculated. If impossible, account for the fact.

(a) Three circles, all of radius 1 cm such that each one passes through the centres of the others.

(b) A circle of radius $1\frac{1}{2}$ cm with a chord that is more than $1\frac{1}{2}$ cm from the centre.

(c) A circle of radius $1\frac{1}{2}$ cm containing a sector whose area is greater than 2π cm².

(d) A triangle, all of whose vertices lie on a circle of radius 2 cm, whose base is the diameter of the circle and whose area is 5 cm².

2. Taking the value of π to be 3·14, use your slide rule to find the volume and the total surface area of a solid cylinder of height 4·45 cm and radius 1·85 cm.

3. Draw a diagram to illustrate the relation 'is a prime factor of' over the set $\{2, 3, 4, 6, 8\}$. Construct the matrix $\mathbf{R}$ for the relation and write down $\mathbf{R}^2$ and the transpose $\mathbf{R}'$. What relations do these matrices represent?

4. Philip, Quentin, Rupert and Simon played one another at chess. P beat Q and S; Q beat S; R beat P and Q; S beat R. Complete matrices showing one- and two-stage dominances and hence put the players in an order of merit.

5. How many 1-nodes, 2-nodes, 3-nodes has:

(a) a line;   (b) a half-line;   (c) a line segment?

6. $ABCD$ is the base and $EFGH$ is the top face of a cube, A and G being opposite vertices. If each edge of the cube is of length 10 cm, calculate AC and AG and so find the angle between AG and the base.

136

7. Find the points with whole-number coordinates which satisfy all three of the orderings $x < 4$, $3y - x \leqslant 6$, $3y + 2x > 6$.

8. It is required to transport 500 troops and 42 tonnes of equipment. Two types of aircraft are available in sufficient numbers; an Albatross can carry 50 men and 5 tonnes of equipment, while a Kestrel can carry 40 men and 3 tonnes of equipment. For the journey, the operating cost for each Albatross is £1050 and for each Kestrel is £900. How many of each are required if the total cost is to be a minimum?

J

1. Find the area of the Meccano piece shown in Figure 1, given that the radii of the large arcs are 2·5 and 3·5 cm, that the ends are semi-circles and the holes have diameters of 0·28 cm. (Take π to be 3·14.)

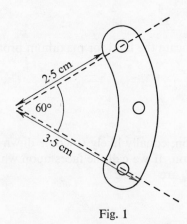

Fig. 1

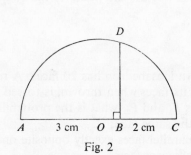

Fig. 2

2. Figure 2 is a semi-circle with centre O. Calculate the lengths of (a) the radius OD, (b) $\angle BOD$, (c) the arc DC (take $\pi = 3\cdot14$).

3. Figure 3 shows three networks. List the number of nodes (N), arcs (A) and regions (R), and so verify Euler's relation $R + N = A + 2$ for each network. Does this relation hold for Figure 3 considered as a whole?

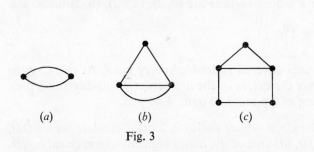

(a)   (b)   (c)

Fig. 3

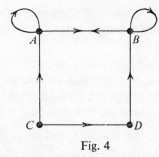

Fig. 4

4. (a) Compile a direct-route matrix S for the network shown in Figure 4. Why is it not symmetrical about the leading diagonal?
(b) Find the matrix S^2. What does it represent?

5. *A, B, C, D* are four points in space. *A, B, C* are in a plane π; *B, C, D* are in a different plane π'. What is $\pi \cap \pi'$?

6. An equilateral triangle *ABC* of edge 4 cm, made of thin cardboard, rests with *AB* on a horizontal table. The plane of the triangle is inclined at 20° to the table. How high is *C* above the table?

7. Find the points with whole-number coordinates that satisfy the orderings

$$-2 \leqslant x+y < 2, \quad 0 \geqslant 3x-y, \quad y-3x \leqslant 2.$$

8. A market gardener intends to split a 10 hectare field between lettuces (*L*) and potatoes (*P*). The relevant details are:

	L	P
Cost per hectare including labour	£10	£6
Labour per hectare (in man days)	4	2
Estimated profit per hectare	£6	£4

If £75 and 30 man days are available, how should he allocate the land for maximum profit? (He need not use the whole of the 10 hectares.)

K

1. An icosahedron has 20 faces. A regular icosahedron, equally likely to come down on any of its faces when thrown, is tossed twice in succession. If we call the faces upon which it lands F_1 and F_2, what is the probability that F_1 and F_2 are
   (*a*) the same face;
   (*b*) parallel faces exactly opposite one another;
   (*c*) adjacent faces;
   (*d*) neither identical nor adjacent?

2. A triangle with vertices at (2, 3), (6, 6), (2, 8) is reflected in the line $y = 0$. Write down the coordinates of the vertices of the image triangle. Are the two triangles congruent? Could the second triangle be the image of the first: (*a*) under a translation; (*b*) under a rotation? Explain briefly.

3. Construct the image of the letter *V* whose vertices are (2, 2), (4, ⁻2), (6, 2) under the transformation whose matrix is

$$\begin{pmatrix} 0 & -\frac{1}{2} \\ \frac{1}{2} & 0 \end{pmatrix}.$$

4. A forest fire spreads so that the area covered is doubled every hour. At mid-day the area is 100 m². Draw a graph to illustrate the extent of the fire between mid-day and 5 p.m. Measure the rate at which it is spreading at 2 p.m., 3.30 p.m., 4.40 p.m.

5. In Figure 5, *O* is the centre of the circle whose radius is 2 cm. Calculate (*a*) $\angle BOD$, (*b*) area of $\triangle BOD$, (*c*) area of sector *BOD*, (*d*) area of the minor segment whose chord is *BD*.

6. The numbers on the network of Figure 6 represent maximum possible traffic flows (in hundreds of cars per hour) for the various roads. Try to work out, giving reasons, the maximum flow possible between *L* and *M*.

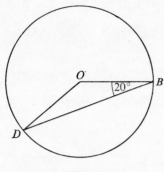

Fig. 5

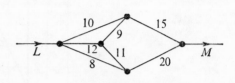

Fig. 6

7. State in each case whether the description is of a line, a half-line or a line segment:

(a) $\{(x, y): x = 0, y \geqslant 0\}$;

(b) $\{(x, y): y = 4\}$;

(c) the longest side of the triangle whose vertices are (2, 1), (3, 7), (5, 4).

Give an example of an equation for a half-plane.

8. A piece of paper is to be cut into the form of a rectangle x cm wide and y cm long, such that

(a) the length is to be more than double the width;

(b) the area is to exceed 48 cm²;

(c) the length of either diagonal is to be less than 15 cm.

Write down three orderings involving x and y, and give one pair of whole numbers satisfying them all.

L

1. *A*, *B* and *C* are three cats sitting on the edge of a goldfish pond (see Figure 7). Copy the figure and shade in the part of the pond in which a goldfish is nearer to *A* than to either *B* or *C*.

2. If possible sketch plane figures with the following specifications, dotting in lines of symmetry and showing centres of rotational symmetry by crosses. Where specifications are impossible, say so.

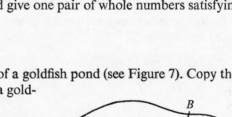

Fig. 7

(a) One line of symmetry, no rotational symmetry.

(b) No line of symmetry, quarter-turn rotational symmetry.

(c) Two different centres of rotational symmetry.

(d) Three lines of symmetry, no rotational symmetry.

(e) An infinite number of lines of symmetry.

3. A machine was valued at £3000 in July 1964. Each year its value has decreased by 7% of its value at the beginning of the year. What is its value in July 1967? (Give your answer to the nearest £10.) Is the total decrease more than, less than or equal to 21% of its July 1964 value?

4. Sketch the triangle whose vertices are (2, 1), (⁻1, 3), (⁻3, ⁻2) and find its area.

139

10-2

5. In Figure 8 what is the equation of the line PP'?

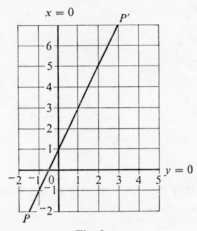

Fig. 8

6. A baby's mass increases steadily from 3·2 kg at birth by 400 g per week for the first ten weeks of its life. Give an algebraic relation to describe this, and sketch a graph illustrating the information.

7. If a solid sphere has a surface area of 50 cm², what is the surface area of another solid sphere with a radius three times as big? If the first has a mass of 70 g, what is the mass of the second assuming they are made of the same material?

8. Say whether each statement is true or false; and where one is false suggest how it could be amended.

(a) π is exactly $\frac{22}{7}$;

(b) $0·9^2 < 0·9$;

(c) in base 5, 302 is an even number;

(d) a cube has three planes of symmetry.

TRIGONOMETRY TABLES: PRACTICE

1. Use tables to find (a) sin 35°, (b) sin 85·5°, (c) cos 47·2°.

2. Use tables to find x where (a) sin $x°$ = 0·421, (b) cos $x°$ = 0·037, (c) cos $x°$ = 0·980.

3. Calculate 2 sin 17° + cos 17°.

4. Find θ if sin $\theta°$ = $\frac{3}{4}$.

5. Calculate 1/sin 20·8°.

6. Calculate, and then add, the squares of (a) sin 64°, (b) cos 64°.

7. Find the coordinates of P, given that $OP = 5$ and OP makes an angle of 40° with $y = 0$.

8. In the triangle ABC, $\angle BAC = 90°$, $ACB = 21°$, $BC = 5$ cm. Find AB and AC.

140

9

WAVES

The winds and waves are always on the side of the ablest of navigators.
EDWARD GIBBON, *Decline and Fall of The Roman Empire*

1. THE SINE AND COSINE FUNCTIONS

So far in our discussion of trigonometry we have only used the sines and cosines of angles of 0°, 10°, 20°, ..., 80° and 90°, and to restrict ourselves to these would clearly be very limiting. In this chapter we shall try to understand better the behaviour of the sine and cosine functions, so that we can free ourselves from this restriction.

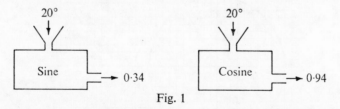

Fig. 1

We know that the sine and cosine functions map angles of 0°, 10°, 20°, ..., 90° onto numbers from 0 to 1, and Figure 2 shows how these mappings can be represented.

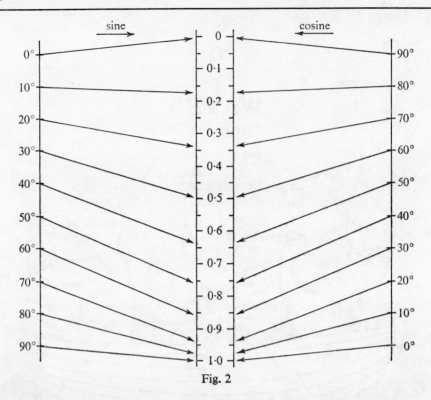

Fig. 2

(a) What does Figure 2 suggest about the value of sin 35°?

(b) Does the figure suggest a value for sin 160° or cos −20°?

To extend our ideas it is necessary to go back to the definition of sine and cosine as sideways and central distances corresponding to a unit displacement.

A convenient way of doing this is to consider a unit displacement from the origin of a Cartesian coordinate system (see Figure 3) and to take the line $y = 0$ as the central direction. In Figure 3 a unit displacement making an angle of 60° with the line $y = 0$ has been drawn.

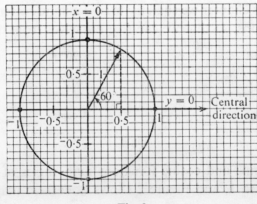

Fig. 3

142

(c) What are the coordinates of the point of the arrow?

(d) Make a copy of Figure 3 and on it mark the points $P(\cos 30°, \sin 30°)$ and $Q(\cos 150°, \sin 150°)$.

(e) Figure 4 shows unit displacements from the origin making angles of 120°, 240° and 300° with the line $y = 0$. What are the values of:

(i) cos 120°, sin 120°;   (ii) cos 240°, sin 240°;

(iii) cos 300°, sin 300°?

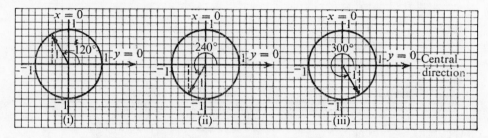

Fig. 4

(f) What meaning would you attach to: sin 420°, cos 480°, cos ⁻60°, sin ⁻300°?

(g) How could you find the value of cos 63° or sin 256° by scale drawing?

By making use of the values of $\sin \theta°$ and $\cos \theta°$ for angles of 0°, 10°, 20°, ..., 90° and diagrams like Figure 4 it is now possible to find values of $\sin \theta°$ and $\cos \theta°$ whenever θ is a multiple of 10.

Example 1

Find the values of sin 150° and cos 150°. A unit displacement **OA** is drawn to make an angle of 150° with the line $y = 0$ which is taken as the central direction (see Figure 5). Cos 150° and sin 150° are the central and sideways distances produced by **OA** and are therefore the coordinates of A. Since angle BOA is 30° and OA is of unit length, it follows that

$$OB = \cos 30° = 0\cdot 87,$$

and

$$BA = \sin 30° = 0\cdot 50.$$

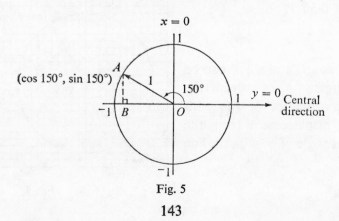

Fig. 5

143

The position of A relative to the lines $x = 0$ and $y = 0$ means that the x coordinate is negative and the y coordinate is positive. Hence A is the point

$$(^-0{\cdot}87, 0{\cdot}50) = (\cos 150°, \sin 150°).$$

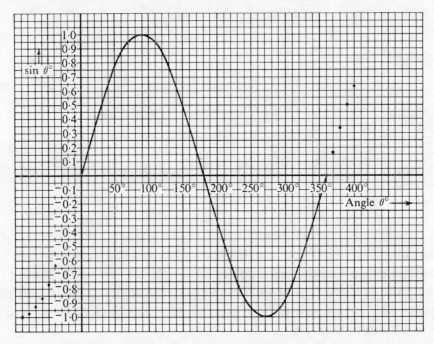

Fig. 6. Graph to show the relation between $\sin \theta°$ and $\theta°$.

Figure 6 has been obtained by plotting the ordered pairs $(\theta°, \sin \theta°)$ for multiples of 10° from 0° to 360° and then joining these points by a smooth curve.

(*h*) Use the graph to find:

    (i) $\sin 110°$ and $\sin 330°$;   (ii) an angle whose sine is 0·5.

(*i*) How many different angles between 0° and 180° does the sine function map onto the number 0·5?

Summary

The values of $\cos \theta°$ and $\sin \theta°$ can be found for any angle of $\theta°$ by considering the Cartesian coordinates of the end-point of a unit displacement from the origin making an angle of $\theta°$ with the line $y = 0$.

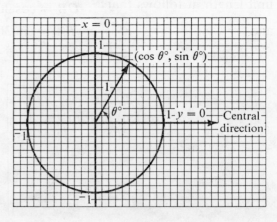

Fig. 7

Exercise A

1. Use the graph in Figure 6 to find:
(a) the values of sin 25°, sin 200°, sin 315°, sin 72°;
(b) the angles whose sines are 0·75, 0·29, ⁻0·97.

2. (a) If $0 < \theta < 30$, what can you say about sin θ°?
(b) Give the range of values for sin θ° when $180 < \theta < 270$.
(c) What can you say about the value of θ if $0 < \sin \theta° < 1$?

3. Graph the function, $\theta° \to \cos \theta°$, for the domain $0 < \theta < 360$ on the same scale as Figure 6.

4. Use the graph you drew when answering Question 3 to find:
(a) the values of cos 15°, cos 67°, cos 135°, cos 284°;
(b) the angles whose cosines are 0·5, 0·85, 0·34, ⁻0·90.

5. A Big Wheel has 36 seats spaced symmetrically around its circumference and you take your seat when the seat is at its lowest point. Suppose you were to take a seat and your friend was then to enter his seat when the wheel had turned through an angle of 40°.
(a) How many seats would there be between you and your friend?
(b) Through what further angle would the wheel have to turn before you were:

   (i)   immediately above your friend;
   (ii) on the same level as your friend;
   (iii) immediately below your friend?

If the radius of the wheel were 7·5 m, how much higher would your friend be than you when he was at the highest point of the wheel?

6. A small nail is picked up by the tyre of a bicycle wheel. If the diameter of the wheel is 65 cm how high above the road is the nail when the wheel has turned through an angle of:

(a) 45°;   (b) 210°;   (c) 480°?

7. A ship's radar picks up the trace of an iceberg 5 kilometres away on a bearing of 220°.
(a) How far is the ship (i) east, (ii) north of the iceberg?
(b) If the iceberg is stationary and the ship is sailing on a bearing of 230°, how near does the ship get to the iceberg?

8. A swimming pool is 1 m deep at one end and 3 m deep at the other. The sloping base of the pool is 20·3 m long (see Figure 8). At approximately what angle does the base of the pool slope away from the horizontal?

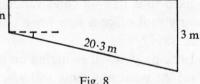

Fig. 8

9. Two sailing dinghys are racing on a course which is due south. While the first dinghy tacks 500 m on a bearing of 120° the second tacks 310 m on a bearing of 220°. Which dinghy progresses farther south in this time?

10. (a) Assuming that $0 < x < 90$, solve the equations:
    (i)   sin $x°$ = cos 60°;   (ii) sin $x°$ = cos 20°;
    (iii) cos $x°$ = sin 40°;   (iv) cos 80° = sin $x°$;
    (v) sin $x°$ = cos 23°.

(b) By considering your answers to (a) suggest a possible connection between x and y if $\sin x° = \cos y°$.

(c) What can you say about x if $\sin x° = \cos x°$?

11. The position of a point A can be described by giving its distance, x, from the origin and the angle, y, which the line joining A to the origin makes with the line $y = 0$. For example, $A(5, 53)$ means that A is 5 units from the origin O and that the line OA makes an angle of 53° with the line $y = 0$.

What are the (x, y) coordinates of:

(a) $A(5, 53)$;   (b) $B(7, 240)$;   (c) $C(12, 310)$?

2. WAVES

The chapter title probably made you think of the seaside and the waves of the sea, and these are related to what we shall be considering. You have seen the shape obtained when the graph of the sine function is plotted. Its similarity to sea waves led to the term 'sine wave'. However, the connection is much deeper than this and modern physics has shown a connection between wave motion and such apparently different topics as heat, light, electricity and sound.

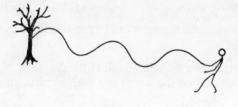 

Fig. 9

In Figure 9 a boy is moving one end of a rope up and down while the other end is fixed to a tree—a child watches him from a swing. The movement of the string clearly looks like a sine wave but what is the connection between the swing and a sine wave?

Imagine yourself swinging on a park swing.

(a) At what moments will you be moving forward fastest?

(b) How does your forward speed change as you swing? Is it ever negative?

Figure 10 shows the result of graphing the function 'time → forward speed'. The sketches above the graph show the appropriate positions of the swing.

The pendulum of a clock has a similar motion and we call the time for one oscillation (that is, a complete swing forwards and back) the *periodic time* of the motion.

(c) What is the periodic time of the swing shown in Figure 10?

146

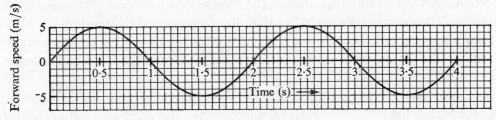

Fig. 10

A pendulum can be made quite simply using a broom handle with a tin filled with concrete, or some similar heavy weight, on the end. If this is pivoted as in Figure 11 and a light pen arm fixed to the pendulum then a sine wave can be obtained by pulling a piece of paper at a steady pace at right-angles to the motion of the pendulum.

(More interesting results can be obtained by having a second pendulum swinging at right-angles to the first: see *Mathematical Models*, by Cundy and Rollett.)

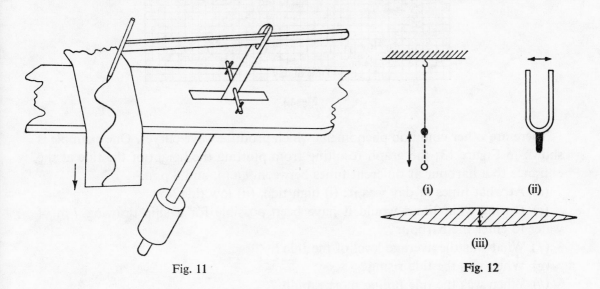

Fig. 11   Fig. 12

Many motions when analysed produce similar graphs, for example (see Figure 12):

(i) the up and down motion of a weight suspended from a piece of elastic or a spring;

(ii) the vibration of a tuning fork;

(iii) the vibration of a violin or piano string.

The main difference between the motion of a tuning fork and a pendulum is that the former has a much shorter periodic time. The pendulum of a clock, for instance, usually has a periodic time of 1 second (or 2 s or $\frac{1}{2}$ s), whereas the periodic time of a tuning fork sounding the note 'middle C' has a periodic time of $\frac{1}{261}$ s. Another way of putting this is to say that the clock pendulum makes 1 (or $\frac{1}{2}$ or 2) oscillations a second whereas the tuning fork makes 261 oscillations a second. The number of complete oscillations made a second is called the *frequency* of the motion.

We hear a musical note because the molecules of air make our ear drums vibrate. This is rather like the waves of the sea hitting a sea wall, only the frequency is much higher.

We can hear notes having frequencies between about 30 and 30,000 waves a second; the higher the note, the greater the frequency. The notes of a bat are about the highest pitched ones we can hear and you will probably find that some of your friends can hear bats while others cannot.

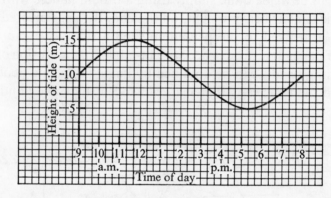

Fig. 13

There are other common phenomena which produce wave curves. One example is shown in Figure 13; the graph resulting from plotting the height of the tide at the entrance to a harbour at different times between 9 a.m. and 8 p.m.

(*d*) At what times of day was it: (i) high tide, (ii) low tide?

(*e*) During what times would it have been possible for a ship drawing 7 m of water to enter the harbour?

(*f*) What was the average level of the tide?

(*g*) When was the tide rising?

(*h*) When was the tide falling most rapidly?

Exercise B

1. The up and down motion of a piston in a car engine and the needle in a sewing machine are examples of oscillations whose variation with time when plotted on a graph lead to curves like the sine wave. Suggest other examples.

2. An electric motor is marked 230 volts a.c. 50 cycles. Find out what is meant by a.c. and 50 cycles.

3. Many radio sets are labelled v.h.f. What do these letters stand for?

4. Look at a gramophone disc through a magnifying glass or find a photograph showing a magnification of a disc. What do you find?

5. The strings which give the note 'middle C' on a piano vibrate with a frequency of 261. The C an octave higher has double the frequency, the frequency of the C above that is doubled again and so on.

(a) What is the frequency of the note which is:
    (i) 3 octaves above middle C,
    (ii) 2 octaves below middle C?

(b) Sketch part of the wave motion of middle C and the wave motion of the C above middle C on the same graph.

6. The 1962 tide tables for Falmouth show the maximum height of each tide measured from a datum level at No. 2 Dock. The figures below show the heights of the morning tides for January measured in metres.

	1st week	2nd week	3rd week	4th week	5th week
Sunday	—	5·31	4·53	5·07	4·50
Monday	4·29	5·43	4·32	5·07	4·32
Tuesday	4·14	5·43	4·38	5·04	4·17
Wednesday	4·35	5·31	4·56	4·98	4·11
Thursday	4·65	5·16	4·74	4·89	—
Friday	4·92	4·95	4·92	4·77	—
Saturday	5·10	4·71	5·01	4·65	—

(a) Graph the function 'day of the month → height of the morning tide'. (It is best to start the height scale from say 4 m as no height is less than this.)

(b) From your graph find the probable height of the afternoon tide on the following days of the month:
    (i) 4th;   (ii) 14th;   (iii) 20th;   (iv) 29th.

(c) Do points between those plotted have any meaning?

7. Most diaries give the times of sunrise and sunset on each Saturday of the year. Preferably on the same graph, plot the sunrise and sunset times (make sure they are all G.M.T.) for each week of the year.

(a) When does the longest day occur and approximately how many hours is the sun up then?

(b) How long is the 'shortest day'?

(c) For how many weeks of the year is the sun up for more than:

    (i) 15 h in a day;   (ii) 12 h in a day;   (iii) 9 h in a day?

(d) For approximately how long is the sun up on your birthday?

8. When a car hits a bump the suspension of the car makes the passenger in the back seat bounce up and down. The graphs in Figure 14 show the effects of two different kinds of suspension. One scale shows the height of the back seat above the road surface when the car hits a bump while the other scale measures the distance travelled along the road.

Explain which suspension you would prefer giving reasons.

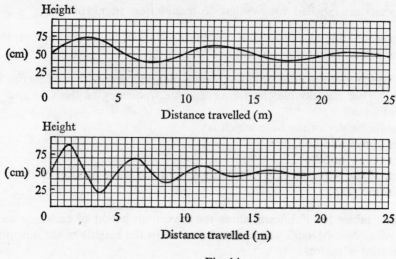

Fig. 14

9. The height of the tide (h m) on a certain day is given by the equation $h = 15 + 3 \cos \theta°$ where $\theta = 30n$, n being the number of hours after 1 a.m. What is the height of the tide on that day at (a) 8 a.m., (b) noon?

Summary

When a displacement **AB** is made at an angle of $\theta°$ to a direction called the central direction, the displacement **AN** parallel to the central direction is called the central displacement. The displacement **NB** at right-angles (to the central direction) is called the sideways displacement. These displacements depend on θ and the length *AB*.

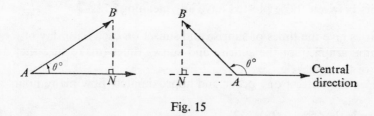

Fig. 15

The lengths of the sideways and central displacements of a unit displacement vector making an angle of $\theta°$ with the central direction are denoted by

$$\sin \theta° \quad \text{and} \quad \cos \theta°.$$

If R is the length of a displacement making an angle of $\theta°$ with some specified direction then the central and sideways distances are respectively

$$R \cos \theta° \quad \text{and} \quad R \sin \theta°.$$

150

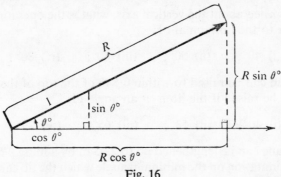

Fig. 16

The values of cos $\theta°$ and sin $\theta°$ can be found for any angle of $\theta°$ by considering the Cartesian coordinates of the end-point of a unit displacement from the origin making an angle of $\theta°$ with the line $y = 0$. The way in which sin $\theta°$ and cos $\theta°$ change as θ changes can be illustrated graphically and one obtains a curve known as a sine wave. Curves of this type occur frequently in physics and engineering.

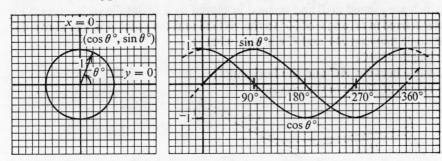

Fig. 17

Exercise C

Miscellaneous

1. Figure 18 shows a sketch of a mobile crane. The jib is 9 m long and at its lower end it is 2·4 m above ground level. The jib can be raised at different angles to the horizontal and can be turned about a vertical axis which is 0·9 m from the bottom of the jib.

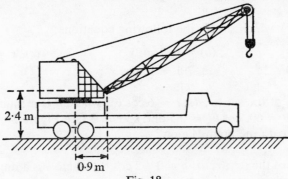

Fig. 18

151

(*a*) When the jib is turned about the vertical axis, what is the operating radius of the crane if the jib is at an angle to the horizontal of:

(i) 40°;   (ii) 50°;   (iii) 60°;   (iv) 80°?

(*b*) In practice, a load can be raised to within 0·5 m of the top of the jib. How high above the ground can a load be raised if the jib is at an angle of:

(i) 40°;   (ii) 53°;   (iii) 65°;   (iv) 79°?

(*c*) The jib of the crane can be lengthened up to 22·5 m by adding 4·5 m sections to it but, in each case, there is a limitation on the minimum angle which the jib can be to the horizontal.

Length of jib in metres	9	13·5	18	22·5
Minimum angle to horizontal	35°	40°	48°	60°

Which jib gives the maximum operating radius?

2. The mechanism for lifting the bucket of a mechanical shovel consists of two rods *AB* and *BC* which are jointed at *B* and opened or closed by a hydraulic jack *AC* (see Figure 19). The rod *AB* is fixed at an angle of 30° to the vertical and the point *A* is 1 m above the ground. When the angle between *BA* and *CA* is 40°, what is:
(*a*) the length of *AC*;
(*b*) the angle between *AC* and the horizontal;
(*c*) the height of *D* above the ground?

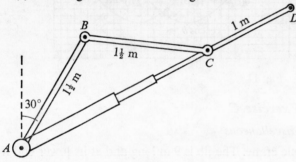

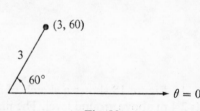

Fig. 19   Fig. 20

3. Find values of *x* which satisfy the following equations:

(*a*) $9 = x \sin 30°$;   (*b*) $4 = 7 \sin x°$;   (*c*) $x = 5 \sin 68°$;
(*d*) $6·4 = x \cos 50°$;   (*e*) $7·5 = 15 \cos x°$;   (*f*) $x = 5·8 \cos 70°$.

4. Plot the points of the set $\{(r, \theta): r = 6 \cos \theta°\}$ where θ is a multiple of 10 up to 180. For example, when $\theta = 60$, $\cos \theta° = 0·5$ and so $r = 3$ (see Figure 20).
What type of curve do the points lie on?

5. Plot the points of the set $\{(r, \theta): r = 1 + 2 \cos \theta°\}$ where θ is a multiple of 10 up to 360. These points lie on a *limaçon*.

6. Figure 21 shows a typical symmetrical roof structure. $AE = 12$ m and $EB = 5$ m. Calculate the size of the angle at A and then use this to calculate the lengths of FB and AC.

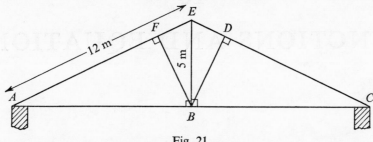

Fig. 21

7. In designing a new village hall an architect found it would be cheaper to build a pointed roof, as shown in Figure 22, than a flat roof.

(*a*) How high is the apex of the roof above the top of the walls?

(*b*) What is the width of the building?

(*c*) The larger roof space will mean increased heating costs. What is the volume of the roof space if the building is 10·5 m long?

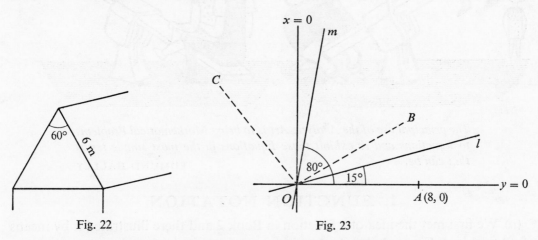

Fig. 22   Fig. 23

8. In Figure 23, the lines *l* and *m* pass through the origin and make angles of 15° and 80° respectively, with the line $y = 0$. B is the image of $A(8, 0)$ after reflection in *l*; C is the image of B after reflection in *m*. Find the angle AOC and the coordinates of C.

10

FUNCTIONS AND EQUATIONS

The principal use of the Analytic Art is to bring Mathematical Problems to Equations and to exhibit those Equations in the most simple terms that can be.

EDMUND HALLEY

1. FUNCTION NOTATION

(*a*) We first met the idea of a function in Book 2 and there illustrated it by means of a 'machine'. Figure 1 shows a machine representing the function

$$x \to x - 4.$$

If the input is 9, then the output is 5.

What would the output be if the input were (i) $^-3$, (ii) 0?

As with transformations it is useful to have a shorthand notation to denote a function and we use letters such as f, g and h.

The function in Figure 1 could be written as shown on the machine

$$f: x \to x - 4$$

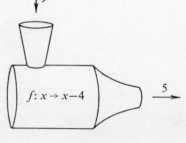

Fig. 1

154

and this is read 'the function f which maps x onto $x-4$'. It is also sometimes written in the form
$$x \xrightarrow{f} x-4.$$

(b) The output of a function machine is written
$$f(x), \quad \text{read as} \quad \text{'} f \text{ of } x \text{'}.$$

$f(x)$ is the image of x under the function f.

You have, of course, already used this type of notation in Chapter 2. There we denoted the image of a point P under the transformation $\mathbf{T}$ by $\mathbf{T}(P)$. Transformations are special types of functions: functions that map points onto points.

In Figure 1, $f(x) = x-4$. What are
$$\text{(i) } f(6), \quad \text{(ii) } f(4), \quad \text{(iii) } f(-2)?$$

(c) For the function $f: x \to 3x+2$, what are
$$\text{(i) } f(3), \quad \text{(ii) } f(0), \quad \text{(iii) } f(-1)?$$

1.1   Composite functions

It is often useful to split up a function into simpler ones and this we have done when solving equations. For example, the function
$$x \to 3x+2$$

can be obtained by combining the two simpler functions
$$x \to 3x \quad \text{and} \quad x \to x+2,$$

or in words,   'multiply by 3'   and   'add 2'.

$x \to 3x+2$ is therefore a *composite* function, composed of two simpler ones.

We can illustrate this by a flow diagram using boxes for machines.

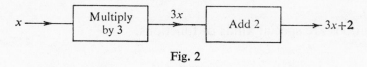

Fig. 2

Calling these functions
$$f: x \to 3x \quad \text{and} \quad g: x \to x+2,$$

we have $f(x) = 3x, \quad g(x) = x+2 \quad \text{and} \quad g(f(x)) = 3x+2.$

Following our notation for combined transformations (see p. 16) we usually write
$$g(f(x)) \quad \text{as} \quad gf(x).$$

It is important to note that, once again, gf means 'f followed by g'.

Figure 3 shows a flow diagram that produces an output $gf(x)$ when the input is x. Draw a similar flow diagram in which the output is $fg(x)$.

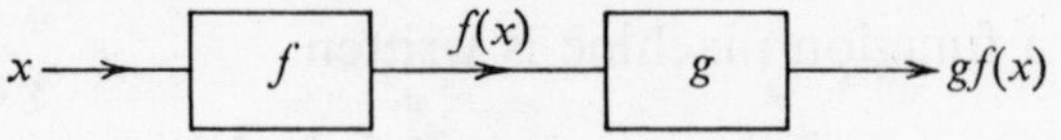

Fig. 3

What are:

(i) $gf(2)$,   (ii) $fg(2)$,   (iii) $gf(-2)$,   (iv) $fg(-2)$?

Is $gf(x) = fg(x)$?

Write the function fg in the form $x \to \dots$.

Could $gf(x)$ and $fg(x)$ be equal for a particular value of x?

1.2 Domain and range

These are words we used in Book 2 and we shall use them again here.

The domain is the set of elements forming the input to a function machine.

The range is the set of elements forming the output of the machine.

Summary

The following notation is used for functions

$$f: x \to px+q.$$

It is read,   'the function f which maps x onto $px+q$'.

The image of x under the function f is written $f(x)$, read 'f of x'.

$$f(x) = px+q.$$

If A denotes the domain and B the range of the function f, we can write

$$B = f(A).$$

If a function f is followed by a function g, we obtain the composite function gf (see Figure 3).

Transformations are special kinds of functions.

Exercise A

1. Describe in words the functions:

     (a) $x \to \frac{1}{2}x$;   (b) $x \to x+2$;   (c) $x \to x^3$.

2. Write the following functions in the form $x \to \dots$:

(a) 'subtract 5';   (b) 'divide by 7';

(c) 'multiply by $\frac{1}{3}$';   (d) 'square and add 2'.

3. For $f: x \to \frac{1}{4}(x-5)$, find:

     (a) $f(9)$;   (b) $f(5)$;   (c) $f(-1)$.

4. For $f: x \to 5-2x$, find:

$$(a) \ f(3); \qquad (b) \ f(\tfrac{1}{2}); \qquad (c) \ f(^-2).$$

5. Given that $f(x) = \dfrac{x+1}{x-1}$, find:

$$(a) \ f(3); \qquad (b) \ f(^-1); \qquad (c) \ f(0); \qquad (d) \ f(4x).$$

Is there a value of x for which $f(x)$ has no meaning?

6. Find the images of (a) 2, (b) 0, under the function $x \to 4^x$.

7. Given that f is the function mapping a number onto its highest prime factor, what are:

$$(a) \ f(10); \qquad (b) \ f(20); \qquad (c) \ f(70)?$$

8. For $f: x \to 2x+3$, find x if:

$$(a) \ f(x) = 7; \qquad (b) \ f(x) = 3.$$

9. Is the function 'square and double' the same as the function 'double and square'? Write both in the form $x \to$ .... Distinguish between $3x^2$ and $(3x)^2$ by referring to functions.

10. Split up the following functions into two simpler ones:

$$(a) \ x \to \tfrac{1}{2}(x-3); \qquad (b) \ x \to (x+7)^2; \qquad (c) \ x \to 5-x.$$

11. Is the function 'subtract 1 and add 6' the same as the function 'add 6 and subtract 1'? Name two other functions for which

$$gf(x) = fg(x)$$

for all values of x.

12. For $f: x \to 4x+1$ and $g: x \to 2-x$, find:

$$(a) \ gf(3); \qquad (b) \ gf(^-1); \qquad (c) \ fg(3); \qquad (d) \ fg(^-1).$$

Express both gf and fg in the form $x \to$ ....

13. For $f: x \to 2x-1$ and $g: x \to 3x-2$, find:

$$(a) \ gf(2) \text{ and } fg(2); \qquad (b) \ gf(0) \text{ and } fg(0); \qquad (c) \ gf(\tfrac{1}{3}) \text{ and } fg(\tfrac{1}{3}).$$

Explain your results by expressing both gf and fg in the form $x \to$ ....

14. For $f: x \to \dfrac{1}{1+x}$ and $g: x \to 2x$, find: (a) $fg(2)$ and $gf(2)$; (b) $fg(^-\tfrac{1}{3})$ and $gf(^-\tfrac{1}{3})$.

15. For the functions $f: x \to 2x+1$ and $g: x \to x^2$, find x if

$$(a) \ fg(x) = 9; \qquad (b) \ gf(x) = 9.$$

16. A function is of the form $x \xrightarrow{f} ax+b$, where a and b are numbers. Given that $f(1) = 5$ and $f(2) = 2$, find $f(3)$ by drawing a graph.

17. Suppose the function f maps the ordered pair (x, y) onto $(x+2, y+3)$ and the function g maps (x, y) onto $(x-1, y+5)$. What are:

$$(a) \ f((1, 1)); \qquad (b) \ g((1, 1)); \qquad (c) \ gf((1, 1)); \qquad (d) \ fg((1, 1))?$$

Would it be generally true to say $gf((x, y)) = fg((x, y))$? Describe f and g in terms of transformations.

18.   The domain of a function is the set of possible inputs to the machine and the range is the set of outputs.

Find the range for $f: x \to x^2 - 1$ with the domain $\{-4, -2, -1, 0, 1, 2, 4\}$.

Mark these points on a graph.

Is it true that $f(-x) = f(x)$ for all values of x? Write down another function for which this is true.

2. INVERSE RELATIONS

The idea of an inverse function is already a familiar one in simple cases. For example, we know that the inverse of 'add 6' is 'subtract 6', and that the inverse of the translation $\binom{2}{3}$ is the translation $\binom{-2}{-3}$.

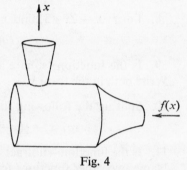

We picture the inverse function as a machine that has been put into reverse. If the action of the machine in Figure 1 were reversed, the result would be as shown in Figure 4.

Inverse functions in general, however, are not always so simple to deal with—there are many functions for which an inverse function cannot be defined. So as to understand more about functions, we shall look once

Fig. 4

again at relations—for you will remember that a function is a special kind of relation.

2.1   Obtaining the inverse relation

In Section 3 of Chapter 6 we considered the relation 'is a parent of' defined on a set of four members of a family $\{a, b, c, d\}$. A mapping diagram illustrating this relation is shown in Figure 5. The diagram tells us that

a is a parent of b,

b is a parent of c,

and b is a parent of d.

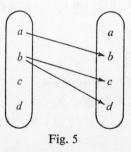

Fig. 5

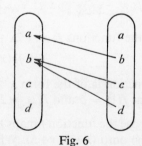

Fig. 6

Figure 6 illustrates the inverse mapping to 'is a parent of'. What relation does this represent?

158

It is easy to see that given any relation we can always find the inverse relation, simply by interchanging the direction of the arrows in the mapping diagram. Also, in Chapter 6 we saw how the matrix describing an inverse relation can be obtained by transposing the matrix that describes the original relation.

2.2 Functions as relations

We learned in Book 2 that a function is a special kind of relation or mapping.

(*a*) Is the relation illustrated in Figure 5 a function? Give your reasons.

(*b*) Is the relation illustrated in Figure 6 a function? Give your reasons.

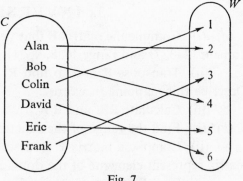

Fig. 7

The mapping illustrated in Figure 7 is a function. It shows how the set C of competitors in a race was mapped onto the set $W = \{1, 2, 3, 4, 5, 6\}$—the positions in which they finished.

Construct the matrix to describe this function.

Compare the matrix you have just constructed with that describing the relation 'is a parent of' in Section 2.1.

How can you tell whether or not the relation described by a matrix is a function?

The following matrices all describe relations, for example, in (i) a is related to a, a is not related to b, and so on. Which of the relations are functions?

(i)

$$
\text{domain} \begin{array}{c} \\ a \\ b \\ c \\ d \end{array}
\begin{array}{c} \text{range} \\ \begin{array}{cccc} a & b & c & d \end{array} \\ \left(\begin{array}{cccc} 1 & 0 & 1 & 0 \\ 1 & 0 & 0 & 0 \\ 0 & 0 & 0 & 1 \\ 0 & 1 & 0 & 0 \end{array} \right) \end{array} ;
$$

(ii)

$$
\text{domain} \begin{array}{c} \\ a \\ b \\ c \\ d \end{array}
\begin{array}{c} \text{range} \\ \begin{array}{ccc} \alpha & \beta & \gamma \end{array} \\ \left(\begin{array}{ccc} 1 & 0 & 0 \\ 0 & 1 & 0 \\ 1 & 0 & 0 \\ 0 & 0 & 1 \end{array} \right) \end{array} ;
$$

(iii)

$$
\text{domain} \begin{array}{c} \\ a \\ b \\ c \\ d \end{array}
\begin{array}{c} \text{range} \\ \begin{array}{cccc} P & Q & R & S \end{array} \\ \left(\begin{array}{cccc} 0 & 0 & 0 & 1 \\ 1 & 0 & 0 & 0 \\ 0 & 1 & 0 & 0 \\ 0 & 0 & 1 & 0 \end{array} \right) \end{array} .
$$

In each case construct the matrix describing the inverse mapping. Which of these are functions?

Summary

A mapping (relation) is a function if *every* member of the domain has one and only one image.

The matrix describing a function will have one and only one non-zero element in each row.

The matrix describing the inverse relation to R is obtained by transposing the matrix that describes R. (To transpose means to interchange rows with columns—to reflect in the leading diagonal.)

Corresponding to every relation there is an inverse relation.

3. INVERSE FUNCTIONS

(a) (i) Compile the matrix R that describes the mapping '$x \rightarrow$ multiple of x' with domain $\{2, 3, 7\}$ and range $\{6, 8, 9, 21\}$.

(ii) Transpose R and so find R' the matrix describing the inverse mapping. Describe this mapping in words.

(iii) Calculate RR' and $R'R$.

(b) (i) Find the range of the function $x \rightarrow 2x$ for clock arithmetic on $\{0, 1, 2\}$.

(ii) Compile a matrix F to describe this function. (Again let the rows of the matrix represent elements of the domain and the columns elements of the range.)

(iii) Find F' the transpose of F.

(iv) Is the relation described by F' a function?

(v) Calculate FF' and $F'F$. What do you find? How do you account for this result?

(c) (i) Find the range of the function $x \rightarrow x^2$ for clock arithmetic on $\{0, 1, 2\}$.

(ii) Compile a matrix G to describe this function.

(iii) Is G a square matrix?

(iv) Find G' the transpose of G.

(v) Is the relation described by G' a function?

(vi) Calculate GG' and $G'G$. Do you obtain a similar result to that you obtained above for FF' and $F'F$?

In answering the various parts of (a), (b) and (c) you have been discovering more and more about the behaviour of functions. Collecting this information, we have:

(i) all functions can be thought of as relations;

(ii) corresponding to every relation there is an inverse relation;

(iii) from (i) and (ii) it follows that corresponding to every function there is an inverse *relation*;

(iv) since not all relations are functions, it does not follow from (iii) that to every function there corresponds an inverse function.

However, we have seen that some functions do possess inverse functions.

If f is a function for which an inverse function can be defined, then we denote the inverse function by f^{-1} read 'f inverse'. For example, if f is the function 'multiply by 2', then f^{-1} is the function 'divide by 2'.

The matrix describing a function has one and only one non-zero element in each row. It follows that the matrix describing a function which possesses an inverse function will have one and only one non-zero element in each column.

Thus, of the three matrices given in Section 2.2, (ii) and (iii) describe functions, but only (iii) describes a function for which an inverse function can be defined.

More generally, a function has an inverse function if and only if every member of the *range* is the image of one and only one member of the domain.

Summary

If an inverse function to the function f exists, then we denote it by f^{-1}, read as 'f inverse'.

If a function maps two or more members of the domain onto the same image, the inverse relation is not a function.

Exercise B

1. What are the inverse functions to:

(a) 'subtract 6';   (b) 'divide by 8';

(c) $x \to x+3$;   (d) $x \to 5x$?

2. With the domains shown, which of the following mappings are functions?

Domain	Mapping
(a) a family of children: Andrew, Brian, Catherine, Deborah	$x \to$ brother of x
(b) houses in a street	house $\to$ number of house
(c) numbers	$x \to$ largest prime factor of x
(d) cars in U.K.	$x \to$ registration number of x

3. Taking f to stand for those mappings of Question 2 you know to be functions, write down (if meaningful):

(a) f(Catherine);   (b) f(your own house);

(c) $f(84)$;   (d) f(your Headteacher's car).

4. Which, if any, of the *functions* in Question 2 have an inverse function? Discuss the existence, or otherwise, of:

(a) f^{-1}(Andrew);   (b) $f^{-1}(104)$;

(c) $f^{-1}(7)$;   (d) $f^{-1}(836\ BJB)$.

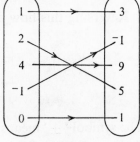

5. Does the mapping shown in Figure 8 define a function f? If so, does it possess an inverse f^{-1}? If appropriate write down:

(a) $f(4)$;   (b) $f^{-1}(f(4))$;

(c) $f^{-1}(3)$;   (d) $f(f^{-1}(3))$.

Describe the function f in words.

6. What is $f^{-1}(x)$ if   (a) $f(x) = \frac{1}{3}x$;   (b) $f(x) = x-4$?   Fig. 8

7. In Section 3 we discovered that there was an inverse function corresponding to the function $x \to 2x$ under clock arithmetic on $\{0, 1, 2\}$.

Is there an inverse function corresponding to $x \to 2x$ under clock arithmetic on $\{0, 1, 2, 3\}$?

Do you think there will be an inverse function to $x \to 2x$ under clock arithmetic on $\{0, 1, 2, 3, 4\}$? Check your opinion by carrying out the necessary working.

8. If f possesses an inverse function f^{-1}, what can you say about $f^{-1}f(x)$ and $ff^{-1}(x)$? How is this connected with what you discovered concerning F'F and FF' in Section 3. What can you say about the inverse of the inverse of a function?

4. FINDING INVERSE FUNCTIONS

(*a*) A composite function can be obtained by combining simple functions. The inverse of a composite function can be obtained from the inverses of the simple functions but the order of combination should be noticed.

Consider the function
$$x \to \frac{x-11}{6}.$$

We can represent it by the flow diagram in Figure 9.

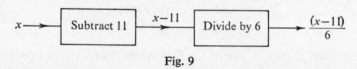

Fig. 9

Put this flow diagram into reverse by replacing each machine by its inverse machine and then by feeding in x *at the right-hand end*. Write the inverse of
$$x \to \frac{(x-11)}{6}$$
in the form $x \to ....$

(*b*) Consider the function $\qquad x \to 3x^2 + 1$.

Splitting up this function we get the flow diagram

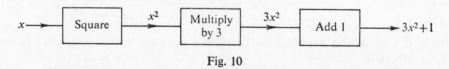

Fig. 10

Reversing this flow diagram and feeding in x we obtain

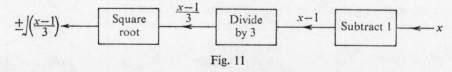

Fig. 11

The symbol '$\pm$' means 'positive or negative'; for example, as $3^2 = 9$ and $(^-3)^2 = 9$, the square root of 9 is either positive or negative 3. This is written ± 3.

162

The inverse mapping is therefore
$$x \to \pm \sqrt{\left(\frac{x-1}{3}\right)}.$$

Is this a function? [Notice that this might be rewritten as $x \to \pm \sqrt{\{\tfrac{1}{3}(x-1)\}}$.]
What is the output in Figure 11, if the input is (i) 4, (ii) 28?
Name two different inputs in Figure 10 that would give rise to the same output.
Taking '$\sqrt{}$' to mean 'the positive square root of', is
$$x \to \sqrt{\{\tfrac{1}{3}(x-1)\}}$$
a function?
Would it be true to say that $x \to \sqrt{\{\tfrac{1}{3}(x-1)\}}$ is the inverse function of $x \to 3x^2+1$?

4.1   Self-inverse functions

(a) Figure 12 shows a graph of the function
$$f: x \to 10-x$$
for the domain
$$\{x: 0 \leqslant x \leqslant 10\}.$$
What are (i) $f(8)$, (ii) $f(2)$? These values are related to the points $A(8, 2)$ and $B(2, 8)$
on the graph, for the points plotted on the graph are those with coordinates $(x, f(x))$.

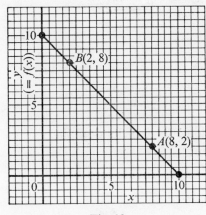

Fig. 12

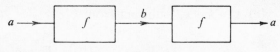

Fig. 13

It is easily seen that $f(7) = 3$ and $f(3) = 7$.
Is it always true that if $f(a) = b$, then $f(b) = a$?
This function is, in fact, its own inverse as is illustrated in Figure 13.
That is, $f^{-1}(x) = f(x) = 10-x$.

(b) Draw the graph of the function
$$f: x \to 12/x$$
for the domain $\{x: 1 \leqslant x \leqslant 12\}$, by first accurately plotting about 8 points.
What are: (i) $f(3)$, (ii) $f(4)$, (iii) $f(8)$, (iv) $f(1\tfrac{1}{2})$?

163

Again we have a function that is self-inverse. What are the equations of the curve you have drawn and of the line in Figure 12?

Do the graphs have a line of symmetry? If so, what is its equation?

It is useful to be able to describe these two functions in words.

$$x \to 10 - x, \text{ we call 'subtract from 10';}$$

and $\qquad\qquad\qquad x \to 12/x, \text{ we call 'divide into 12'.}$

Example 1

Find the inverse of $\qquad\qquad f: x \to 5 - 2x.$

A flow diagram for this is shown in Figure 14.

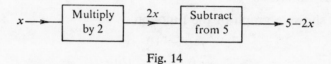

Fig. 14

Reversing this flow diagram and feeding in x we obtain

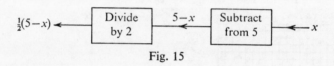

Fig. 15

The inverse function is $\qquad\qquad x \to \frac{1}{2}(5 - x).$

Summary

A function f is self-inverse if $ff(x) = x$ for all elements x of its domain.
Two important functions that are self-inverse are:

(a) $x \to k - x$, 'subtract from k'; $\qquad$ (b) $x \to k/x$, 'divide into k'.

Exercise C

1. Draw flow diagrams to illustrate the functions:

$$(a) \ x \to \frac{x+3}{5}; \qquad (b) \ x \to \frac{5}{x+3}.$$

Are these inverse to one another? Work out the inverse functions in the form $x \to \dots$

2. Given that f is the function $x \to 4/x$, write down $f(2)$ and $f^{-1}(2)$, $f(10)$ and $f^{-1}(10)$. What do you notice? What is $f(f(x))$? If g is any function and $g(g(x)) = x$, what can you say about g^{-1}?

3. Find, by using flow diagrams, the inverses of:

(a) $x \to 2x - 1$; $\qquad$ (b) $x \to 3x + 2$; $\qquad$ (c) $x \to 5 - \frac{1}{3}x$;
(d) $x \to \frac{1}{2}(3x + 7)$; $\qquad$ (e) $x \to 5(2x - 1)$; $\qquad$ (f) $x \to 4(1 - 5x)$.

164

4. What is the inverse of $x \to {}^-x$? We can call this function 'multiply by $^-1$'. Draw a flow diagram showing
$$f: x \to 3 - x$$
as a combination of $x \to {}^-x$ and $x \to x + 3$. Reverse the flow diagram and hence show that f is self-inverse.

5. f and g are two functions having inverses. Express $(fg)^{-1}$ in terms of f^{-1} and g^{-1}, and draw a flow diagram and its reverse to illustrate this relation.

6. Find, by drawing flow diagrams, whether or not inverse functions exist for:

(a) $x \to 3/x^2$;   (b) $x \to 1 - \frac{1}{4}x^2$.

7. Find the inverse of
$$x \to 1 - \frac{1}{1-x}.$$
What sort of function is this?

8. The function f maps acute angles, measured in degrees, onto the sines of the angles. Use your tables to write down $f(40)$ and $f^{-1}(0.45)$. Why is the word 'acute' necessary in the first sentence? What is the range of this function?

9. Taking all the points in the Cartesian plane as domain does the mapping
$$P \to (\text{reflection in } x = 0 \text{ of } P)$$
define a function? Do you have to leave out any of the points of the plane? Does this function have the properties of g in Question 2?

10. Find examples of functions that are self-inverse and have the following domains:

(a) numbers;   (b) points of a plane;   (c) people.

11. Sketch the graph $x° \to \cos x°$. Is this a function? Discuss the possible meaning of $\cos^{-1} x°$. Is this a function?

12. Define a domain for which the function $x \to 4 - x^2$ has an inverse function. Illustrate your answer by drawing a graph.

5. EQUATIONS

(a) Consider how we solve the equation
$$\tfrac{1}{8}(3t + 4) = 2.$$

A flow diagram for the function $t \to \frac{1}{8}(3t + 4)$ is shown in Figure 16.

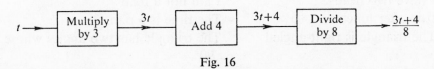

Fig. 16

Figure 17 illustrates the result of feeding $\frac{1}{8}(3t + 4)$ and 2 into reversed flow diagrams.

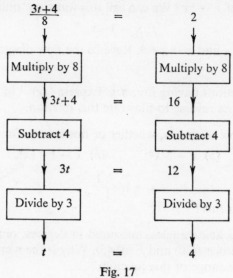

Fig. 17

We normally do not draw the complete flow diagram, but write

$$\tfrac{1}{8}(3t+4) = 2,$$
$$\Rightarrow \quad 3t+4 = 16,$$
$$\Rightarrow \quad 3t = 12,$$
$$\Rightarrow \quad t = 4,$$

that is, we write down the intermediate stages in the reversal procedure.

As you can see, $\qquad \tfrac{1}{8}(3t+4) = 2 \Rightarrow t = 4.$

Find by substitution whether or not it is true that

$$t = 4 \Rightarrow \tfrac{1}{8}(3t+4) = 2.$$

This is plainly so.

The symbol $\Rightarrow$ (implies) could be replaced by the symbol $\Leftarrow$ (is implied by) or, better still, by the symbol $\Leftrightarrow$ which means 'implies *and* is implied by'.

Which of the symbols $\Rightarrow$, $\Leftarrow$, or $\Leftrightarrow$ are appropriate links between the following pairs of statements?

  (i) I have two heads   I am not a man
  (ii) It is after lunch   The time is 3 p.m.
  (iii) The triangle is right-angled   The triangle has two angles whose sum is 90°.

When you have solved an equation using '$\Leftrightarrow$' at every step, then it is good sense to check your answer by substituting in the original relation. For if you are right, the relation will be satisfied and if you are wrong the relation will not be satisfied.

166

The two examples which follow demonstrate these methods of solution applied to different forms of equations.

Example 2

Solve the equation $\qquad 5 = \dfrac{2}{x+3}.$

The function $\qquad\qquad x \rightarrow \dfrac{2}{x+3}$

is illustrated by the flow diagram in Figure 18. Note that the function 'divide into 2' is self inverse.

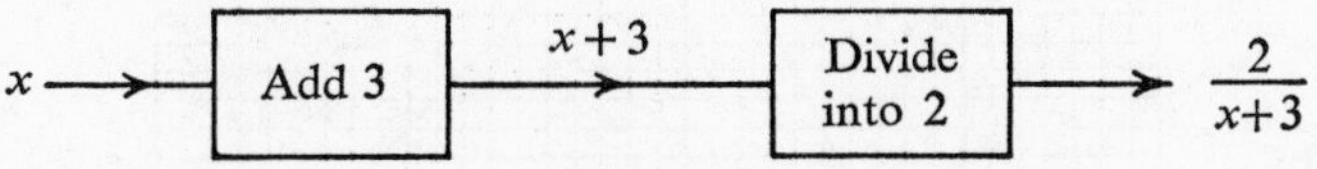

$$x \longrightarrow \boxed{\text{Add 3}} \xrightarrow{\;x+3\;} \boxed{\begin{array}{c}\text{Divide}\\\text{into 2}\end{array}} \longrightarrow \dfrac{2}{x+3}$$

Fig. 18

The images of each side of the equation under the inverse functions applied in the reverse order are given by:

$$5 = \frac{2}{x+3};$$

divide into 2,

$$\tfrac{2}{5} = x+3;$$

subtract 3,

$$-2\tfrac{3}{5} = x.$$

Example 3

Solve the equation $\qquad 12 = 2\left(8 - \dfrac{3}{x}\right).$

The right-hand side of the equation is the image of x under the function composed of, in order:

divide into 3 (self-inverse), subtract from 8 (self-inverse) and multiply by 2.

The images of each side of the equation under the inverse functions applied in the reverse order are given by:

$$12 = 2\left(8 - \frac{3}{x}\right);$$

divide by 2,

$$6 = 8 - \frac{3}{x};$$

subtract from 8

$$2 = \frac{3}{x};$$

divide into 3

$$\tfrac{3}{2} = x.$$

The method of 'inverse function' can be used to solve equations only when x appears once; that is, when of side of the equation is the image of a compound function in x. If x appears more often, as in the equation

$$2x-1 = 5-x,$$

it is necessary to use ideas connected with inverse elements and these are discussed in the next chapter and in Book 4. The graphical method is easy and can immediately be demonstrated. The graphical solution of the equation $2x-1 = 5-x$ is illustrated in Figure 19.

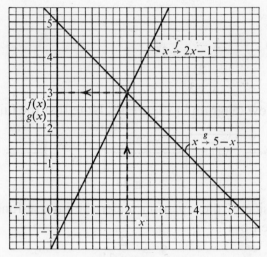

Fig. 19

The functions $f: x \to 2x-1$ and $g: x \to 5-x$

are represented by straight lines. We wish to find x when

$$f(x) = g(x);$$

that is, we wish to find the value of x that is mapped onto the same number (y co-ordinate) by both functions.

From the graph we see, for example, that $f(1) = 1$ but $g(1) = 4$; $f(3) = 5$ but $g(3) = 2$. In fact, it is clear that the point in which we are interested, is the point where the lines meet, that is, $(2, 3)$. At this point $f(x) = g(x) = 3$. The solution to our problem, therefore, is $x = 2$.

When using the 'inverse function' method to solve simple orderings, you must be especially careful to notice any change in the direction of the ordering sign. Copy and complete the right-hand column of the following; sketch graphs to illustrate each ordering and check your algebraic answers (particularly in (v) and (vi)).

(i) $x + 2 > 3$ Apply $x \to x+2$ $x > 1$

(ii) $x - 9 \leqslant {}^-5$ Apply $x \to x+9$ $x \quad 4$

(iii) $2x > 1$ Apply $x \to \dfrac{x}{2}$ x

(iv) ${}^-5x \geqslant 20$ Apply $x \to \dfrac{x}{{}^-5}$ x

(v) $1-x \leqslant 2$ Apply $x \to 1-x$ x

(vi) $\dfrac{1}{x} \leqslant 7$ Apply $x \to \dfrac{1}{x}$ x

168

Example 4

Solve the ordering

$$1-2x \leqslant 2.$$

Sketching the graph of the composite function $x \rightarrow 1-2x$ gives Figure 20. When the image of x is less than 2, x must be greater than $\frac{1}{2}$.

Using the method of inverse functions: the composite function consists of 'multiply by 2' and 'subtract from 1'. Applying the inverse functions in the reverse order:

$$1-2x \leqslant 2;$$

subtract from 1,

$$2x \geqslant {}^{-}1;$$

divide by 2,

$$x \geqslant {}^{-}\tfrac{1}{2}.$$

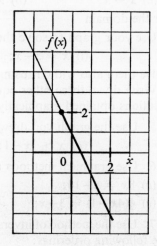

Fig. 20

Note that the ordering sign changes when 'multiplying or dividing by a negative quantity, when applying the self-inverse function $x \rightarrow k-x$ and, for positive x the self-inverse function $x \rightarrow k/x$. When x is negative in the latter case, you must work out what happens.

Exercise D

1. Use reversed flow diagrams to solve

(a) $3x+5 = 12;$ (b) $3(x+5) = 12;$ (c) $\dfrac{x+5}{3} = 12;$ (d) $\dfrac{3}{x+5} = 12.$

2. Use the method of inverse functions to solve the following equations. List the simple functions needed and set out the application of the inverse functions as in *Example* 3.

(a) $5x+2 = 11;$ (b) $8 = a-14;$ (c) $2-p = 6;$
(d) $^{-}4 = 3-2h;$ (e) $0 = \frac{1}{2}e-3;$ (f) $\frac{2}{3}+\frac{1}{3}m = 2;$
(g) $\frac{1}{2}(b+2) = 1;$ (h) $(1/s)+3 = 22.$

3. Use the method of inverse functions to solve the following equations. List the simple functions needed and set out the application of the inverse functions as in *Example* 3.

(a) $7+4y = 9;$ (b) $1 = 5-3r;$ (c) $13 = \dfrac{1}{2q} -3;$

(d) $9 = 1-\dfrac{4}{d};$ (e) $3 = \dfrac{6}{2+b};$ (f) $\dfrac{5x+13}{2} = 9;$

(g) $\dfrac{1}{2} = \dfrac{3}{1 \div v};$ (h) $37-\dfrac{2}{n} = 19.$

4. On the same diagram graph the functions:

(a) $x \rightarrow x$; (b) $x \rightarrow 3-x$; (c) $x \rightarrow 3x-1$; (d) $x \rightarrow \frac{1}{3}x-1$,

for the domain $\{x: ^-4 \leqslant x \leqslant 4\}$.

Use your graph to solve the equations:

(i) $x = 3-x$; (ii) $3x-1 = \frac{1}{3}x-1$; (iii) $3-x = 3x-1$.

Solve them also without using the graph and compare your results.

Write down three other equations that can be solved using your graphs. Check that the solutions obtained graphically are correct.

5. Use the graph you drew in Question 4 to solve the orderings:

(a) $x > \frac{1}{3}x-1$; (b) $3-x > 3x-1$; (c) $\frac{1}{3}x-1 \leqslant 3-x$.

6. Use graphical methods to solve the following:

(a) $8x = x-14$; (b) $2x-1 = 5-x$;

(c) $\frac{1}{2}(4x-1) = 3+x$; (d) $2x-(3x+4) = 4x-(3x-2)$.

7. Use the method of inverse functions, checking each answer with a sketch graph, to solve the following orderings:

(a) $7+2x < 5$; (b) $10 < 3-x$; (c) $\frac{2}{3}(4x-6) \leqslant 12$;

(d) $\frac{3}{x} \leqslant 6$; (e) $\frac{4}{x+1} > 1$.

8. Could the flow diagram in Figure 17 be used to justify this argument:

$$\frac{1}{8}(3t+4) \text{ is a multiple of } 2 \quad \Leftrightarrow \quad t \text{ is a multiple of } 4?$$

If this is not true, at what stage in the flow diagram is the argument faulty?

6. FORMULAE

Algebraic relations are sometimes referred to as 'formulae' particularly when they are an expression of physical laws. It is often necessary to rearrange the letters in a formula in order to make calculation easier.

A well-known formula occurs in physics when a gas expands on being heated,

$$V = V_0(1+\gamma t).$$

V_0 and V are the numbers of units of volume of the gas at the beginning and end of the period during which the gas is heated and t is the number of degrees by which the temperature has risen. γ is usually known as the coefficient of cubic expansion.

Suppose we measure V, V_0 and t and wish to find γ. It would be more useful to have the formula in the form $\gamma = ...$

When the brackets are removed the formula becomes

$$V = V_0+\gamma t V_0.$$

We can see this as a mapping of $\gamma \rightarrow V$ illustrated by the flow diagram in Figure 21.

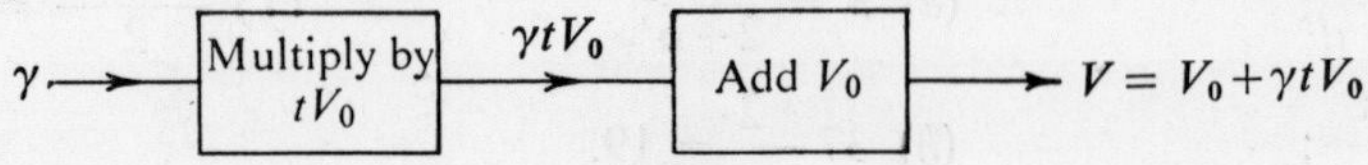

Fig. 21

Reversing this flow diagram we have the function that maps V onto γ.

$$\gamma = \frac{V-V_0}{tV_0} \longleftarrow \boxed{\begin{array}{c}\text{Divide}\\\text{by } tV_0\end{array}} \xleftarrow{V-V_0} \boxed{\begin{array}{c}\text{Subtract}\\V_0\end{array}} \longleftarrow V$$

Fig. 22

The rearranged formula is $\gamma = \dfrac{V-V_0}{tV_0}.$

Written in the form $V = V_0(1+\gamma t)$

we say that the formula has V as *subject*.

In the form

$$\gamma = \frac{V-V_0}{tV_0}$$

the subject is γ, and so the process described above is known as 'changing the subject of a formula'.

Example 5

Figure 23 shows a section through an instrument used to measure the speed V of air in a wind tunnel. p_0 is the pressure due to the movement of the air and p the static pressure. Provided the units of measurement have been selected correctly, the formula

$$p_0 = p + \tfrac{1}{2}\rho V^2$$

relates p, p_0, V and ρ, the density of the air.

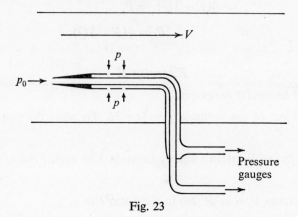

Fig. 23

Change the subject of this formula to V and find V if $p_0 - p = 550$ and $\rho = 0\cdot0765$. Representing the formula by a flow diagram we have

$$V \longrightarrow \boxed{\text{Square}} \xrightarrow{V^2} \boxed{\begin{array}{c}\text{Multiply}\\\text{by } \rho\end{array}} \xrightarrow{\rho V^2} \boxed{\begin{array}{c}\text{Divide}\\\text{by } 2\end{array}} \xrightarrow{\frac{1}{2}\rho V^2} \boxed{\text{Add } p} \longrightarrow p_0 = p + \tfrac{1}{2}\rho V^2$$

Fig. 24

171

Reversing this we have

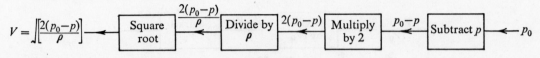

Fig. 25

With subject V the formula is

$$V = \sqrt{\left(\frac{2(p_0-p)}{\rho}\right)}.$$

[In examples such as this, one can generally reject negative square roots on physical considerations.]

Given that $p_0-p = 550$ and $\rho = 0.0765$,

$$V = \sqrt{\left(\frac{2 \times 5\cdot 5 \times 10^2}{7\cdot 65 \times 10^{-2}}\right)} = \sqrt{(1\cdot 44 \times 10^4)}$$

$$= 1\cdot 20 \times 10^2$$

$$= 120 \text{ to 3 s.f. (by slide rule).}$$

Example 6

Make P the subject of the formula $R = 3Q+2P$. In this case we dispense with the flow diagram.

$$R = 3Q+2P,$$

$$\Leftrightarrow \quad R-3Q = 2P,$$

$$\Leftrightarrow \tfrac{1}{2}(R-3Q) = P,$$

that is,
$$P = \tfrac{1}{2}(R-3Q).$$

Exercise E

Flow diagrams should be used if necessary.

1. Make c the subject of the formula $f = \tfrac{9}{5}c + 32$. To what do you think this formula relates?

2. Make c the subject of Einstein's energy formula $E = mc^2$. Find c, when $m = 0\cdot 03$ and $E = 2\cdot 7 \times 10^{19}$.

3. Arrange the formula $V = er^2B^2/2m$ in the form $e/m = \dots$.

4. Figure 26 shows a *closed* box.
(*a*) Calculate P, the total length of its edges. Show that

$$b = \frac{P-8a}{4}$$

and rearrange the formula in the form $a = \dots$.
(*b*) Calculate S, the total area of the faces of the box. Make b the subject of this formula.
(*c*) Calculate V, the volume of the box. Make a the subject of this formula.

(*d*) Use the formulae to find:
   (i)   the value of *b* when $P = 32$ and $a = 1\frac{1}{2}$;
  (ii)   the value of *b* when $S = 137$ and $a = 5$;
 (iii)   the value of *a* when $V = 80$ and $b = 5$.

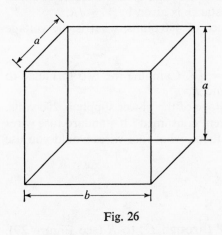

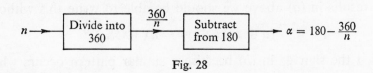

Fig. 26   Fig. 27

5. A weight *P* is hung from the end of a beam of length *l* embedded in a wall (see Figure 27). The deflection *d* of the end of the beam is given by the formula

$$d = \frac{Pl^3}{3EI},$$

where *I* depends on the shape of the cross-section of the beam and *E* on the material of which it is made.
Make *E* the subject of this formula.
Find *E* when $P = 150$, $l = 40$, $I = 1$ and $d = 1 \cdot 5$.

6. The number of degrees (α) in the angle of a regular polygon of *n* sides is given by

$$\alpha = 180 - \frac{360}{n}.$$

This formula can be represented by the flow diagram in Figure 28.
What is special about the two operations in this flow diagram? Reverse the diagram to make *n* the subject of the formula. Check your result by putting $\alpha = 90$.

$$n \longrightarrow \boxed{\begin{array}{c} \text{Divide into} \\ 360 \end{array}} \xrightarrow{\frac{360}{n}} \boxed{\begin{array}{c} \text{Subtract} \\ \text{from } 180 \end{array}} \longrightarrow \alpha = 180 - \frac{360}{n}$$

Fig. 28

7. Make *R* the subject of the formula $a = 6 - 12/R$. What is *R* when (*a*) $a = 5$; (*b*) $a = 5\frac{1}{4}$?

8. On a dry road, the shortest braking distance (*d* metres) of my car is given approximately by dividing the square of the speed (*v* km/h) by 200.
  (*a*) Write this as a formula, with *d* as subject.
  (*b*) Find the shortest braking distances from speeds of 30 km/h and 60 km/h.

(c) Change the subject of the formula to v.

(d) On a misty evening visibility is down to 45 m. What speeds are safe (use ordering signs)?

9. Ohm's law states that if a current of I amps flows through a resistance of R ohms, then the difference in potential V volts, across the resistance is given by $V = IR$.

(a) If a current of 5 amps flows through a resistance of 480 ohms, what is the voltage difference across the resistance?

(b) Make I the subject of the formula.

(c) The power consumed, W watts, is given by $W = IV$. Combine the two formulae to find W, first in terms of I and R, then in terms of V and R.

(d) An electric fire consumes 2000 watts and the voltage of the power supply is 250 volts. What are: (i) the resistance of the fire, and (ii) the current consumed? If standard fuse wires melt when currents of 5, 10 or 15 amps flow through them, what fuse wires would you use with this fire to guard against overloading?

7. BRACKETS

(a) Suppose we wish to make a journey from P through Q, to R (see Figure 29). Two routes are possible from P to Q and two from Q to R. We could, for example, take route a, and then route y. Suppose we write this ay.

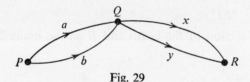

Fig. 29

	x	y
a		ay
b		

Fig. 30

What other possible combinations are there? Copy and complete Figure 30.

(b) In going from P to Q we made the choice 'a or b'. Suppose we write this $a \oplus b$. The choice for the whole route from P to R would then be written

$$(a \oplus b)(x \oplus y),$$

that is,   (a or b)   and then   (x or y).

Using the results in (a) above we should be able to write this without brackets. Complete

$$(a \oplus b)(x \oplus y) = ax \oplus \ldots.$$

(c) We used the sign $\oplus$ in (b) because a similar pattern occurs when using $+$ and numbers.

In Figure 31 the multiplication 17×13 is illustrated as

$$(10+7) \times (10+3).$$

The multiplication sign between the brackets is usually omitted and we write

$$(10+7)(10+3).$$

174

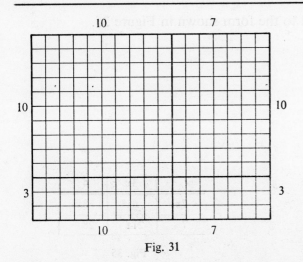

Fig. 31   Fig. 32

Copy and complete $(10+7)(10+3) = (10 \times 10) + \dots$

Copy and complete the multiplication table in Figure 32 and compare it with Figure 30.

(*d*) Replacing 10 in Figure 31 by *a* we get Figure 33 which represents $(a+7)(a+3)$. The second part of the figure shows the four products that occur when the brackets are removed.

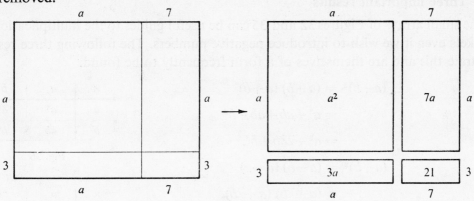

Fig. 33

Check that $(a+7)(a+3) = a^2 + 10a + 21.$

Example 7

What is $(2x+7)(3x+4)$? Check your answer by putting $x = 10$.

From Figure 34, $(2x+7)(3x+4)$

$$= 6x^2 + 8x + 21x + 28$$

$$= 6x^2 + 29x + 28.$$

175

Figure 34 is conveniently shortened to the form shown in Figure 35.

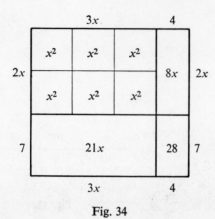

Fig. 34

×	3x	4
2x	6x²	8x
7	21x	28

Fig. 35

Put $x = 10$. Then

$$2x+7 = 27 \quad \text{and} \quad 3x+4 = 34,$$

$$27 \times 34 = 918 \quad \text{and} \quad 6x^2+29x+28 = 600+290+28 = 918.$$

7.1 Three important results

The small arrays of Figures 32 and 35 can be useful guides to the multiplication of brackets even if we wish to introduce negative numbers. The following three results illustrate this and are themselves of a form frequently to be found.

$$(a+b)^2 = (a+b)(a+b)$$
$$= a^2+ab+ab+b^2$$
$$= a^2+2ab+b^2.$$

×	a	b
a	a²	ab
b	ab	b²

Fig. 36

$$(a-b)^2 = (a-b)(a-b)$$
$$= (a+{}^-b)(a+{}^-b)$$
$$= a^2+{}^-ab+{}^-ab+({}^-b)^2$$
$$= a^2+2{}^-ab+({}^-b)^2$$
$$= a^2-2ab+b^2.$$

×	a	⁻b
a	a²	⁻ab
⁻b	⁻ab	b²

Fig. 37

$$(a+b)(a-b) = (a+b)(a+{}^-b)$$
$$= a^2+ab+{}^-ab+{}^-bb$$
$$= a^2+0+{}^-(b^2)$$
$$= a^2-b^2.$$

×	a	⁻b
a	a²	⁻ab
b	ab	⁻(b²)

Fig. 38

176

Notice that $(a+b)^2$ does not equal a^2+b^2. So, for example

$$(x+3)^2 \neq x^2+9, \qquad (2+k)^2 \neq 4+k^2, \qquad 11^2 = (10+1)^2 \neq 100+1.$$

Which of the following are correct:

(i) $2(a+b) = 2a+2b$;

(ii) $(a \times b)^2 = a^2 \times b^2$;

(iii) $\dfrac{(a+b)}{2} = \dfrac{a}{2}+\dfrac{b}{2}$;

(iv) $\dfrac{2}{(a+b)} = \dfrac{2}{a}+\dfrac{2}{b}$?

Exercise F

1. Copy and complete the following tables.

(a)
×	a	3b
2a		
b		

; (b)
×	c	3d
c		
3d		

; (c)
×	p	⁻5q
p		
⁻4q		

Write without brackets

(a) $(2a+b)(a+3b)$;

(b) $(c+3d)^2$;

(c) $(p-4q)(p-5q)$.

2. A menu offers sausage or egg with chips or beans or spaghetti. Write out all the possible combinations.

3. Write without brackets, using tables similar to those in Question 1 if necessary:

(a) $(x+2)(x+3)$;

(b) $(x+7)(x+11)$;

(c) $(2x+5)(x+1)$;

(d) $(3x+7)(5x+8)$;

(e) $(x+2)(x-3)$;

(f) $(3x-2)(2x+1)$;

(g) $(x-4)(4x-1)$;

(h) $(2+a)(5-2a)$.

4. Draw a diagram similar to Figure 29 but add a third route z from Q to R. How many different routes are now possible from P to R?

Complete $(a+b)(x+y+z) = ax+\dots$.

Write without brackets:

(a) $(x+1)(a+b+c)$;

(b) $(x-1)(a-b+c)$;

(c) $(x+2)(2x-y+3)$;

(d) $(x+y+z)(2x+3y+4z)$.

5. Copy the following and fill in the missing operation symbols, letters or numbers:

(a) $(p+q)^2 = p^2+2pq+\quad$;

(b) $(p-q)^2 = p^2 \quad 2pq \quad q^2$;

(c) $(d+e)(d\quad) = d^2-e^2$;

(d) $(j+k)(j+k) = j^2+\quad+\quad$;

(e) $(x-\quad)(x+\quad) = \quad-y^2$;

(f) $(\quad+v)(\quad-v) = u^2 \quad$.

6. Copy the following and fill in the missing operation symbols, letters or numbers:

(a) $(x+2y)^2 = x^2+4xy+\quad$;

(b) $(r-2s)(r-2s) = \quad -4rs+\quad$;

(c) $(2m+\quad)^2 = 4m^2+12mn+9n^2$;

(d) $(2a-5b)(2a+5b) = 4a^2 \quad 25b^2$;

(e) $(\quad-4)(\quad-4) = 9y^2-24y+16$;

(f) $10,401^2 = 10,000^2+2\times\quad\times\quad+401^2$.

7. Calculate 975^2 by regarding it as $(1000-25)^2$. Calculate also 1000^2-25^2. Is this greater or smaller than $(1000-25)^2$?

8. We can calculate $(2 \cdot 005)^2$ in the following manner.

$$(2 \cdot 005)^2 = (2 + 0 \cdot 005)^2 = 2^2 + 2(2 \times 0 \cdot 005) + 0 \cdot 005^2$$
$$= 4 + 0 \cdot 02 + 0 \cdot 000025$$
$$= 4 \cdot 020025.$$

Use a similar method to calculate:

(a) 1002^2; (b) 99^2; (c) $1 \cdot 04^2$;
(d) 408^2; (e) 793^2; (f) $0 \cdot 79^2$.

9. Calculate in the neatest way:

(a) $25 \times 978 \times 4$; (b) 978×1022; (c) $3615^2 - 3615 \times 3515$;

(d) $4 \cdot 72^2 - 3 \cdot 22^2$; (e) $1 \cdot 25 \times 4 \times 1697 \times 2$; (f) $\dfrac{0 \cdot 814^2 - 0 \cdot 186^2}{0 \cdot 814 - 0 \cdot 186}$.

10. From a square of side a units is cut a square of side b units, as shown in Figure 39. Write down an expression for the shaded area, A square units, and show that $A = (a-b)(a+b)$.

Calculate A if the side of the larger square is 12·57 cm, and that of the smaller one 2·57 cm. Why is this formula for the area easier to work with even if the sides of the squares are less conveniently chosen than in this question?

11. A rocket is accelerating upwards and h, its height in metres t s after blast-off, is given approximately by the formula

$$h = 12t^2.$$

Fig. 39

Write down its height after 2 s and after 22 s. Find its average velocity during these 20 s. Why is it a good idea not to multiply out at the beginning of the problem? Write down and simplify a formula for the average velocity for the period t_1 s to t_2 s after blast off.

12. $(a \ b) \begin{pmatrix} x \\ y \end{pmatrix} = (ax + by)$ is a familiar result. Can $\begin{pmatrix} a \\ b \end{pmatrix} (x \ y)$ be worked out? If so, compare the result with Figure 30.

13. (a) Complete the following:

(i) $(2a + b) = (a \ b) \begin{pmatrix} \ \ \end{pmatrix}$; (ii) $(3a + 7b) = (\quad) \begin{pmatrix} a \\ b \end{pmatrix}$.

(b) Copy and complete

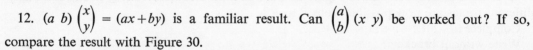

$$(2a + b)(3a + 7b) = (a \ b) \begin{pmatrix} 2 \\ 1 \end{pmatrix} (3 \ \ 7) \begin{pmatrix} a \\ b \end{pmatrix} = (a \ b) \begin{pmatrix} \cdot & \cdot \\ \cdot & \cdot \end{pmatrix} \begin{pmatrix} a \\ b \end{pmatrix}.$$

By first combining $(a \ b)$ with the 2×2 matrix and then the result with $\begin{pmatrix} a \\ b \end{pmatrix}$, find an expression for $(2a + b)(3a + 7b)$ without brackets.

How does this method compare with the one we already have?

(c) Complete the following:

(i) $(p + 3q)(5p - q) = (p \ q) \begin{pmatrix} \ \ \end{pmatrix} \begin{pmatrix} p \\ q \end{pmatrix}$;

(ii) $(a + b)^2 = (a \ b) \begin{pmatrix} \ \ \end{pmatrix} \begin{pmatrix} a \\ b \end{pmatrix}$.

Summary

Expressions of the form $(p+q)(r+s)$ may be written without brackets by using a table as shown in Figure 40

$$(p+q)(r+s) = pr+qr+ps+qs.$$

×	r	s
p	pr	ps
q	qr	qs

Fig. 40

Three important cases are:

$$(a+b)^2 = (a+b)(a+b) = a^2+2ab+b^2,$$
$$(a-b)^2 = (a-b)(a-b) = a^2-2ab+b^2,$$
$$(a+b)(a-b) = a^2-b^2.$$

11
IDENTITY AND INVERSE

He marched them up to the top of the hill,
And he marched them down again.
ANONYMOUS, *The Noble Duke of York*

1. SETS

1.1 Universal sets

I| A = {children born in August}

and B = {children who come to school on a bicycle},

describe the set $A \cap B$. How many members has this intersection set? Before you can answer this question you will have to decide what complete set of children we are thinking about. For instance, we might have to consider all the children in one class, all the children in one school, all the children who enjoy dancing, or many other possible sets. In each case the complete set under consideration is called the *universal set*. It is denoted by the letter $\mathscr{E}$, written in curly script. It is the initial letter of the French word for a set, which is 'Ensemble'.

180

Example

Let $E = \{$even numbers$\}$. Write out the members of E in the following cases.

(*a*) $\mathscr{E} = \{5, 6, 7\}$. The only even number is 6, so $E = \{6\}$.

(*b*) $\mathscr{E} = \{$positive whole numbers$\}$. There are infinitely many even positive whole numbers, so we have to indicate the members of E by means of a row of dots, $E = \{2, 4, 6, ...\}$.

(*c*) $\mathscr{E} = \{$whole numbers n satisfying $10 < n < 20\}$. Then $E = \{12, 14, 16, 18\}$.

In most cases in which we talk of sets it is necessary to be quite clear before starting what set we are taking as $\mathscr{E}$. All the sets involved will then be subsets of $\mathscr{E}$. It is useful to have a special symbol to mean 'is a subset of' and we write $\subset$. The sentence
$$\text{`}A \subset \mathscr{E} \quad \text{and} \quad B \subset \mathscr{E}\text{'}$$
is read

'A is a subset of the Universal Set   and B is a subset of the Universal Set'.

It is possible to write the symbol the other way round also. $\mathscr{E} \supset A$ has the same meaning as $A \subset \mathscr{E}$. How would you read '$\mathscr{E} \supset A$'?

1.2   Complementary sets

Let $\mathscr{E} = \{$children in your class$\}$ and $G = \{$children wearing glasses$\}$. All the members of $\mathscr{E}$ *not* in G also form a subset of $\mathscr{E}$. We call this set the *complement* of G in $\mathscr{E}$ and denote it by G'. What can you say about

$$G \cap G'?$$

Figure 1 shows a Venn diagram of a universal set $\mathscr{E}$ and two subsets. If we denote these subsets by A and B, what can one say about A, B, $\mathscr{E}$ and ø. Does it matter which subset is labelled A?

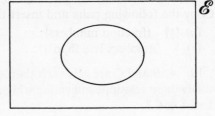

Fig. 1

Exercise A

1. $\mathscr{E} = \{{}^-3, {}^-2, {}^-1, 0, 1, 2, 3\}$.
(*a*) Write down A' if $A = \{{}^-2, {}^-1, 0\}$.
(*b*) Write down B if $B' = \{$numbers $> 0\}$.
(*c*) Write down $(P \cap Q)'$ if $P = \{{}^-1\}$ and $Q = \{{}^-1, 1\}$.

2 Let $\mathscr{E} = \{$positive even numbers less than 10$\}$ and $A = \{$multiple of 4$\}$. Write down A'.

3. If $P = \{1, 3\}$ and $P' = \{2, 7, 8\}$, write down $\mathscr{E}$.

4. Name three possible sets $\mathscr{E}$ having $\{1, 3\}$ and $\{2, 7, 8\}$ as subsets.

5. Let
$$\mathscr{E} = \{\text{letters of the English alphabet}\}$$
and
$A = \{$letters used in the sentence 'The quick brown fox jumps over the lazy dog.'$\}$.
Write down A'. We still say A is a subset of $\mathscr{E}$ and write $A \subset \mathscr{E}$. In what way is this a special kind of subset?

6. What is the complement of the complement of the set K in $\mathscr{E}$?

7. What is the difference between a complement and a compliment?

8. *The symbol* $\in$. We use the symbol $\in$ to denote 'is a member of', or 'is an element of'. If

$$\mathscr{E} = \{\text{British coins}\} \quad \text{and} \quad S = \{\text{silver coins}\},$$

then we can write

a 10p piece $\in S$;

a penny $\in S'$;

a button $\notin \mathscr{E}$ ($\notin$ indicates 'is not a member of').

In the following cases state whether the element in the first column belongs to the set in the second column, to its complement, or to neither. Write your answers using the symbol $\in$.

Element	Set (A)	Universal set ($\mathscr{E}$)
(a) 5	Even numbers	Whole numbers
(b) Square	Figures with 4 sides	Polygons
(c) Mauve	Primary colours	Colours
(d) π	Positive numbers	Fraction numbers
(e) >	Ordering symbols	Mathematical symbols

9. Sometimes it is necessary to distinguish between, for example, the number 3 and the set {3}. Within the universal set, Z, of integers (whole numbers), for instance,

the ordering $1 < 5-x < 3$ has a solution set $\{x : 2 < x < 4\}$,

the equation $5-x = 2$ has a solution set $\{3\}$.

Both $\{x : 2 < x < 4\} \subset Z$ and $\{3\} \subset Z$ but also, of course, $3 \in Z$.
Copy the following pairs and insert the correct symbol $\in$, $\notin$ $\subset$ or $\not\subset$ between them.

(a) $\{\frac{1}{2}\}$ {fraction numbers};

(b) $\frac{1}{2}$ {integers};

(c) $\frac{1}{2}$ {numbers less than 1};

(d) $\{4, 5\}$ $\{3, 4, 5\}$.

10. A, B and C are sets such that $A \subset B$ and $B \subset C$. Give an example of three sets which satisfy these relations indicating which are A, B and C. Is it always, sometimes, or never true that $A \subset C$?

11. Given that $a \in A$ and $a \in B$, write down a single statement connecting a, A and B.

12. Can one find b, A and $\mathscr{E}$ such that $b \in A$ and $b \in A'$?

1.3 Union of sets

Let $\mathscr{E} = \{\text{new cars for sale at this year's Motor Show}\}$, $A = \{\text{Austin cars}\}$ and $B = \{\text{blue cars}\}$. The shaded region in Figure 2 represents the cars which are possible buys for a man who says 'I am looking for a blue car, but I wouldn't mind having an Austin, whatever its colour'. The region represents the members of $\mathscr{E}$ that are Austins *or* blue *or both*. This subset of $\mathscr{E}$ is called the *union* of the two sets A and B, and is denoted by $A \cup B$. A simple way of reading this is 'A cup B'.

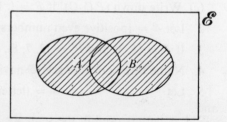

Fig. 2

182

Exercise B

1. Given that $A = \{a, b, c, d\}$ and $B = \{a, c, e\}$, list the members of (a) $A \cap B$; (b) $A \cup B$.

2. Given that $E = \{2, 4, 6, 8\}$ and $Y = \{2, 2^2, 2^3\}$, list the members of (a) $E \cap Y$; (b) $E \cup Y$.
Write down a relation satisfied by E and Y.

3. Let $\mathscr{E} = \{$letters in the word CUSHION$\}$, $S = \{$letters in the word SHUN$\}$, $V = \{$I, O, U$\}$.
List the members of: (a) V'; (b) $V \cup S$; (c) $V' \cup S$; (d) $V \cup S'$.

4. Given that $S = \{$squares$\}$ and $T = \{$rectangles$\}$, define a suitable universal set $\mathscr{E}$.

(a) Write down a relation satisfied by S and T.
(b) What is $S \cap T$?   (c) What is $S \cup T$?

5. Let $\mathscr{E} = \{$types of mechanically propelled vehicles$\}$. Describe three subsets of $\mathscr{E}$ such that the intersection of any two is empty. Is it possible to find three sets such that the union of any two is empty?

6. Is it always, sometimes or never true that $A \cap B \subset A \cup B$?

7. What can you say about sets P and Q if

$$(a) \; P \cap Q = P; \qquad (b) \; P \cup Q = Q?$$

Are these statements equivalent to each other?

8. (a) List all the subsets of $\{$Alan, Betty, Charles$\}$. (Remember to count the empty set and original set as subsets.)

(b) How many subsets has a set containing:

(i) one member,   (ii) two members,   (iii) three members?

What do you notice about your answers? Guess the number of subsets of a set with four members and check your answer. Can you extend the pattern?

9. Simplify:

(a) $A \cup A$;   (b) $A \cap A$;   (c) $A \cup \mathscr{E}$;   (d) $A \cap \mathscr{E}$;

(e) $A \cup \emptyset$;   (f) $A \cap \emptyset$;   (g) $\emptyset \cup \mathscr{E}$;   (h) $\emptyset \cap \mathscr{E}$.

10. What can you say about the sets L and M in Figure 3? Simplify: (a) $L \cap M$; (b) $M \cup L$.

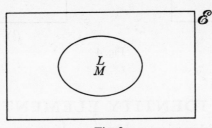

Fig. 3

11. Copy the following statements and state which are always true, which are sometimes true (when?) and which are never true. If any are meaningless, then say so.

(a) $P \cup Q = Q \cup P$;   (b) $P \cap Q = Q \cap P'$;   (c) $P \cup P = 2P$;

(d) $P \cap P = P^2$;   (e) $P \cup Q = P \cap Q$.

D12. Let $\mathscr{E}$ = {birds alive at this moment}; C = {canaries}; S = {singing birds}; W = {well-fed birds}. Change the following statements of relations between sets into English sentences. For example, (a) tells us that 'the set of all canaries is a subset of the set of singing birds' or, more briefly (and in more day-to-day language) 'all canaries sing'. (The truth of the sentences does not matter!)

(a) $C \subset S$; (b) $S \subset C$; (c) $C \subset S'$;

(d) $S = C \cap W$; (e) $S \cap W \cap C' = \varnothing$.

Write the following sentences in symbols.

(f) Some canaries are well-fed.
(g) Some singing canaries are not well-fed.
(h) All canaries that do not sing are ill-fed.

Summary

1. *Subsets.* A is a subset of B if every member of A is also a member of B. We write this $A \subset B$.

2. *Universal sets.* The universal set for sets $A, B, C, \ldots$ is a set of which each of $A, B, C, \ldots$ is a subset. We write this $\mathscr{E}$.

3. *Complementary sets.* The complement of a set A in $\mathscr{E}$ is the set of all members of $\mathscr{E}$ which are not members of A. We write this A'.

4. *Union of sets.* The union of two sets A and B is the set of all members of $\mathscr{E}$ which are members of A, or of B, or of *both* A and B. We write this $A \cup B$.

5. *'is a member of'* or *'is an element of'*. The symbol for this is $\in$.

6. *Venn diagrams*

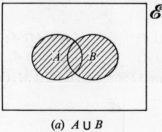

(a) $A \cup B$

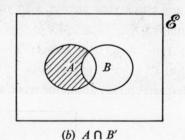

(b) $A \cap B'$

Fig. 4

2. IDENTITY ELEMENTS

2.1 Closed sets. An arithmetic teacher is making up exercises for her class of eight-year-old children. They have met the positive integers and know how to add, subtract, multiply and divide. She is working quickly and writes down the following:

(1) $6+4$; (2) $6-4$; (3) $14+6$;

(4) $14-6$; (5) $5+8$; (6) $5-8$.

Why does she have to stop and cross out one of these? Leaving aside questions of difficulty, are there any additions that she would not be able to use?

The set of positive integers is said to be *closed* under the operation of addition since the sum of any two positive integers must also be a positive integer. Formally, if $P = \{\text{positive integers}\}$, then $a \in P$ and $b \in P$ implies $(a+b) \in P$.

The set is *not* closed under subtraction, however, since a subtraction may result in a negative integer. If $a \in P$ and $b \in P$, then it is not necessarily true that $a-b \in P$.

Is the set of positive integers closed under multiplication? Is it closed under division?

2.2 Operation tables

(*a*) Let us use E to stand for 'any even number' and O to stand for 'any odd number'. (Can the numbers be any other than integers?) By $E+O$ we denote 'any even number added to any odd number'. What can you say about the answer? Is the set $\{E, O\}$ closed under the operation of addition? To confirm your answer, copy and complete the following table:

		Second number	
+		E	O
First number {	E		O
	O		

This table is called an *operation table*. An ordinary multiplication table is an example of an operation table. You will remember that one advantage of using binary arithmetic is that you do not have to learn complicated tables. All that it is necessary to know is contained in two tables. Copy and complete the following in binary:

(i) for addition (put-down digit only)

		Second number	
+		0	1
First number {	0	0	
	1		

(ii) for multiplication

		Second number	
×		0	1
First number {	0		0
	1		

Is the set $\{0, 1\}$ closed under multiplication? Is it closed under addition (be careful!)? Which of tables (i) and (ii) resembles the table for O and E under addition? Try to explain why. Make a guess regarding the table for O and E under multiplication and confirm or reject it by compiling the table.

(*b*) Even and odd are really words which describe numbers according to their relationship to the number 2.

E is exactly divisible by 2.

O leaves a remainder of 1 when divided by 2.

In a similar way we can classify integers by the way in which they are related to 3, though we will have no special names for them. Figure 5 shows how this can be done.

This is a spiral divided into three sections.

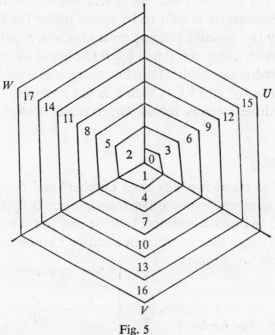

Fig. 5

U denotes 'any integer exactly divisible by 3',
V denotes 'integers that when divided by 3 leave a remainder of 1',
W denotes 'any integer that when divided by 3 leaves a remainder of 2'.

Is the set {*U*, *V*, *W*} closed under the operation of addition? Copy and complete the operation table for *U*, *V*, *W*

+	*U*	*V*	*W*
U			
V			*U*
W			

Now form an addition table for clock arithmetic with the set {0, 1, 2} and compare it with the table for {*U*, *V*, *W*}. Why does the same pattern arise?

Make tables in each case for the operation of multiplication and again compare the patterns that arise.

2.3   Identity elements

In the addition table for *E* and *O* (see Section 2.2(*a*))

+	*E*	*O*
E	*E*	*O*
O	*O*	*E*

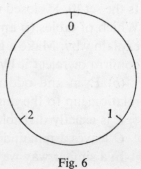

Fig. 6

E has an interesting and important role. You will see it more clearly from the following relations:

$$E+O = O,$$
$$E+E = E,$$
$$O+E = O.$$

The addition of *E* has no effect (whether *E* is the first or second number); added to *E* it gives *E*, added to *O* it gives *O*. We say that *E* is the *identity element* in this table, it leaves things unaltered.

By inspection find the identity element of the following table for the operation o on the set $\{K, L, M\}$

o	K	L	M
K	L	M	K
L	M	K	L
M	K	L	M

Notice that we need not know anything about *K*, *L*, *M* or about the operation o in order to be able to spot the identity.

Find the identity element for the set $\{E, O\}$ under multiplication.

Look at the tables you constructed for $\{U, V, W\}$ under the operations + and × and decide which is the identity element in each case. Do you expect them to be the same element?

What is the identity element when ordinary numbers are (i) added, (ii) multiplied? Since these are again different we sometimes distinguish them by calling the former the additive identity and the latter the multiplicative identity.

What is the identity element when transformations are combined?

Exercise C

1. State which of the following sets are closed under the operation stated:
(*a*) {translations} under 'followed by';   (*b*) {fractions} under division;
(*c*) {numbers greater than 1000} under addition.

2. Let the symbol ~ (read 'twiddles') represent the operation 'find the positive difference between'. Thus 19 ~ 8 and 8 ~ 19 are both 11. State which of the following sets are closed under ~ :

(*a*) {positive integers};   (*b*) {rational numbers};   (*c*) {square numbers}.

3. Let **Q** denote a rotation through a quarter-turn, **H** denote a rotation through a half-turn and **T** denote a rotation through a three-quarter-turn, the centre of rotation in all three cases being (0, 0). If **I** is the identity transformation, complete the following operation table for the set $\{Q, H, T, I\}$ under the operation 'followed by'. Is the set closed under the operation?

'Followed by'	Q	H	T	I
Q	H			
H				
T			T	
I				

187

4. Is the set {{1, 2}, {2, 3}, {3, 1}} closed under the operation ∩?

5. (a) Name an operation under which the set of even numbers is closed but the set of odd numbers is not closed.

(b) Name an operation under which they are both closed.

6. Let F denote the operation 'take the highest common factor of'. For example, $30 \, F \, 12 = 6$, since $30 = 2 \times 3 \times 5$ and $12 = 2 \times 2 \times 3$, showing that $2 \times 3 = 6$ is the required factor. Is F commutative? Find a set of integers with at least three members that is closed under the operation F.

7. An equilateral triangle can be mapped onto itself by rotations of 120° and 240° about its centre. How can **I**, the identity transformation, be thought of as a rotation?

Suppose: **I** denotes the identity transformation,

P denotes a rotation of 120° about the centre of the triangle,

Q denotes a rotation of 240° about the centre of the triangle.

Copy and complete the table for the operation 'followed by'. Is the set {**I, P, Q**} closed under this operation?

'Followed by'	I	P	Q
I			
P		Q	
Q			

Compare this table with the ones for {U, V, W}. To which of them does it have a similar pattern?

8. A girl counted the plumstones on her plate at dinner time with the rhyme

cottage, palace, mansion, pigsty, cottage, palace, ...

A plate with 3 stones on it would give 'mansion', and one with 6 stones on it would give 'palace'.

If the stones on the two plates were combined there would be 9 stones giving 'cottage'. If we write ⊕ to stand for combination, then

mansion ⊕ palace = cottage.

Copy and complete the following table. Which is the identity element?

⊕	Cottage	Palace	Mansion	Pigsty
Cottage				
Palace				
Mansion		Cottage		
Pigsty				

Compare the table with that in Question 3. What do you notice?

9. Make up operation tables for a clock arithmetic on the set {0, 1, 2, 3} for the operations + and ×.

In each case state the identity element.

Rearrange the first table with the numbers in the order 1, 2, 3, 0 and compare the pattern with those of the tables in Questions 3 and 8. What do you notice? Why is it necessary to rearrange the table?

10. Place two pennies side by side on the table. They can be 'altered' in four ways:

(a) leave them as they are, **I**;

(b) turn the right one over, **R**;

(c) turn the left one over, **L**;

(d) turn them both over, **B**.

What single alteration is equivalent to **R** followed by **L**? Is the set {**I, R, L, B**} closed under the operation ' followed by'?

Construct the operation table.

Could this table be made to have a similar pattern to those in Questions 3, 8 and 9 by altering the order of the letters **I, R, L** and **B**? Give reasons.

11. Reflection in the longer line of symmetry maps a rectangle onto itself. What other single transformations will do this? There are four altogether. Using letters to denote these four transformations, construct a table for the operation 'followed by' and compare it with that obtained in Question 10.

12. Copy and complete the following operation tables for intersection and union between the empty set ø, $A = \{a\}$, $B = \{b\}$ and $P = \{a, b\}$.

∩	ø	A	B	P
ø				
A			A	
B				
P				

∪	ø	A	B	P
ø				
A			P	
B				
P				

Which is the identity element in each case? Rearrange the second table with the letters in the order $P, B, A,$ ø and compare the new pattern with that of the first table. State what you notice.

D 13. Clock arithmetic with the set {0, 1, 2, 3, 4, 5} is also referred to as arithmetic modulo 6 or mod 6; one with the set {0, 1, 2, 3} is mod 4.

(a) Find identity elements for:

(i) {1, 5} under the operation × mod 6;

(ii) {0, 2, 4} under the operation × mod 6.

(b) Compare the patterns of combination tables for:

(i) {1, 2, 3, 4} under × mod 5;

(ii) {1, 3, 7, 9} under × mod 10;

(iii) {0, 1, 2, 3} under + mod 4.

What rearrangements of the numbers are necessary in order to produce similar patterns?

14. Have all the operation tables constructed so far a line of symmetry from top left to bottom right (along the leading diagonal)? What does this imply about the operations involved? Construct a table for {0, 1, 2, 3} for the operation of subtraction mod 4. Is this set closed under subtraction? Explain why the leading diagonal is not a line of symmetry. Discuss whether an identity element exists in this case.

Summary

A set P is said to be *closed* under an operation o if,

whenever $a \in P$ and $b \in P$, it follows that $a \circ b \in P$.

A table showing the results of an operation on pairs of members of a set is called an *operation table*, for example,

+	E	O
E	E	O
O	O	E

The table for a certain operation on a set may sometimes have the same pattern as the table for a second operation on that set, or on a different set.

The *identity element* of a set P under an operation o is a member i of P such that

whenever $a \in P$ then $a \circ i = i \circ a = a.$

3. INVERSE ELEMENTS

(*a*) Consider the table for the set {0, 1, 2, 3} under the operation of addition mod 4.

+	0	1	2	3
0	0	1	2	3
1	1	2	3	0
2	2	3	0	1
3	3	0	1	2

The identity element is 0 and it occurs inside the table four times, corresponding to the four additions:

$$0+0 = 0,$$
$$1+3 = 0,$$
$$2+2 = 0,$$
$$3+1 = 0.$$

When two elements can be combined in this way to yield the identity element they are called *inverses* of each other, or an *inverse pair*.

In this example, 3 is the inverse of 1 and 1 is the inverse of 3. 2 is the inverse of itself and is called *self-inverse*.

What about 0 itself? Is it also self-inverse?

If **A** is a transformation, what is meant by the inverse of **A**? Name two transformations that are self-inverse.

(*b*) Now consider the table for the same set under multiplication mod 4. Which is the identity element? Do any elements have no inverse? Are any elements self-inverse?

×	0	1	2	3
0	0	0	0	0
1	0	1	2	3
2	0	2	0	2
3	0	3	2	1

190

(c) Construct a table for multiplication mod 5 on the set {1, 2, 3, 4}. Which is the identity element? Do any elements have no inverse? Are any elements self-inverse?

(d) In ordinary arithmetic what is the inverse of 5 for the operation of (i) addition, (ii) multiplication? (That is, what are the additive and multiplicative inverses of 5?)

Exercise D

1. Use the operation table for the set {U, V, W} under addition (see p. 186) to answer the following questions.

(a) What is the additive identity?

(b) What are the inverses (if any) of U, V and W?

(c) Which elements (if any) are self-inverse?

2. The operation table for the set {0, 1, 2} under subtraction mod 3 is as follows:

Second number

−	0	1	2
0	0	2	1
1	1	0	2
2	2	1	0

First number {0, 1, 2}

(a) Is there an identity element?

(b) What are the inverses (if any) of 0, 1, 2?

D3. In the table for a certain set under the operation ∘ there are two elements A and B. We can see that $A \circ B = I$ (the identity element) and that $B \circ A = C$ (a third element, different from I). Discuss whether or not A and B form an inverse pair under this operation. Is A the inverse of B? Is B the inverse of A?

4. Construct the table for {1, 2, 3} under multiplication mod 4.

(a) Is the set closed under this operation?

(b) What is the identity element?

(c) Which (if any) of the following are inverse pairs: (1, 2), (2, 3), (3, 1)?

(d) Which elements are self-inverse?

5. Use the operation table for the set {ø, A, B, P} under ∩ (Exercise C, Question 12), to answer the following.

(a) What are the inverses (if any) of ø, A, B and P?

(b) Are there any self-inverse elements, if so, which?

Summary

If a is any member of a set and ∘ denotes an operation which combines two members of the set for which i is the identity element, and if another member, b, of the set can be found such that

$$a \circ b = b \circ a = i,$$

then a and b are called an *inverse pair*.

191

Note that *a* is the inverse of *b* and *b* is the inverse of *a*. Some examples of inverse pairs are:

  (i) 6 and ⁻6 under addition;

 (ii) 6 and 1/6 under multiplication;

(iii) 'turn left' and 'turn right' under the operation 'followed by'.

Exercise E

Miscellaneous

1. Use your previous work or construct new tables for the following:

(*a*) {1, 2} under multiplication mod 3;   (*b*) {1, 2, 3} under multiplication mod 4;

(*c*) {1, 2, 3, 4} under multiplication mod 5;

(*d*) {1, 2, 3, 4, 5} under multiplication mod 6;

(*e*) {1, 2, 3, 4, 5, 6} under multiplication mod 7.

In which cases do some elements have no inverse? Try to state a general rule which tells us whether or not all elements will have inverses.

2. Since division is the *inverse operation* to multiplication we can use multiplication tables to help us compile division tables. For example, working mod 5, we see that $2 \times 3 = 1$. We can then define $1 \div 3 = 2$, and $1 \div 2 = 3$. Use the table for the set {1, 2, 3, 4} under multiplication mod 5 to draw up the table for division mod 5. Try to repeat this with the set {1, 2, 3} under multiplication and division mod 4. What do you find?

3. Draw a Venn diagram to illustrate the relationships between

$$\mathscr{E} = \{\text{relations}\}, \qquad F = \{\text{functions}\},$$

$$G = \{\text{functions for which an inverse function can be defined}\}$$

and $$T = \{\text{translations}\}.$$

4. Three playing cards, Ace, King and Queen are placed in a column of 3:

A

K

Q

How many different arrangements are possible?

The order may be changed in various ways called *permutations*. Suppose permutation **L** means that the *bottom two cards* (whichever they are) are interchanged. Then we can illustrate **L** as shown in Figure 7(*a*).

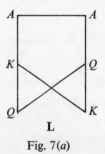

L

Fig. 7(*a*)

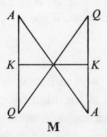

M

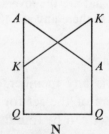

N

Fig. 7(*b*)

Two permutations of the same type are shown in Figure 7(*b*). Describe them in words.

Figure 7(c) shows how permutation **L** may be followed by permutation **M** resulting in a new permutation which we will call **V**. Describe **V** in words.

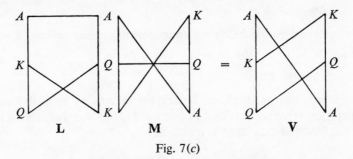

Fig. 7(c)

A permutation of the same type as **V** is the permutation **U** in which each card is moved down one, the bottom card being replaced at the top. Illustrate **U** in the same style as above and describe it in words. Are any other permutations possible? If so, describe and illustrate them. Construct an operation table for the permutations under the operation 'followed by' and including **I** the identity permutation.

(a) Which permutations are self-inverse?   (b) Which pairs are not commutative?
(c) Name any inverse pairs that there are.

5. Using the tables constructed for Question 1(c) and (d), find solution sets for the following equations: (i) in arithmetic mod 5, (ii) in arithmetic mod 6.

(a) $x^2 = 1$;   (b) $x^2 = 3$;   (c) $x^2 = 4$;   (d) $x^3 = 2$.

6. Construct the operation table for the set $\{A, B, P, \emptyset\}$ defined in Question 12 of Exercise C under the operation $\triangle$, where $A \triangle B$ (for example) means the set whose elements belong either to A or to B but *not* to both. What can you say about inverses under this operation?

D7. If f is the function $x \to 1/x$, then $f(3) = \frac{1}{3}$, etc.
(a) Write down $ff(3)$ and $fff(3)$. What different answers can be obtained by operating on 3 with combinations of the function f only?
Suppose also that g is the function $x \to 1-x$, so that $g(3) = {}^-2$, etc.
(b) Write down $gg(3)$ and $ggg(3)$. What different answers can be obtained by operating on 3 with combinations of the function g only?
(c) What can you say about the inverses of f and g?
(d) fg denotes g followed by f so that $fg(3) = f({}^-2) = {}^-\frac{1}{2}$. Write down $gfg(3)$, $fgfg(3)$, $gfgfg(3)$, $fgfgfg(3)$. What do you find? Write down the next few in the sequence.
(e) Write down also $gf(3)$, $fgf(3)$, $gfgf(3)$, $fgfgf(3)$, $gfgfgf(3)$. What do you find?
(f) How many different answers can be obtained by using *any* combination of the functions f and g? How many rows and columns will a complete operation table have to have?
(g) By comparing the numerical values obtained from operations on 3, build up the operation table, in terms of f's and g's keeping the entries as simple as possible.

D8. In ordinary arithmetic, what is the multiplicative inverse of 3? What is the inverse function of $x \to 3x$?
In arithmetic modulo 5 on the set $\{1, 2, 3, 4\}$, what is the multiplicative inverse of 3? What is the inverse function of $x \to 3x$ in this arithmetic?
We can use this inverse function to solve equations in arithmetic modulo 5.

For example, $3x = 2$

$$\Leftrightarrow 2 \times 3x = 2 \times 2 \quad \text{(since } x \to 2x \text{ is inverse to } x \to 3x\text{).}$$

$$\Leftrightarrow \quad x = 4.$$

In a similar manner solve the following equations in arithmetic mod 5.

        (a) $3x = 1$;   (b) $3x = 4$;   (c) $2x = 3$;   (d) $4x = 3$.

Check your answer in each case.

D9. Some mathematicians think of binary operations as special kinds of functions. Consider an operation table such as that in Section 3 (a). If this describes a function, what is the domain of the function and what is its range?

12

SHEARING

Change is not made without inconvenience.

JOHNSON, *Preface to the 'English Dictionary'*
as from Hooker

1. THE SHEARING TRANSFORMATION

In our study of geometry so far we have dealt with rotations, reflections, enlargements and translations. Now we shall consider another transformation, shearing, which, amongst other things, has important applications to areas and volumes. We shall also extend the work on transformation matrices which we met in Chapter 3.

(*a*) In Figure 1(*a*) we see a side view of a pile of 30 exercise books. In Figure 1(*b*) we see the same pile but this time pushed sideways.

Approximately what shape is Figure 1(*b*)?

If you measured the heights of the two piles, what would you expect to find? Are any parts of the books visible in one pile but not in the other? Are the areas of the parts of the two piles you can see the same? What other features of the pile of books have remained unaltered? Such features are said to be *invariant*.

(*b*) Figure 2 shows another example of the same idea, this time with a pile of thin cards such as a pack of playing cards.

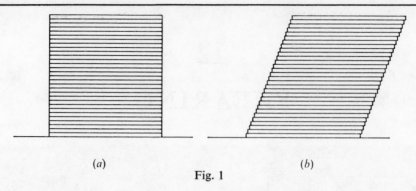

(a)   (b)

Fig. 1

In Figure 2(b) the jagged edges of Figure 1(b) have virtually disappeared and what we see is almost exactly a parallelogram.

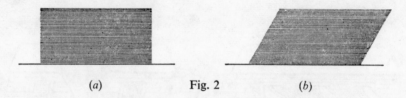

(a)   Fig. 2   (b)

The idea of shearing is illustrated by Figures 1 and 2 and one of the most important features of this transformation is that it preserves area. This point will be considered in greater detail in Section 2.

First, we shall examine other aspects of the shearing transformation.

1.1   Describing a shear

Make a copy of Figure 3 and, in order to help you answer the questions of this section, shade the various parallelograms and triangles using different colours.

(a) Suppose that in the tessellation in Figure 3, we represent the 'pile of books' by the parallelogram $BFKE$. Keeping EK fixed, that is, like the bottom book in the pile, we can shear parallelogram $BFKE$ onto parallelogram $FLKE$. Similarly, keeping RQ fixed we can shear parallelogram $RQVW$ onto parallelogram $RQUV$. Find two other parallelograms onto which $RQVW$ can be sheared and state the side which is kept fixed in each case.

We can see that under a shear one line remains fixed in position, as, for example, the bottom book of the pile does in Figure 1. This line is called *the invariant line*. So far it has always coincided with one side of the object which has been sheared. However, this need not be the case.

(b) Consider how the parallelogram $LSRK$ in Figure 3 could be mapped onto parallelogram $JPNH$.

It could, for example, be done by combining two shears of the type discussed in (a) above.   (i) $LSRK \rightarrow LPNK$ with the line LK invariant,
                      (ii) $LPNK \rightarrow JPNH$ with the line PN invariant,

196

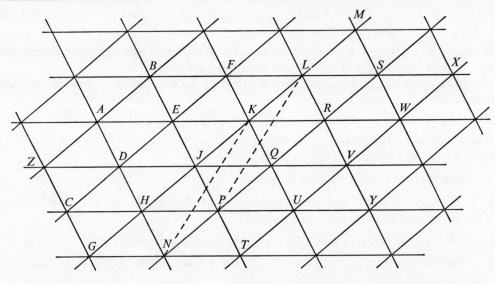

Fig. 3

the intermediate position, *LPNK*, being shown dotted. However, by considering where *SL* meets *PJ* and *RK* meets *NH*, can you see how the mapping can be accomplished using only one shear?

What would be the invariant line of this shear?

(*c*) Where is the invariant line of the single shear which maps triangle *EFJ* onto triangle *DEJ*?

(*d*) Where is the invariant line of the shear which maps parallelogram *BFUP* onto parallelogram *LSPH*?

What can you say about points on opposite sides of the invariant line in a shearing transformation?

(*e*) If *FE* is the invariant line of a shear, find the images of

(i)   parallelogram *PQUT* if $P \to R$,

(ii) parallelogram *AFKD* if $A \to B$.

This shows us that a shear is defined if we are given its invariant line and the image of one point not on that line.

Exercise A

1. If the top book of 30 in Figure 1 (*b*) has been pushed 6 cm to the right, approximately how far have the following books been moved:

(*a*) tenth from the bottom;   (*b*) twentieth from the bottom?

2. When a figure is sheared, a point 4 cm from the invariant line moves 3 cm. How far does a point 6 cm from the invariant line move?

Questions 3–10 refer to Figure 3 and require a copy of this figure without the dotted lines. Extra lines may be required in some questions.

3. Show, by marking the intermediate position in red, how two successive shears could be used to map parallelogram *ABFE* onto parallelogram *AEJD*.

Show also, using different colours, how it could be done by combining (*a*) three shears, (*b*) four shears.

4. Construct a sequence of shears (using as few as possible) which would:

(*a*) map triangle *CHG* onto triangle *NHG*;

(*b*) map triangle *LRW* onto triangle *RQU*.

Indicate intermediate images on your diagram.

5. Parallelogram *HPTN* can be mapped onto parallelogram *JQUP* by a translation. How can it be done by combining two shears?

6. Show on your diagram how *LSRK* can be mapped onto *JQUP* by:

(*a*) a shear followed by a translation;   (*b*) a shear followed by a rotation.

Give at least two methods in each case.

In (*a*) state the invariant line of the shear and a vector defining the translation.

In (*b*) state the invariant line of the shear and the centre and angle of rotation.

7. Describe the invariant line of the shears which map:

(*a*) *FLRK* onto *DKRJ*,   and   (*b*) *FDQ* onto *FGL*.

8. Find the image under a shear of:

(*a*) *BFKE*, if *FE* is the invariant line and $B \to A$;

(*b*) *KHU*, if *JQ* is the invariant line and $K \to E$.

9. Describe four quadrilaterals onto which parallelogram *EKQJ* can be mapped by a single shear.

Are they all parallelograms?

Do you think you could shear a parallelogram onto a quadrilateral which is not a parallelogram?

What geometrical property does this suggest to be invariant under shearing?

10. We saw in Section 1.1(*b*) how the combination of the two shears

$$LSRK \to LPNK, \text{ with the line } LK \text{ invariant, and}$$

$$LPNK \to JPNH \text{ with the line } PN \text{ invariant}$$

is equivalent to the single shear

$$LSRK \to JPNH \text{ with the line } AB \text{ invariant.}$$

Give another example in which the combination of two shears is equivalent to a single shear.

What conditions must the invariant lines satisfy in each case?

11. In a shear the line $y = 0$ is invariant and the point $(0, 1)$ is mapped onto $(2, 1)$. What is the image of the line $x = 0$? What is the image of $(0, 3)$?

12. In a shear the line $x = 0$ is invariant and the line $y = 0$ is mapped onto the line $y = x$. Find the images of $(0, 0)$, $(0, 1)$, $(1, 0)$ and $(1, 1)$. What is the image of the square formed by these four points? Find also the images of the points $(2, 2)$, $(3, 1)$, $(0, 4)$, $(-1, 2)$ and $(-1, -1)$.

13. In Figure 4, the parallelogram *ABML* is sheared onto the parallelogram *A'B'ML*. By reference to the pile of books, and using the properties of enlargement, can you explain why the line segment *LB* is mapped onto the line segment *LB'*?

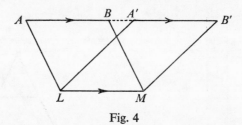

Fig. 4

Does the mid-point of *AB* map onto the mid-point *A'B'*?
Does the mid-point of *LB* map onto the mid-point of *LB'*?
Do all mid-points map onto mid-points?

14. A shear has $y = 0$ as its invariant line What can you say about the images of lines parallel to $y = 0$? Can you say that such lines are also in some way invariant? If so, how does this way differ from the invariance of *the* invariant line?

1.2   Shearing constructions

We have seen that a shear is defined once we know the invariant line and the image of a point not on that line.

In Figure 5, *l* is the invariant line of a shear which maps *A* onto *A'*.

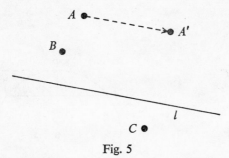

Fig. 5

Can we find the image of *B*?

Copy the figure and extend *AB* to meet *l* at *O*.

Assuming that straight lines map onto straight lines, can you say why *OA'* is the image of *OA*?

Using a straight-edge and set-square to draw parallel lines, you should now be able to find *B'*.

Find *C'*, the image of *C*, in a similar manner. State two other fractions which are equal to *AA'/BB'*.

199

Exercise B

1. Shear the 'man' in Figure 6 keeping $y = 1$ invariant and mapping A onto $(7, 6)$.

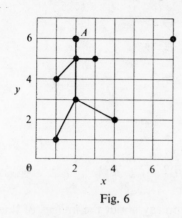

Fig. 6

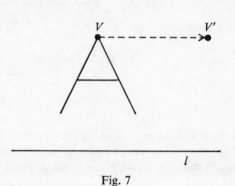

Fig. 7

2. Copy Figure 7 and, using only a straight-edge and set-square, draw the image of the letter A under the shear which has invariant line l and maps V onto V'.

3. Repeat Question 2 but this time consider a shear whose invariant line is not parallel to the cross bar of the letter A.

4. Copy Figure 8 and find its image under the shear with invariant line l which maps T onto T'.

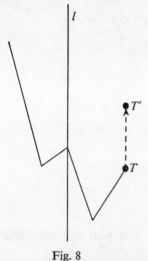

Fig. 8

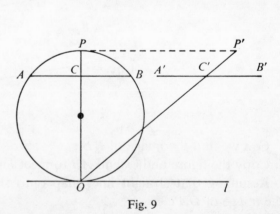

Fig. 9

5. Draw a diagram to show how a rectangle could be sheared onto another congruent rectangle by using one diagonal as the invariant line.

6. Shear a circle by the method indicated in Figure 9. If $P \to P'$, then $ACB \to A'C'B'$. AB and $A'B'$ are the same length and at the same distance from the invariant line l.

C is the mid-point of AB and C' is the mid-point of $A'B'$. Draw about 15–20 chords parallel to AB and draw in their new positions. By joining up the ends of these chords, sketch the figure onto which the circle is mapped. Has this new figure any lines of symmetry? (This example is best done on graph paper.)

7. Draw a face (about 3 cm high) in profile on a $\frac{1}{2}$ cm grid of squares. Construct the image of this grid of squares under a shear with the base of the grid as invariant line (compare Figure 17), and, with the aid of this new grid, draw the image of the face.

8. In Figure 10 the point P is mapped onto P' by a shear with invariant line l and then P' is mapped onto P'' by a shear with invariant line m. Copy the figure and, by joining P and P' to a point O on l, find a point in the diagram which is mapped onto itself by the combination of the two shears. Hence find the invariant line of a single shear equivalent to the combination of these two shears.

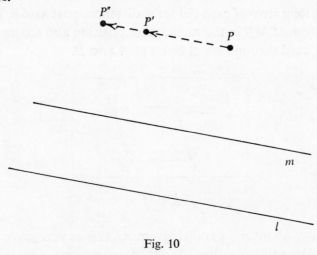

Fig. 10

9. In Question 8, two shears were combined and the resulting transformation was found to be a shear. Does it matter in which order the shears are combined, that is, do the shears commute?

Summary

A shear is a transformation in which:

(*a*) the points of a certain line, for example, l in Figure 11, are invariant;

(*b*) all other points move parallel to the invariant line—the lines PP' and QQ' are parallel to l;

(*c*) the distance moved by points is proportional to their distance from the invariant line;

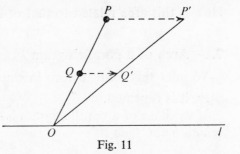

Fig. 11

(*d*) straight lines map onto straight lines, for example, the line PQ onto the line $P'Q'$. A line and its image will meet on the invariant line unless parallel to it.

A shear is defined once we know:

(i) the invariant line,

(ii) the image of a point not on this line.

2. AREA

We have seen that, in spite of the distortion of shape that takes place in a shear, the area of a figure is preserved.

We can make a simple model which illustrates the action of shearing dynamically.

Take two pieces of card one about 18×12 cm and the other 30×3 cm. Cut a long slot about 0·3 cm wide in one of the pieces as shown in Figure 12. Draw AB about 6 cm long, parallel to the slot. Through the slot push two split paper-fasteners and attach them to the long strip of card the same distance apart as AB. Fasten a piece of shirring elastic round $ALMB$ in the rectangular position and secure it by knotting it at the back of the card through small holes at A and B.

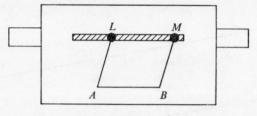

Fig. 12

What can you say about the parallelogram $ALMB$ as you move the long strip of card to and fro? Does its area alter? What measurements would you make to find this area?

Remove the elastic from over M and tighten it, if necessary, to form the triangle ALB.

State what you can about the area of this triangle as L is moved along the slot. How is this area related to that of the parallelogram $ALMB$?

2.1   Area of a parallelogram

We met this result before in Book 1 but, as shearing illustrates it in a dynamic way, it is repeated.

If the base of a parallelogram is of length b cm and the perpendicular height is of length h cm, then its

$$\text{area} = b \times h \text{ cm}^2.$$

This can be found in two different ways. Any one of the sides can be regarded as the base. Figure 13(a) shows the two rectangles onto which the parallelogram $ABCD$ can be sheared. One base and height are labelled. Notice that the directions of the shears are not across the page in this case.

2.2   Area of a triangle

In Figure 13(*b*) triangle *PQR* can be sheared onto triangle *PMR*. Its area is therefore one-half of that of the rectangle *PRML*.

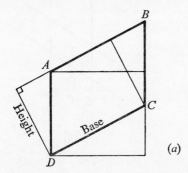

(*a*)   (*b*)

Fig. 13

If the base is of length *b* cm and the perpendicular height is of length *h* cm, then its

$$\text{area} = \frac{b \times h}{2} \text{ cm}^2.$$

This can be found in three different ways. One case is shown in Figure 13(*b*).

Exercise C

1. Figure 14 shows a side view of a ream of 500 sheets of paper. The edges of the paper seen are 30 cm long and each sheet is 0·015 cm thick. What is the area of the shaded region? How does the transformation from the original rectangular shape differ from what we have called a shear?

Fig. 14

2. Draw a parallelogram with sides 9 and 12 cm and one angle 64°. Measure the distance between each pair of opposite sides and calculate the area of the parallelogram in two ways.

3. Draw a triangle with sides 6, 7 and 10 cm. Draw three 'heights', measure them and calculate the area of the triangle in three different ways. How accurate are these answers? How would you obtain a better estimate of the actual area from these answers?

4. *ABCD* is a rectangle in which *AB* = 7·8 cm and *AD* = 10·4 cm. *P* and *Q* lie on *AB* and *AD* respectively, with *AP* = 4·3 cm and *AQ* = 3·9 cm. Calculate the area of triangle *CPQ*. (This can be done without drawing or measurement.)

5. Draw accurately a quadrilateral *ABCD* in which *AB* = 9 cm, *BC* = 4·8 cm, *CD* = 8·4 cm, ∠*B* = 104° and ∠*C* = 136°. Find the area of *ABCD*.

6. A trapezium has sides of length 3, 10, 24 and 17 cm, with the shortest and longest sides parallel and 8 cm apart. Calculate its area.

7. Express the area of the parallelogram in Figure 15(a) in two ways and so find x. This parallelogram may be sheared into a rectangle in two different ways. What will be the dimensions of the rectangles?

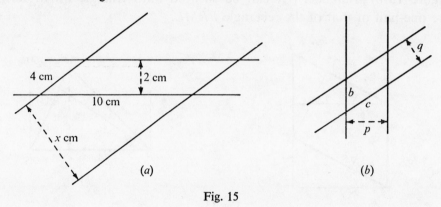

(a)   (b)

Fig. 15

8. What formula connects b, c, p and q from the two pairs of parallel lines in Figure 15(b)?

3. PYTHAGORAS'S THEOREM

We are familiar with this famous theorem but shearing offers a demonstration of the result.

Make a copy of Figure 16 on graph paper. It is a large square with four lines drawn across it so that the corners are also squares.

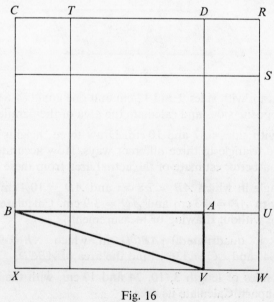

Fig. 16

ABV is a right-angled triangle. Square *AVWU* can be sheared onto a parallelogram with *A*, *V* and *R* as three of its vertices. Draw in this parallelogram and shade
it red.

Square *ABCD* can be sheared onto a parallelogram with *A*, *B* and *R* as three of
its vertices. Draw in this parallelogram and shade it red also. Outline *BTSV* in
another colour. Why is it a square? How can the two red parallelograms be sheared
so that together their images form the square *BTSV*?

What is the relationship between the areas of squares *ABCD*, *AUWV* and *BTSV*?

If *AB* is *x* cm, *AV* is *y* cm and *BV* is *z* cm, state the relation between *x*, *y* and *z*.

4. THE SHEARING MATRIX

When answering Question 7 of Exercise B we used the fact that a tessellation of
squares is transformed into a tessellation of parallelograms by shearing.

Figure 17 shows a tessellation of six squares sheared into six parallelograms. It is
important to think in terms of every point of the diagram being mapped—we have
only illustrated what happens to a few particular points.

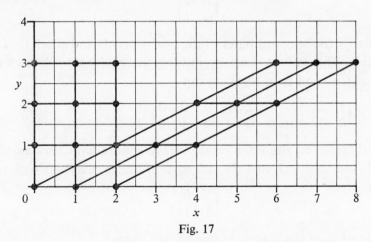

Fig. 17

In Chapter 3 we saw that a 2×2 matrix could be used to describe some transformations. We shall find out what matrix describes a shear.

(*a*) What is the equation of the invariant line in Figure 17?

Considering the vertices of the squares, they are transformed as follows, listing
them in threes:

$$
\begin{aligned}
(0, 0) &\to (0, 0) \\
(1, 0) &\to (1, 0) \\
(2, 0) &\to (2, 0)
\end{aligned}
\quad
\begin{aligned}
(0, 1) &\to (2, 1) \\
(1, 1) &\to (3, 1) \\
(2, 1) &\to (4, 1)
\end{aligned}
\quad
\begin{aligned}
(0, 2) &\to (4, 2) \\
(1, 2) &\to (5, 2) \\
(2, 2) &\to (6, 2)
\end{aligned}
\quad
\begin{aligned}
(0, 3) &\to (6, 3) \\
(1, 3) &\to (7, 3) \\
(2, 3) &\to (8, 3)
\end{aligned}.
$$

In each set of three, what happens to the *y* coordinate?

Since the y coordinate remains unaltered, the bottom row of the transformation matrix must be 0   1. That is,

$$y = (0 \times x) + (1 \times y), \quad \text{so we need} \quad \begin{pmatrix} \cdot & \cdot \\ 0 & 1 \end{pmatrix} \begin{pmatrix} x \\ y \end{pmatrix} = \begin{pmatrix} \cdot \\ y \end{pmatrix}.$$

Notice that the matrix is operating on the coordinates (x, y) written as a column matrix $\begin{pmatrix} x \\ y \end{pmatrix}$.

What happens to the x coordinates?

For the first three points, for which $y = 0$, the x coordinates are unaltered;

for the second three, on $y = 1$, the x coordinates increase by 2;

for the third three, on $y = 2$, the x coordinates increase by 4;

for the fourth three, on $y = 3$, the x coordinates increase by 6;

and so on.

What would be the images of $(0, 4)$, $(1, 4)$ and $(2, 4)$?

In each case the x coordinates increase by double the y coordinate. Thus the top row of the matrix is 1   2, and the complete matrix is

$$\begin{pmatrix} 1 & 2 \\ 0 & 1 \end{pmatrix}.$$

Apply this matrix to the coordinates of the twelve points and check that it produces the correct result. This is best done by putting the twelve coordinates together to form a 2×12 matrix, and then working out

$$\begin{pmatrix} 1 & 2 \\ 0 & 1 \end{pmatrix} \begin{pmatrix} 0 & 1 & 2 & 0 & 1 & 2 & 0 & 1 & 2 & 0 & 1 & 2 \\ 0 & 0 & 0 & 1 & 1 & 1 & 2 & 2 & 2 & 3 & 3 & 3 \end{pmatrix}.$$

(b) Draw a diagram to show the image of the square with vertices $(0, 0)$, $(1, 0)$, $(1, 1)$ and $(0, 1)$ (we shall call this *the unit square*) under the shear with matrix

$$\begin{pmatrix} 1 & 0 \\ 2 & 1 \end{pmatrix}.$$

What is the equation of the invariant line of this shear?

Exercise D

1. Apply the shear described by the matrix

$$\begin{pmatrix} 1 & 1\frac{1}{2} \\ 0 & 1 \end{pmatrix}$$

to the following figures and show each object and image pair on a separate diagram:

(a) the square with vertices $(0, 0)$, $(1, 0)$, $(1, 1)$ and $(0, 1)$;

(b) the parallelogram with vertices $(^-1, 0)$, $(2, 0)$, $(0, 3)$ and $(^-3, 3)$;

(c) the parallelogram with vertices $(4, 1)$, $(7, 1)$, $(3, 3)$ and $(6, 3)$.

2. Apply the shear described by the matrix

$$\begin{pmatrix} 1 & 1\frac{1}{2} \\ 0 & 1 \end{pmatrix}$$

to the quadrilateral with vertices (0, 2), (2, 1), (2, 3) and (4, 2).
What shape are the object and image figures?
Find the areas of these figures.

3. Find two matrices to describe the shears which would map the unit square onto the two parallelograms in Figure 18.

4. Apply the shear described by the matrix

$$\begin{pmatrix} 1 & 1 \\ 0 & 1 \end{pmatrix}$$

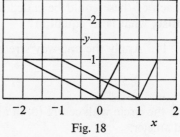

to the rectangle with vertices (1, 0), (4, 0), (1, 1) and (4, 1). Now find the image of the resulting figure under the shear with matrix $\begin{pmatrix} 1 & -2 \\ 0 & 1 \end{pmatrix}$.

Fig. 18

What would be the matrix of the shear equivalent to the combination of these two shears? How can this matrix be obtained from the two given matrices?

5. Find the matrix of the shear which would map the square $ABCD$ onto the parallelogram $PQRS$, in Figure 19.

6. Transform the rectangle with vertices (‾1, 3), (‾3, 1), (‾2, 0) and (0, 2) using the matrix $\begin{pmatrix} \frac{1}{2} & \frac{1}{2} \\ -\frac{1}{2} & \frac{3}{2} \end{pmatrix}$.

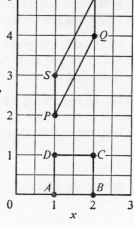

Describe your result geometrically. Is the transformation a shear? If so, what is the equation of the invariant line?

7. Transform the square with vertices (0, 0), (5, 0), (5, 5) and (0, 5) using the matrix $\begin{pmatrix} 0\cdot6 & 0\cdot8 \\ -0\cdot2 & 1\cdot4 \end{pmatrix}$.

Is the transformation a shear?
If it is, find the equation of the invariant line by finding two invariant points of the transformation, that is, points that map onto themselves.

Fig. 19

8. The square with vertices (1, 1), (1, ‾1), (‾1, ‾1) and (‾1, 1) is to be transformed by the shear with matrix

$$\begin{pmatrix} 3 & 2 \\ -2 & -1 \end{pmatrix}$$

By finding the coordinates of the points onto which the four vertices are mapped, find two invariant points and hence the equation of the invariant line. Only draw a diagram if you find it necessary.

9. Transform the unit square by the shear with matrix

$$\begin{pmatrix} 1 & \frac{1}{2} \\ 0 & 1 \end{pmatrix}$$

and then shear its image by the shear with matrix

$$\begin{pmatrix} 1 & 0 \\ 1 & 1 \end{pmatrix}.$$

Is the combination of these two shears equivalent to a single shear?

10. Draw separate diagrams to show the images of the unit square under transformations with matrices

(a) $\begin{pmatrix} 3 & 0 \\ 0 & 1 \end{pmatrix}$; and (b) $\begin{pmatrix} 1 & 0 \\ 0 & 2 \end{pmatrix}$.

Each of these could be called a 'one-way stretch'. Is there an invariant line in each case? If so, what is its equation?

11. Apply the one-way stretch whose matrix is

$$\begin{pmatrix} 1 & 0 \\ 0 & 3 \end{pmatrix}$$

to the circle with centre $(0, 0)$ and radius 2. Show the result in a sketch. Mark the invariant diameter.

12. Draw a diagram to show the result of applying the two transformations of Question 10 in succession. Does the order in which the transformations are applied matter? The resulting transformation could be called a 'two-way stretch'. What is the matrix that describes it? What would be the result of two 'two-way stretches'?

What name do we give to the particular case of a two-way stretch in which the amounts of stretch in each direction are the same?

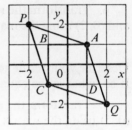

13. Sketch the image of the unit square under an enlargement with centre $(0, 0)$ and scale factor (a) 2, and (b) $^-1\frac{1}{2}$.

Write down the matrices which describe these two enlargements.

*14. In Figure 20, $ABCD$ is stretched to $APCQ$. What is the equation of the invariant line?

Find the matrix that describes this transformation.

Fig. 20

Summary

A matrix which describes a shear keeping each point of $y = 0$ fixed is of the form

$$\begin{pmatrix} 1 & K \\ 0 & 1 \end{pmatrix}.$$

The effect of this shear is to map *the unit square* with vertices $(0, 0)$, $(1, 0)$, $(1, 1)$ and $(0, 1)$ onto the parallelogram with vertices $(0, 0)$, $(1, 0)$, $(1 + K, 1)$ and $(K, 1)$ (see Figure 21).

$$\begin{pmatrix} 1 & K \\ 0 & 1 \end{pmatrix} \begin{pmatrix} 0 & 1 & 1 & 0 \\ 0 & 0 & 1 & 1 \end{pmatrix} = \begin{pmatrix} 0 & 1 & 1+K & K \\ 0 & 0 & 1 & 1 \end{pmatrix}.$$

Similarly the matrix

$$\begin{pmatrix} 1 & 0 \\ K & 1 \end{pmatrix}$$

describes a shear which keeps each point of $x = 0$ fixed.

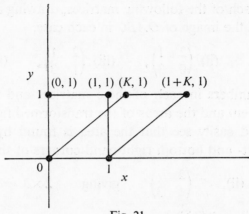

Fig. 21

5. AREA AND MATRICES

Under rotations, reflections and translations both shape and area are preserved. We have also seen that although shearing does not preserve shape, it does preserve area. Do enlargements preserve shape? Do enlargements preserve area?

In this section we shall meet transformations which preserve neither shape nor area.

(*a*) Find the image of the unit square under the transformations described by the following three matrices:

$$\text{(i) } \begin{pmatrix} 2 & 0 \\ 0 & 2 \end{pmatrix}, \qquad \text{(ii) } \begin{pmatrix} 2 & 0 \\ 1 & 2 \end{pmatrix}, \qquad \text{(iii) } \begin{pmatrix} 2 & 3 \\ 0 & 2 \end{pmatrix}.$$

In each case sketch the image on graph paper and find its area using the unit square as the unit of area.

We can find the areas of these images in terms of the area of the unit square by using the formula for the area of a parallelogram.

Provided one pair of the sides of the parallelogram is parallel to either $x = 0$ or $y = 0$ this is straightforward, but if this is not the case we have to fall back on other methods.

Figure 22 shows how the unit square $OABC$ is mapped onto the parallelogram $OA'B'C'$ by the transformation with matrix

$$\begin{array}{cccc} & O & A & B & C \\ \end{array} \qquad \begin{array}{cccc} O & A' & B' & C' \\ \end{array}$$

$$\begin{pmatrix} 5 & 1 \\ 3 & 2 \end{pmatrix}, \text{ i.e. } \begin{pmatrix} 5 & 1 \\ 3 & 2 \end{pmatrix} \begin{pmatrix} 0 & 1 & 1 & 0 \\ 0 & 0 & 1 & 1 \end{pmatrix} = \begin{pmatrix} 0 & 5 & 6 & 1 \\ 0 & 3 & 5 & 2 \end{pmatrix}.$$

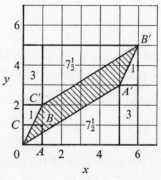

By enclosing the parallelogram in a rectangle of area 30 units and dividing up the rectangle as shown, the area of $OA'B'C'$ can be seen to be

$$30-(2\times3)-(2\times1)-(2\times7\tfrac{1}{2}) = 7 \text{ units.}$$

Fig. 22

209

(b) Repeat (a) for each of the following matrices, drawing a separate diagram for each. Find the area of the image of *OABC* in each case.

(i) $\begin{pmatrix} 2 & 0 \\ 0 & 3 \end{pmatrix}$,   (ii) $\begin{pmatrix} 2 & 1 \\ 0 & 3 \end{pmatrix}$,   (iii) $\begin{pmatrix} 2 & 1 \\ 1 & 3 \end{pmatrix}$,   (iv) $\begin{pmatrix} 2 & 2 \\ \frac{1}{2} & 3 \end{pmatrix}$.

(c) Examine the numbers in each of these matrices and see if you can spot a connection between them and the areas of the transformed figures. For example, in (i) and (ii) you should easily see that the area is found by multiplying the two numbers in the top left- and bottom right-hand corners of the matrix, that is,

in (ii), $\begin{pmatrix} 2 & \\ & 3 \end{pmatrix}$ giving $2 \times 3 = 6.$

What happens in (iii) and (iv)?

Exercise E

1. Find the image of the unit square under the transformations described by the following matrices. In each case find the area of the transformed figure and check your result by examining the numbers in the matrix.

(a) $\begin{pmatrix} 4 & 0 \\ 0 & 2 \end{pmatrix}$;   (b) $\begin{pmatrix} 4 & 2 \\ 1 & 3 \end{pmatrix}$;   (c) $\begin{pmatrix} 3 & 3 \\ -2 & 2 \end{pmatrix}$.

2. Find the image of the unit square under the transformation with matrix

$$\begin{pmatrix} 3 & 1 \\ 1 & 2 \end{pmatrix}.$$

Draw a figure showing the unit square in black and its image in red.

Now find the image of the square with vertices (1, 0), (2, 0), (2, 1) and (1, 1) under the same transformation and show your result on the same diagram.

Repeat this for all the nine unit squares enclosed by the square with vertices (0, 0), (3, 0), (3, 3) and (0, 3), showing all nine images on the same diagram.

3. Repeat Question 2 for a matrix of your own and transform a tessellation of six rectangles.

4. Find the image of the unit square under the transformation with matrix

$$\begin{pmatrix} 4 & -1 \\ 1 & 4 \end{pmatrix}.$$

What shape is the image? What is its area? Use the area to find the length of each side and check your result by using Pythagoras's theorem.

5. Find the image of the unit square under the transformation with matrix

$$\begin{pmatrix} 4 & 1 \\ 3 & 4 \end{pmatrix}.$$

What is the area of the image? What is the length of the longer pair of parallel sides? (Take the length of side of the unit square as the unit of length.) Find the perpendicular distance between this pair of sides.

6. A triangle has vertices (0, 0), (3, 0) and (0, 2). What is its area? Find the image of the triangle under the transformation with matrix

$$\begin{pmatrix} 2 & \frac{1}{2} \\ 1 & 1\frac{1}{2} \end{pmatrix}.$$

By referring to the numbers in this matrix find the area of the image. Check your result by the method shown in Figure 22.

7. Find the image of the rectangle with vertices (4, 2), (10, 0), (11, 3) and (5, 5) under the transformation with matrix

$$\begin{pmatrix} 0.3 & -0.1 \\ 0.1 & 0.3 \end{pmatrix}.$$

Hence find the area of the rectangle.

8. Write down a matrix that describes:
(a) an enlargement with centre (0, 0) and scale factor h;
(b) a two-way stretch with scale factor h parallel to $y = 0$ and scale factor k parallel to $x = 0$.
Use the numbers in the matrix to find the area scale factor in each case.

9. Draw $OA'B'C'$, the image of the unit square under the transformation with matrix

$$\begin{pmatrix} 5 & 3 \\ 2 & 4 \end{pmatrix}.$$

How do the coordinates of the points A' and C' match with the numbers in the matrix? What matrix describes the transformation which maps the unit square onto a parallelogram with vertices (0, 0), (4, 1), (6, 6) and (2, 5)?

10. (a) The coordinates of the vertices O, P and R of the parallelogram $OPQR$ are (0, 0), (h, k) and (u, v).
What are the coordinates of Q?
What matrix would map the unit square onto $OPQR$?
What is the area of $OPQR$?
(b) Use this last result to find the areas of triangles with vertices at:

(i) (0, 0), (7, 2), (2, 5);
(ii) (0, 0), (5, 1), (−1, 2);
(iii) (0, 0), (2, −3), (5, 2).

11. Draw on the same diagram the images of the unit square under the transformations with matrices

$$(a) \begin{pmatrix} 4 & 2 \\ 1 & 1 \end{pmatrix} \quad \text{and} \quad (b) \begin{pmatrix} 1 & 1 \\ 4 & 2 \end{pmatrix}.$$

What is the relationship between the two images?
Use the numbers in each matrix to find the area of each image.
What significance has the negative number that arises in (b)?

12. Explain why (0, 0) is an invariant point for the transformation described by

$$\begin{pmatrix} a & b \\ c & d \end{pmatrix}.$$

211

Summary

The transformation described by the general 2×2 matrix

$$\begin{pmatrix} a & b \\ c & d \end{pmatrix}$$

maps the unit square onto a parallelogram as shown in Figure 23.

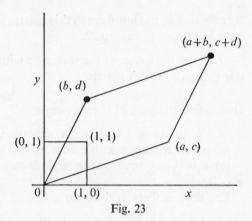

$$\begin{pmatrix} a & b \\ c & d \end{pmatrix}\begin{pmatrix} 0 & 1 & 1 & 0 \\ 0 & 0 & 1 & 1 \end{pmatrix} = \begin{pmatrix} 0 & a & a+b & b \\ 0 & c & c+d & d \end{pmatrix}.$$

The origin is an invariant point.

There is an important number associated with this matrix, namely $ad - bc$.

When the matrix describes a geometrical transformation, then this number gives the *area scale factor* of the transformation. In Figure 23 the area of the parallelogram is $(ad-bc)$ square units.

An enlargement with scale factor k and centre $(0, 0)$ is described by the matrix

$$\begin{pmatrix} k & 0 \\ 0 & k \end{pmatrix}.$$

6. SHEARING IN THREE DIMENSIONS

In Section 1 we considered the side view of a pile of books. We now apply the same idea to the pile of books as a whole.

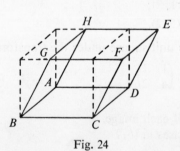

Fig. 24

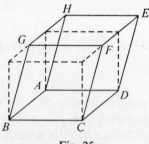

Fig. 25

Figure 24 shows how a rectangular cuboid is sheared parallel to one of its faces. Has the volume altered? Is the height still the same? Which faces are still rectangles? What are the shapes of the other faces? We can also shear the cuboid parallel to another face (see Figure 25). The cuboid could be sheared obliquely (see

212

Figure 26). Which faces are now still rectangles? How would you have to saw through this sheared cuboid to obtain a rectangular cross-section?

These cuboids are all prisms, that is, they have a constant cross-section parallel to a pair of end faces. They all have the same base area, the same perpendicular height and the same volume.

In particular:

$$\text{volume} = (\text{area of base}) \times (\text{perpendicular height}).$$

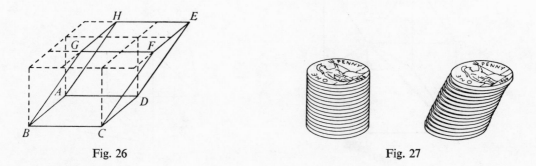

Fig. 26   Fig. 27

6.1 Cylinders

In a similar manner we can shear a cylinder. In Figure 27 the sheared pile of pennies on the right has the same volume as the pile on the left. The volume of both cylinders is the same, namely,

$$(\text{area of base}) \times (\text{perpendicular height}),$$

or $\pi r^2 h$ where the radius is r units and the height h units.

The results of this section—prisms on the same base and with the same height are equal in volume—is a special case of Cavalieri's Principle. This states that if two solids have equal areas of cross-section at the same distances from the base then they have equal volumes. Even if the sides of the pile of pennies are not straight the volume is still the same.

6.2 Pyramids

(a) In Figure 28 we see three congruent square-based pyramids folding together to form a cube.

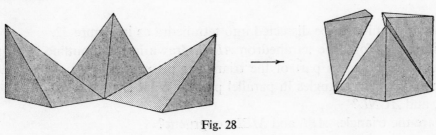

Fig. 28

213

Figure 29 shows how they fit together (one is shown in heavy outline).

The net for one of these pyramids is shown on a small scale in Figure 30. The lengths marked are all equal to the length of edge of the cube. (Tabs need adding. The net is easily marked out on graph paper and with some adjustment of the triangular faces three pyramids can be made together as a single net.)

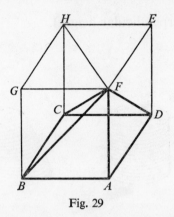
Fig. 29

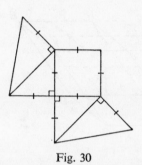
Fig. 30

Make three such pyramids to form a 5 cm cube. Since the volume of the cube is

$$\text{(area of } ABCD) \times \text{(height } AF),$$

the volume of each pyramid must be

$$\tfrac{1}{3}\text{(area of base)} \times \text{(perpendicular height)}.$$

(*b*) Is this true for all pyramids? Before answering this question we note the following two facts.

(i) By shearing we can see that pyramids with the same base *ABC* and equal heights have equal volume (see Figure 31).

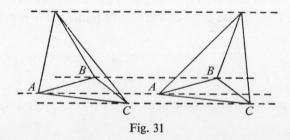
Fig. 31

(ii) Any pyramid can be dissected into tetrahedra as in Figure 32.

Consider, therefore, the tetrahedron *ABCL* drawn in thick outline in Figure 33. This can be regarded as part of the triangular prism *ABCNML* where *ABC* and *LMN* are congruent triangles in parallel planes. What shape are the faces *ABML*, *BCNM*, and *ACNL*?

Why are the triangles *ABL* and *MBL* congruent?

214

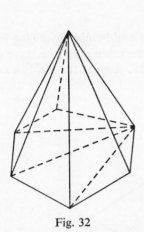

Fig. 32

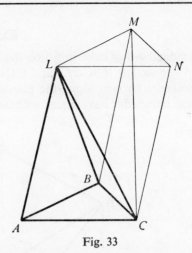

Fig. 33

The prism is divided into the three tetrahedra *ABCL*, *LBMC* and *LMNC*. The tetrahedra *ABCL* and *LBMC* have congruent bases *ALB* and *LBM*. They have the same vertex *C* and, hence, the same height.

This implies they have the same volume.

Why do the tetrahedra *ABCL* and *LMNC* have equal volume?

If the three tetrahedra are equal in volume and together they make the prism, then the volume of each tetrahedron is

$$\tfrac{1}{3}(\text{area of base}) \times (\text{perpendicular height}).$$

This, using facts (i) and (ii) above, implies that the same is true for all pyramids.

6.3   Cones

Just as in Chapter 5 we thought of the circle as the limiting form of a polygon with many sides, in a similar way a cone can be regarded as the limiting form of a pyramid with many faces. Its volume can therefore be found in a similar manner to that of the pyramids which approximate to it. Figure 34 shows a right circular cone and its volume is

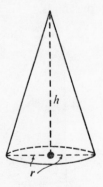

$$\tfrac{1}{3}(\text{area of base}) \times (\text{perpendicular height}) = \tfrac{1}{3}\pi r^2 h.$$

Fig. 34

Summary

Volume of prism	= (area of base) ×(perpendicular height).
Volume of cylinder	$= \pi r^2 h.$
Volume of pyramid	$= \tfrac{1}{3}(\text{area of base}) \times (\text{perpendicular height}).$
Volume of circular cone	$= \tfrac{1}{3}\pi r^2 h.$

Exercise F

1. Take a cuboid of cake in which the length, breadth and height differ (see Figure 35). Slice it into two wedges $ABCDEF$ and $CDHEFG$. Divide the top wedge into three *differently* shaped tetrahedra by cuts along the planes CAE and CAF. Repeat for the bottom wedge. Why will the tetrahedra have equal volumes?

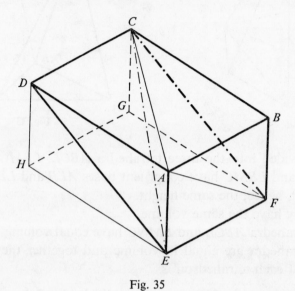

Fig. 35

2. Figure 36 shows a cuboid $9 \times 6 \times 3$ cm made out of three different rectangular-based pyramids.

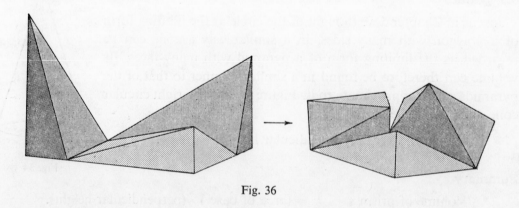

Fig. 36

Figure 37 shows the net for the tall pyramid on the left of Figure 36.

Design nets for the other two and so construct the model. (With care the three nets can be made as one piece.)

Why are the three pyramids of equal volume?

216

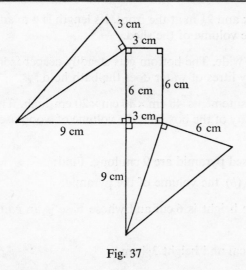

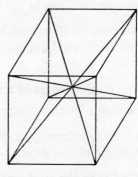

Fig. 37   Fig. 38

3. Each edge of the cube in Figure 38 is 6 cm long. How many square-based pyramids 3 cm high make up the cube?

Figure 40 shows the net for a pyramid; the equal sides of the triangle are roughly 5·1 cm long.

Make six of these and join them together in such a way that they fold up to make a cube.

(If the triangles are arranged round the net of a cube shown in Figure 39, then a net giving much of Figure 38 can be made as a single piece.)

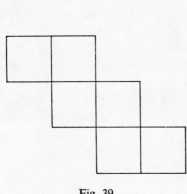

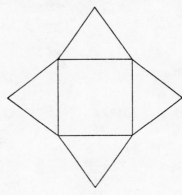

Fig. 39   Fig. 40

4. How many packets of butter $12 \times 5 \times 3$ cm can fit into a box $60 \times 54 \times 36$ cm? Explain which way they would have to fit for your answer to be correct.

5. A water tank has a base 3 m square, and contains water to a depth of 2 m. How far will the water level rise if a rock of volume 3 m³ is put in the tank and is completely submerged?

6. A drainpipe has external diameter 15 cm and internal diameter $13\frac{1}{2}$ cm. Find the volume of metal in a 7·20 m length of pipe.

7. A lean-to shed has height 3 m at the back and $2\frac{1}{6}$ m at the front. Its length is 4 m and its breadth from front to back is $2\frac{2}{3}$ m. Find the volume of the shed.

8. A swimming bath is 25 m long and 15 m wide. The bottom gets steadily deeper from 1 m at one end to $2\frac{2}{3}$ m at the other. How many litres of water does the bath hold?

9. An open wooden box has external measurements 48 cm × 40 cm × 20 cm high. The bottom and sides are 1 cm thick. Find the capacity of the box, and the volume of wood used to make it.

10. The slanting edges of an 8 cm square-based pyramid are 9 cm long. Find:

(a) the area of each slanting face;   (b) the volume of the pyramid.

11. Find the volume of a tetrahedron whose height is 6 cm and whose base is an equilateral triangle of side 4 cm.

12. Find the volume of a cone of radius 1·7 cm and height 3·4 cm.

13. Find the height of a cone of radius 3·2 cm³ and volume 39 cm³.

14. A cone has volume 400 cm³ and height 12·1 cm. Find:

(a) the area of its base;   (b) the radius of its base.

REVISION EXERCISES

SLIDE RULE SESSION NO. 5

Give all answers as accurately as you can.

1. $3\cdot3 \times 24\cdot5$.
2. $19\cdot2 \times 7\cdot6$.
3. $9\cdot44^2$.
4. $17 \times 28\cdot9$.
5. $0\cdot59 \times 32$.
6. $24\cdot5 \div 3\cdot3$.
7. $7\cdot6 \div 19\cdot2$.
8. $9\cdot44 \div 1\cdot2$.
9. $28\cdot9 \div 17$.
10. $0\cdot59 \div 32$.

SLIDE RULE SESSION NO. 6

Give all answers as accurately as you can.

1. $\sqrt{51\cdot3}$.
2. $\sqrt{75,000}$.
3. $1\cdot91^3$.
4. $\pi \times 2\cdot7^2$.
5. $37 \times 0\cdot81^2$.
6. $\pi \times \sqrt{\frac{100}{981}}$.
7. $\frac{4}{3}\pi \times 1\cdot2^3$.
8. $\dfrac{19 \times 23^2}{64\cdot4}$.
9. $3\cdot1 \times 10^3 \times 1\cdot7 \times 10^{-4}$.
10. $\dfrac{4\cdot2 \times 10^7}{1\cdot5 \times 10^{-3}}$.

M

1. Give the value of cos 60° without using tables.

2. Find the angle made with the line $y = 0$ by the line joining $(2, ^-1)$ to $(4, 1)$.

3. Solve $2m - 7 = 3$.   4. Solve $9(k + 3) = 18$.

5. If $f(x) = 2 + x$, find $f^{-1}(0)$.   6. If $f(x) = x^2 + 3x + 1$, find $f(4)$.

7. Simplify $\emptyset \cap \mathscr{E}$.   8. Simplify $A \cup A'$.

9. Make c the subject of the formula $T = 3/\sqrt{c}$.

10. Solve the equation $11x = 1001$, the numbers being in binary, giving the solution in binary.

N

1. $(2, 1), (2, ^-1), (^-2, ^-1), (^-2, 1)$ are the vertices of a quadrilateral. Find its area.

2. Find the distances of the other vertices of the quadrilateral in Question 1 from the vertex $(2, 1)$.

3. Describe the shape of the region $\{(x, y): 3 < x < 5\} \cap \{(x, y): 0 < y < 2\}$.

4. Is it true that $x = 1 \Leftrightarrow x^2 = 1$?

5. If a square and a circle have the same perimeter, which has the greater area?

6. $ABCD$ is a square, with the diagonals AC and BD drawn in. Is the figure traversable?

7. Simplify $\frac{7}{8} \div \frac{3}{4}$.

8. Write $2x^2 + 2x + x^2 - 5x + x(2 - x) + 7$ in a shorter form.

219

9. Express 1111_2 in base 8.

10. One side of a right-angled triangle is 4 cm long and the hypotenuse is 5 cm long. Find the area of the triangle.

O

1. At Mahiti International Airport a building 18 m high is 180 m from the end of the main runway. Assuming that a plane is to climb along a straight path once it has taken off, find, by scale drawing, the minimum safe angle of ascent. If the angle of ascent is 10°, use another drawing to estimate by what vertical distance the plane will clear the top of the building if it leaves the ground 30 m before the end of the runway.

2. The height of the tide (h m) on a certain day is given by $h = 15 + 4 \cos x°$, where $x = 30n$, n being the number of hours after midnight. Make out a table of values for h for the period midnight to noon the same day, and graph the function $n \to h$.
   At what times on that day will the height of the tide be 13 m?

3. If $g: x \to 1 + \dfrac{x}{2}$, express the function g^{-1} in the same form and find the value of $g^{-1}g^{-1}(2)$.
Check your answer by finding the function gg and using the fact that $(gg)^{-1} = g^{-1}g^{-1}$.
   For what value of x does $gg(x) = 101$?

4. Represent on number lines, the intersection of the solution sets for each of the following pairs:

(a) $3 - x < 5$ and $5 < 4 - x$.   (b) $\dfrac{x+1}{2} \leqslant 1$ and $1 \leqslant x + 3$,

5. A P-matrix is of the form $\begin{pmatrix} a & 0 \\ 0 & b \end{pmatrix}$ and a Q-matrix is of the form $\begin{pmatrix} 0 & c \\ d & 0 \end{pmatrix}$. Form the operation table for the P-matrices and Q-matrices under matrix multiplication. State the identity element (if any).

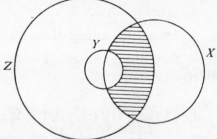

6. Is the shaded area in Figure 1:

(a) $(X \cup Y) \cap Z$;   (b) $(X \cap Y) \cup Z$;
(c) $(X \cap Y') \cap Z$;   (d) $(X \cap Y)' \cap Z$?

7. If $\mathscr{E} = \{10, 11, 12, 13, 14, 15, 16, 17, 18, 19\}$, list the members of the following subsets of $\mathscr{E}$:

(a) {prime numbers};   (b) {multiples of 3};
(c) {numbers such that $55 - 2x < 25$};
(d) {numbers such that $(x - 13)^2 = 4$}.

Fig. 1

List the members of any two subsets A and B of $\mathscr{E}$ such that $A \cap B = \varnothing$, and $A \cup B = \mathscr{E}$.

8. The volume of a spherical soap bubble is increasing at a steady rate of 7 cm³ per s. At a certain instant the volume is 1 cm³.

(a) If the volume of the bubble is v cm³, t s after that instant, write down a formula for v in terms of t,
(b) Find the ratio of the volume when $t = 1$ to the volume when $t = 9$.
(c) Find the ratio of the radius when $t = 1$ to the radius when $t = 9$.

P

1. If $\cos A = \frac{5}{13}$ and $270° < A < 360°$, find the value of $\sin A$ without using tables.

2. Show that the matrices $\mathbf{M}$ and $\mathbf{I}$ where $\mathbf{M} = \begin{pmatrix} -1 & 2 \\ 0 & 3 \end{pmatrix}$ and $\mathbf{I} = \begin{pmatrix} 1 & 0 \\ 0 & 1 \end{pmatrix}$ satisfy the equation $\mathbf{M}^2 - 2\mathbf{M} - 3\mathbf{I} = 0$.

3. If the matrices $\mathbf{X} = \begin{pmatrix} 1 & 1 \\ 0 & 1 \end{pmatrix}$ and $\mathbf{Y} = \begin{pmatrix} 1 & 0 \\ 1 & 1 \end{pmatrix}$, represent transformations, find the matrices $\mathbf{X}^2$, $\mathbf{Y}^2$, $\mathbf{XY}$ and $\mathbf{YX}$. Use a graph to show the effect of these combined transformations on the unit square.

4. (a) Write down all the subsets with three elements of the set $\{b_1, b_2, b_3, b_4\}$ and the subsets with two elements of the set $\{g_1, g_2, g_3\}$.

(b) If three boys are chosen at random from Bryan, Basil, Benjamin and Bartholomew and two girls from Gloria, Grace and Gladys, what is the probability that neither Bryan nor Grace are chosen? What is the probability that Bryan, Basil, Gloria and Grace are chosen?

5. A rocket rises 15 km vertically, 20 km at 30° from the vertical, and then 50 km at 35° from the vertical. Calculate to the nearest kilometre how high it then is above the launching pad.

6. Here are the brands of toothpaste used by the boys of one form: 12 use Bitewite, 9 use Shynodent, 6 use Tusko, 4 use Formula XT 5, 3 use Molarcare, 2 use Toothine. Illustrate this information by: (a) a bar chart, (b) a pie chart.

7. The police compiled a list of 15 men suspected of having committed a certain crime. 10 suspects were right-handed. 9 were *either* left-handed *or* brown-eyed *or* both; of these 3 were left-handed but not brown-eyed.

In the Venn Diagram (Figure 2) S is the set of all suspects, R is the set of right-handers amongst them and B is the set with brown eyes. Use this diagram to find the number of men who can now be crossed from the list of suspects if it is later discovered that the criminal must be both right-handed and brown-eyed. (Start by supposing that the number of men in the set $R \cap B$ is x, and work from there.)

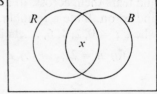

Fig. 2

8. A greedy boy is told by a kind uncle that he may have up to 25p, provided he spends it only on Munchy Bars (2p each) and Nutty Bars (3p each).

(a) If the boy buys x of the former and y of the latter, write down the ordering which must be satisfied.

(b) List the different ways he could spend the 25p without having any change given to him.

(c) If he decided to buy twice as many Nutty Bars as Munchy Bars, what is his greatest possible expenditure?

Q

1. A circle has a radius of 4 cm and a centre O. Two parallel chords are 4 cm apart. What is the total length of arc between these chords when
(a) one chord passes through the centre.
(b) the chords are symmetrical about the centre?

2. In a car that does 11 km to the litre, my petrol bill is £120 per annum. How much less would it be if the consumption were 15 km to the litre?

3. (a) Does $x = 3$ satisfy the relation $3x - 5 < \frac{1}{2}(2x + 1)$?
(b) What can you say about x if $2x + 5 > 5x + 17$?
(c) Solve $4(3 - x) < 30$.

4. Draw a freehand pattern (not composed entirely of straight lines) which has exactly three axes of symmetry.

5. In a village of 176 houses it is discovered that the only newspapers that anyone buys are the *Daily Telegraph*, *Daily Mail* and the *Sketch*. The newsagent delivers at least one paper to every house, but never 2 copies of the same paper to one house. Altogether they deliver 40 copies of the *Sketch*, 71 *Telegraphs* and 98 *Mails*. Including those houses that take all three papers, 12 take the *Sketch* and the *Mail*, 13 take the *Mail* and the *Telegraph*, and 15 take the *Telegraph* and the *Sketch*. Draw a Venn diagram and hence find how many take all three.

6. *A* is a solid cylinder, *B* is a cylinder with the same height as *A* but with twice *A*'s diameter. *C* is a cylinder geometrically similar to *A* (that is, an enlargement of *A*) with the same diameter as *B*. How many times *A*'s volume is: (a) the volume of *B*; (b) the volume of *C*?

7. A straight line segment connects $O(0, 0)$ and $P(3, 0)$. It is rotated about O through an angle of $\theta°$. What are the new coordinates of P? Make a table of the coordinates of P for the values $\theta = 30, 45, 60, 90, 120, 135, 180$.

8. A man takes a sheet of paper and tears it across. In 2 s he puts the two pieces together and tears them across. In another 2 s he puts the four pieces together and tears them across, and so on. State a formula which gives the number of sheets to be torn across at time t s, where $t = 0, 2, 4, 6, \ldots$. Is it:

(a) $n = 2t$;   (b) $n = 2^t$;   (c) $n = 2^{2t}$;   (d) $n = t$;   (e) $n = 2^{\frac{1}{2}t}$?

R

1. Find the solution set of each of the following:

(a) $2(3x - 1) + 8 = 6(x + 1)$;   (b) $1 - (4 - x) > x - 2$;   (c) $(x - 3)^2 = x(x - 6)$.

2. Mark the points $A(4, 5)$, $B(2, 1)$ and $C(4, 0)$ on graph paper.

(a) Show on your diagram the result of applying the translation $\begin{pmatrix} -2 \\ 1 \end{pmatrix}$ to *ABC*. Label this $A'B'C'$.

(b) $A'B'C'$ maps onto $A''B''C''$ when rotated 60° anticlockwise about O. Show $A''B''C''$ on the diagram.

(c) Find by construction the centre of the rotation that maps *ABC* straight onto $A''B''C''$.

3. Similar shaped bottles in a chemists shop, with heights 10, 14, 16 cm sell for 25p, 60p, 90p respectively. Arrange these in order of 'best buy'.

4. Draw a figure, like an F, in an equilateral triangle. Draw its images under reflection in the three sides of the triangle. What transformations connect these images?

222

5. A helicopter flies due north at 96 km/h for 1 h. It then changes course to due east and continues for 20 min. On what course should it fly to return directly to the starting point and how long will this take if the same speed is maintained?

6. AB is the spine of a book. The covers are $ABPQ$ and $ABXY$. The book is opened through a right-angle, so that $\angle XBP = \angle YAQ = 90°$. Using only the letters A, B, P, Q, X, Y write down the angle, or an equivalent angle,
   (a) between plane XAQ and plane $ABPQ$;
   (b) that XQ makes with $ABPQ$;
   (c) that XQ makes with AB.
If the book had been opened through an angle which was not a right-angle, would any of your answers still be correct?

7. Teletown is in a fringe area. $A = \{$houses receiving BBC 1 clearly$\}$, $B = \{$houses receiving BBC 2 clearly$\}$, $C = \{$houses receiving ITV clearly$\}$. Describe the sets $A \cap B$, $A' \cap B'$, $A \cup B$, $A \cup B \cup C$. If A, B, $C \subset \mathscr{E}$, $n(\mathscr{E}) = 1000$, $n(A) = 500$, $n(B) = 400$, give the greatest and least values of $n(A \cup B)$ and $n(A \cap B)$. If $n(A \cap C) = 200$, what (if anything) can you say about $n(C)$?

8. A man has a straight hedge 80 m long, and he buys an electrical cutter with which to trim it. The nearest electricity point is 30 m away from the hedge, half-way along. Unfortunately the cable on the cutter is only 40 m long. What length of the hedge can the man reach? How much should he extend the cable so that he can trim the whole hedge?

223

13
STATISTICS

*He uses statistics as a drunken man uses lamp-posts—for support rather
than illumination.*

ANDREW LANG

1. MISREPRESENTATION

'There are three kinds of lies: lies, damned lies and statistics.' Disraeli.

It is often said that anything can be proved using statistics. Although this is not
quite true, statistics can be used to deceive.

(*a*) The graph in Figure 1 supposedly shows the increase in sales of Whoosh over
a period of 4 years. Are you convinced of the phenomenal success of Whoosh? Give
your reasons.

(*b*) The following table gives the sales of the *Daily Wail*:

Year	Sales in millions
1965	11
1966	$11\frac{1}{2}$
1967	$12\frac{1}{4}$
1968	$13\frac{1}{4}$

Represent this information on a graph:

(i) with the scale up the page marked from 0 to 16 million and with 2 cm representing 4 million;

(ii) with the scale up the page marked from 10 to 14 million and with 2 cm representing 1 million.

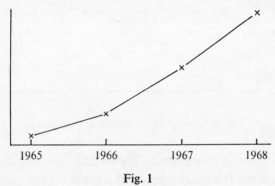

Fig. 1

Compare the visual effect of the two graphs.

(c) Figure 2 shows the vitamin/mineral content of 1 kg of Doggo compared with that of 1 kg of shin of beef.

What are the misleading features?

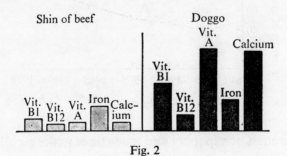

Fig. 2

(d) Figure 3 illustrates the company Chairman's statement: 'Profit this year is double that of last year.' Is it a fair representation? What is the ratio of:

(i) the heights of the money bags;
(ii) their areas?

Last year   This year

Fig. 3

225

(*e*) Look carefully at Figure 4. How does it differ from graphs you have drawn before?

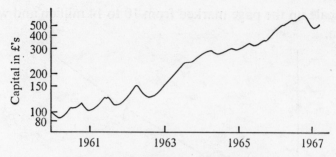

Fig. 4. Growth of an investment of £100.

This graph is not intended to mislead. Try to find out why this particular type of graph is used. Of what do the markings on the scale up the page remind you?

(*f*) Figure 5 shows the results of the school hockey team over five seasons up to 1968. The dotted line is a prediction for the future. Is this justified?

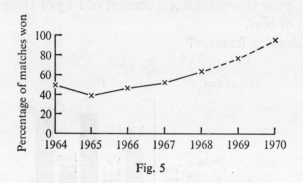

Fig. 5

(*g*) By looking through newspapers and magazines make a collection of statistical representations that mislead.

2. FREQUENCY FUNCTIONS

2.1 Frequency tables

You already know how to represent information diagrammatically using:

> bar charts,
> pictograms,
> pie charts,
> frequency diagrams.

In this section we shall consider the last of these methods in more detail.

A function which maps a set of possible events onto the number of times each event occurs, i.e. the frequency of each event, is called a *frequency function*.

For example, the following table gives information about the clutch sizes (number of eggs) in 100 tree-sparrow nests. It represents the frequency function

$$\text{size of clutch} \rightarrow \text{number of nests of that size.}$$

Size of clutch (eggs)	2	3	4	5	6	7
Frequency (nests)	2	7	25	53	12	1

A graphical representation of this function is shown in Figure 6.

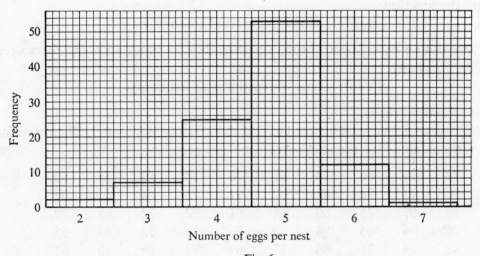

Number of eggs per nest

Fig. 6

Notice that each number is placed under the centre of a column. Strictly speaking this graph should consist of lines straight up the page from the points 2, 3, 4, etc., but it is more useful to draw it in the way shown. In this case we are, in a sense, saying that 4 covers the whole interval from the marks 3·5 to 4·5.

(*a*) A postman noted how many letters he delivered at each house in a road containing 40 houses.

The frequency function is described by this table:

Number of letters delivered at a house	0	1	2	3	4	5	6	7
Frequency (houses)	8	13	10	7	1	0	0	1

Thus 8 houses received no letters, 13 houses 1 letter and so on.

Graph this function and compare it with Figure 6. Try to explain the reason for their different shapes.

(*b*) The two frequency functions above are based on observations. It is also possible to construct functions based on *expected* frequencies, in the same way that we had expected probabilities in Chapter 1.

Suppose, as in Monopoly, that two dice, say a red and a green, are thrown to determine the score. We can form a frequency function mapping the possible scores onto the number of ways in which they can be obtained.

For example, there is only 1 way of scoring 2, that is a '1' on each die; but there are 2 ways of scoring 3, a '1' on the red die and a '2' on the green, or a '1' on the green die and a '2' on the red.

Copy and complete this frequency table for 36 throws of the two dice.

Possible scores	2	3	4	5	6	7	8	9	10	11	12
Expected frequency	1	2	3								

Graph the function:

$$\text{possible scores} \to \text{expected frequency.}$$

Now carry out an experiment, throw a pair of dice 36 times and note the scores. Graph the function:

$$\text{possible scores} \to \text{experimental frequency.}$$

Compare the two graphs.

(c) 60 15-year-old boys were tested to find their resting pulse-rates. The following figures were obtained for the number of beats per minute:

72	70	66	74	81	70	74	53	57	62
58	92	74	67	62	91	73	68	65	80
78	67	75	80	84	61	72	72	69	70
76	74	65	84	79	80	76	72	68	65
82	79	71	86	77	69	72	56	70	62
76	56	86	63	73	70	75	73	89	64

A collection of observations like this is often referred to as a *population*.

Form a frequency function by separating the different pulse rates into *classes*, 50–54, 55–59, 60–64, etc., and considering the function:

$$\text{class} \to \text{number of boys in that class.}$$

In this case we say the *class interval* is 5. Had we taken classes 50–59, 60–69, etc., ..., then the class interval would have been 10.

It will help you to construct the mapping if you draw up a table like the following, and use tally marks:

Class	Tally marks	Frequency
50–54	/	1
55–59	////	4
60–64		
65–69		
70–74		
75–79		
80–84		
85–89		

This is called a *grouped* frequency table, because, instead of considering every pulse rate separately, we have *grouped* the pulse rates into classes.

Graph the frequency function and comment on its shape in comparison with the ones in (*a*) and (*b*).

2.2   Span of intervals

(*a*) The number of eggs in a clutch, the number of letters delivered, the number of spots on a die are all whole numbers. When drawing a frequency diagram, the columns, whatever their width, must be centred on the whole number marks.

(*b*) Measurements of length or mass are usually given to the nearest suitable unit. 'This box is 10·5 cm long, as near as I can see.' 'The mass of the letter is 90 g to the nearest ten grams', meaning that its mass is between 85 g and 95 g. When constructing the frequency diagram, for a collection of letter masses given to the nearest ten grams, it would be necessary to take the 80, 90, 100, ... gram marks as the centres of the intervals. In these cases the column *must* stretch from 75 to 85, from 85 to 95 etc., so that the whole number line is covered. (A specific decision has to be made about those objects that are thought to have a reading that lies exactly on the interval line.)

(*c*) Different from (*a*) and (*b*), are collections of ages of people and of dates. Though for some reason it might be best to take peoples' ages to the nearest year, it is usual for anyone between their 5th and 6th birthdays to call themselves 5 years old. The centre of the column in this case would be $5\frac{1}{2}$ and it would stretch from 5 to 6. Similarly with dates; considering the monthly rainfall at a town, the line across the page would be marked in months and the columns would be centred over the month centres and would stretch from the beginning to the end of the month.

(*d*) Pulse rates might be given in two ways. If you are calling out the numbers while watching a clock, then you might take the reading called just *before* the minute was up, or you might take the reading called *nearest* to the time when the minute was up. Which do you think is better? Using the second method, the reading 50 would mean the actual rate was between 49·5 and 50·5 pulses per minute. The class interval named 50–54 would stand for an interval of from 49·5–54·5.

2.3   Normal frequency functions

Many diagrams of frequency functions are similar to that in Section 2.1 (*c*) above; that is, they have bilateral symmetry with a central hump. Figure 7 shows another example: the reaction times of a timekeeper in 500 tests with a stopwatch.

If the population is large and the class intervals are small, the graph of such a frequency function approaches a bell-shape (see Figure 8). Frequency functions having such a bell-shaped graph are called *Normal*.

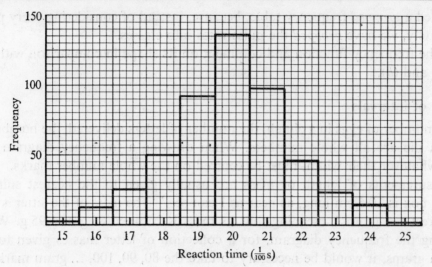

Fig. 7

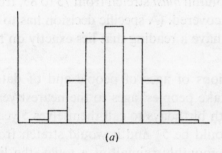
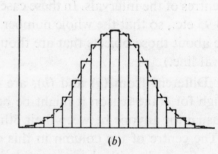

(a)   (b)

Fig. 8

Exercise A

1. The following table describes the frequency function for the number of words in two samples of 100 sentences from books by each of two authors, Enid Blyton and P. G. Wodehouse. The samples were taken from descriptive passages only and are not necessarily in the correct order.

Number of words	1–5	6–10	11–15	16–20	21–25	26–30	31–35	36–40	41–45	46–50
Sample 1	18	24	30	14	8	3	1	0	2	0
Sample 2	15	22	17	11	12	9	8	2	2	2
Sample 3	22	18	10	14	7	9	6	5	5	4
Sample 4	15	27	32	15	7	3	1	0	0	0

Graph the frequency function for each sample. By examining the shape of the graphs find which samples are taken from the same author.

Why would you not expect the graphs of the frequency functions to be symmetrical in this case?

2. The table below describes another frequency function relating to the lengths of 100 sentences from a book.

Number of words	1–5	6–10	11–15	16–20	21–25	26–30	31–35	36–40	41–45	46–50
Frequency	5	20	25	16	16	7	6	3	1	1

Graph the frequency function. Compare this graph with those you drew when answering Question 1.

Can you say whether or not the author in this example is the same as one of those in Question 1?

3. Project: take samples of 100 sentences from various books, taking several from books by the same author. Draw graphs and comment on your results.

4. On 2 June 1965, 100 batsmen in first-class cricket matches made scores of less than 100 runs.

Number of runs	0–9	10–19	20–29	30–39	40–49	50–59	60–69	70–79	80–89	90–99
Number of batsmen	43	23	9	10	4	5	4	0	2	0

Graph the frequency function.

Compile a similar table for another day (it is best to choose a day which will be the first day of many matches; possibly a Saturday or a Wednesday).

Graph this second function and compare the graph with the one previously drawn.

Comment on any similarities or differences.

5. Compile a frequency function table for 100 throws of a die as follows:

Score	I	2	3	4	5	6
Frequency						

Graph this function.

What would be the shape of the graph of the function

$$\text{score} \to \text{expected frequency?}$$

6. Discuss the likely shape of the graphs of frequency functions in the following cases.

(a) Number of teams scoring 0, 1, 2, 3, 4, etc., goals in football matches on a particular Saturday.

(b) Number of children with different shoe sizes in your class.

(c) Number of children in 100 families.

7. Project: draw frequency function graphs for sizes of shoe, heights, masses and ages for a group of 50–100 people in your school. Would a graph for the whole school be the same sort of shape as the graph for your sample?

8. Meteorologists measure the cloudiness of the sky in eighths. A clear sky is $\frac{0}{8}$ and an overcast sky is $\frac{8}{8}$.

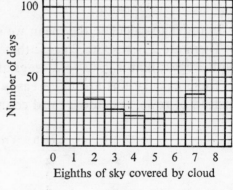

Fig. 9

Figure 9 shows the sort of graph that might be obtained if records were kept for noon on each day for a year. Explain the significance of the shape of this graph. Keep records of your own for a period of, say, two months and compare the graph you get with Figure 9.

9. Using the information in Section 2, approximately what would be the probability of the number of eggs in a tree-sparrow's nest being

(a) 5;   (b) 3 or 4?

10. The masses of a large group of students involved in a particular sporting activity were recorded and the graph of the function

mass → number of students

approached the shape shown in Figure 10. What was the sport?

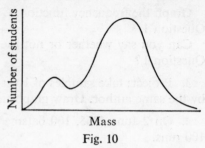

Fig. 10

3. THE MEAN

In Section 2 we compared the shapes of the graphs of frequency functions.

We are now going to look at more precise methods of comparison.

You have already done some work on this in Book 2 where you met two measures of *average*:

(i) the *mode* (the most 'popular class');

(ii) the *mean* (the everyday 'average', for example, a batting average).

What is the mode for the number of eggs in a clutch (see p. 227)? If a batsman scores 11, 32, 7 and 50 in four innings and is out every time, what is his mean score?

In which of these two measures of average would a shoe manufacturer be interested?

3.1   Finding the mean from a frequency table

It is easy to find the mean when the population is small, as in the cricket example above, but when the population is large a systematic method is necessary.

Here again is the frequency function table for clutch sizes in 100 tree-sparrow nests.

Size of clutch (eggs)	2	3	4	5	6	7
Frequency	2	7	25	53	12	1

In order to calculate the mean we shall need to find the total number of eggs.

There are 2 nests with 2 eggs; that is $2 \times 2 = 4$ eggs altogether. There are 7 nests with 3 eggs; that is $7 \times 3 = 21$ eggs altogether, and so on.

These calculations are more easily made if we rewrite the table using columns instead of rows, and add a third column that is formed as shown.

Size of clutch	Frequency	Size × frequency
2	2	4
3	7	21
4	25	100
5	53	265
6	12	72
7	1	7
	100	469

The mean is $\dfrac{\text{the total number of eggs}}{\text{the total number of nests}} = \dfrac{469}{100} = 4 \cdot 69.$

Find the mean number of letters delivered to a house in the example in Section 2.1 (a).

3.2 Finding the mean from a grouped frequency table

Look back at Exercise A, Question 1, Sample 1. There are:

18 sentences with 1–5 words,

24 sentences with 6–10 words,

and so on.

Is it possible to say how many words there are altogether in the 1–5 class?

Can you suggest a way out of this difficulty?

What usually happens is that the mid-interval value is used, for example,

is regarded as

18 sentences with 1–5 words,

18 sentences with 3 words, that is $18 \times 3 = 54$ words altogether.

3 is the *mid-interval* value for the class 1–5.

What is the mid-interval value for the 6–10 class?

The calculation is usually set out like this:

Sentence length	Frequency	Mid-interval value	Mid-interval value × frequency
1–5	18	3	54
6–10	24	8	192
11–15	30	13	390
16–20	14	18	252
21–25	8	23	184
26–30	3	28	84
31–35	1	33	33
36–40	0	38	0
41–45	2	43	86
	100		1275

The mean length of sentence is

$$\frac{\text{total number of words}}{\text{total number of sentences}} = \frac{1275}{100} = 12 \cdot 75 \text{ words.}$$

Is the result exact?

It is important to realize that it is only possible to give an *approximate* value for the mean of a grouped frequency function.

Exercise B

1. A darts player made the following scores in 12 throws: 11, 20, 6, 9, 17, 13, 1, 5, 14, 7, 10, 19. Find his mean score.

2. Find the mean number of children per household in Barchester at the last two censuses.

Number of children per household	0	1	2	3	4	5	6	> 6 (av. 8)	Total
Frequency (thousands of households)									
1951 census	81	25	20	10	5	3	1	0	145
1961 census	89	28	23	11	6	4	2	1	164

3. In a year's entry of 182 boys for G.C.E. O level examinations, 6 boys had no passes; 10 boys one pass; 40 boys two or three passes; 103 boys four, five or six passes; 23 boys seven or eight passes. What is the approximate mean number of passes?

4. The masses of a group of children at 6 months were as follows:

Mass (kg)	6–7	7–8	8–9	9–10	10–11	Total
Frequency (children)	5	11	18	8	3	45

Find the approximate mean mass.

5. (a) Using your form's results in a recent examination, find the mean mark.
   (b) Now form a grouped frequency function by taking classes

$$1\text{–}10$$
$$11\text{–}20, \text{ etc.}$$

What is the mid-interval mark for the 1–10 class? Find the approximate value of the mean from the grouped frequency table.
   (c) Compare the two answers that you have obtained for the mean.

6. The mean length of sentence for Exercise A, Question 1, Sample 1 was found on p. 233. Find the mean lengths for the other samples, and also for the samples you recorded yourself.

7. The ages in years and months of a form of 30 boys are as follows:

Age	13.0–13.2	13.2–13.4	13.4–13.6	13.6–13.8	13.8–13.10	13.10–14.0
Frequency (boys)	4	7	5	5	3	6

Find the approximate mean age by multiplying 13 years 1 month by 4 and so on.
Can you see a way of simplifying the working?

8. A timekeeper tests his reaction time with a stopwatch, and records the following results (see Figure 7):

Reaction time ($\frac{1}{100}$ s)	15	16	17	18	19	20	21	22	23	24	25
Frequency	2	12	25	50	92	136	98	46	23	14	2

Rewrite this table as follows:

Number of $\frac{1}{100}$ seconds by which reaction time exceeds $\frac{15}{100}$ s	0	1	2	3	4	...
Frequency		2	12	25		...

Find an appropriate value of the mean from this table.
Deduce the mean reaction time of the timekeeper.

9. Using the information you collected in Question 7 of Exercise A, calculate the mean shoe size, height, mass, etc. (You may find it useful in some cases to use the technique of Questions 7 and 8.)

10. Before the final game of the season two cricketers A and B had both taken 16 wickets at 9 runs per wicket.
In the final game A took 1 for 26 and B took 4 for 56.
Who had the best average for the whole season?

234

4. THE MEDIAN

(*a*) The shares in a company are held by 100 members:

1 shareholder has £1010,
99 shareholders have £10 each.

What is the mean shareholding?

Is it fair to advertise that the average shareholding is £20?

As you see in this example, it can be misleading to quote the mean: the large shareholding of £1010 affects the mean.

A type of average which does not depend on the 'freak' values is the *median*. If all the members of a population (of letters delivered, clutch sizes, pulse rates, ...) are set out in order of magnitude, then the middle member is the median of the population. The median shareholding is £10 though the mean is £20.

(*b*) The heights in centimetres of 11 boys are:

160   157   178   155   165   135   160   165   157   160   163

Rearrange these in ascending numerical order, and pick out the middle one. This is the median of the population. The median height is 160 cm.

(*c*) If you have five men arranged 'shortest on the left, tallest on the right', which man has median height?

What would you do if there were only four men?

How would you find the median of *N* numbers arranged in ascending order?

5. SPREAD

(*a*) Two batsmen are being considered for selection for a cricket team. Their last 15 scores are:

| Batsman A | 1 | 115 | 94 | 3 | 42 | 2 | 88 | 102 | 15 | 40 | 18 | 97 | 6 | 50 | 77 |
| Batsman B | 40 | 71 | 18 | 49 | 61 | 46 | 57 | 80 | 51 | 27 | 55 | 51 | 68 | 36 | 40 |

Work out the mean score for each batsman.

Which batsman would you select? Certainly *B* is more consistent. His scores vary from 18 to 80: the *range* of his scores is said to be 62.

What is the range of *A*'s scores?

(*b*) What is the range of the heights given in Section 4(*b*)? Do you think this is a fair measure of the spread of the heights?

Like the mean, the range is affected by the 'dwarfs and giants'. Can you suggest a fairer way of describing the spread? We want a way which will help us to see how the population is 'bunched' within the range and which will not be affected by extreme cases.

One method is to extend the idea we used in finding the median. Suppose again that the population of the heights of the eleven boys in Section 4(*b*), is arranged in

235

ascending order and that now, instead of taking the number mid-way along the line, we take those one-quarter and three-quarters of the way along.

The values taken by these elements are called the *lower quartile* and the *upper quartile* respectively.

135   155   (157)   157   160   160   160   163   (165)   165   178

lower
quartile

upper
quartile

The difference between them is the *inter-quartile* range. It is the spread of the 'middle half' of the population. In the case of heights, the inter-quartile range is $165 - 157 = 8$.

(c) Arrange the scores of each batsman in (a) in ascending order. Put a ring around the lower and upper quartiles. Find the inter-quartile ranges.

Do you think that the inter-quartile range gives a better idea of the consistency of the batsmen than the full range?

6. CUMULATIVE FREQUENCY

(a) To find the median for a frequency function, it is easiest to use a column of *cumulative* (meaning 'piling up') frequencies.

Here again is the table for clutch sizes of tree-sparrow nests.

Size of clutch	Frequency	Cumulative frequency	Clutch sizes represented by C.F.
2	2	2	Not more than 2
3	7	9	Not more than 3
4	25	34	Not more than 4
5	53	87	Not more than 5
6	12	99	Not more than 6
7	1	100	Not more than 7

Each number in the cumulative frequency column except the first, is best found by adding together two other numbers. Which two numbers?

With 100 nests there is no middle one. To which class do the two centre ones, the 50th and 51st, both belong? This is the median clutch size.

(b) If the information is grouped, as with the sentence lengths, we proceed as follows:

Sentence length	Frequency	C.F.	Sentence length represented by C.F.
1–5	18	18	Not more than 5
6–10	24	42	Not more than 10
11–15	30	72	Not more than 15
16–20	14	86	Not more than 20
21–25	8	94	Not more than 25
26–30	3	97	Not more than 30
31–35	1	98	Not more than 35
36–40	0	98	Not more than 40
41–45	2	100	Not more than 45

Quite clearly the 50th and 51st sentences are in the 11–15 class: this is the median class.

If we wish to estimate the median a little more accurately we can plot a *cumulative frequency diagram*.

In this frequency diagram the intervals are: 0·5–5·5, 5·5–10·5, 10·5–15·5, etc., as in Figure 11.

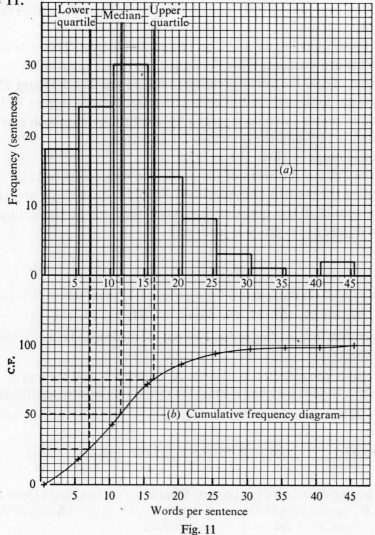

Fig. 11

The cumulative frequencies are plotted at the end of the interval because not until the end of an interval are all the members in that interval necessarily included.

Thus we plot the points: (0·5, 0), (5·5, 18), (10·5, 42), ...

To find the quartiles we need to know the quarter and three-quarter positions in a population of 100. Of course, these are approximately the 25th and 75th position. Why approximately?

Consider again the 11 heights on Page 236. In order they are:

135   155   157   157   160   160   160   163   165   165   178

↑	↑	↑
lower	median	upper
quartile		quartile

The median is found by adding 1 to 11 and dividing by 2. This tells us that the median is the 6th element.

To obtain the lower quartile, we add 1 to 11 and divide by 4. This tells us that the lower quartile is the 3rd element. How do we get the upper quartile?

For a population of 100 the corresponding numbers are $25\frac{1}{4}$, $50\frac{1}{2}$ and $75\frac{3}{4}$.

These positions are indicated on the cumulative frequency diagram in Figure 11 in which the plotted points have been joined by a continuous smooth curve.

Thus the median is 11·8 and the quartiles 7·1 and 16·4.

The inter-quartile range is $16·4 - 7·1 = 9·3$.

What can you say about the areas of the parts into which Figure 11 (a) is divided by lines representing the median and quartiles? Would it have made any significant difference to the results if the quartiles had been read off at the 25th and 75th positions? What degree of accuracy is justified?

Exercise C

1. The annual rainfall (in centimetres) for a period of 15 years was as follows:

64, 97, 69, 99, 107, 87, 69, 66, 61, 84, 81, 89, 89, 112, 74

Rearrange these numbers in ascending order. Pick out the median and the quartiles. What is the inter-quartile range?

2. Using the results you collected in Exercise A, Question 7, find the median shoe size, height, mass, age, etc. In each case find also (a) the range; (b) the inter-quartile range.

3. A 5 kg bag of new potatoes is found to contain 50 potatoes with a distribution of masses as follows:

Mass (g)	0–30	30–60	60–90	90–120	120–150	Total
Frequency	14	23	8	4	1	50

Draw up a table showing cumulative frequencies. What is the median class? Draw frequency and cumulative frequency diagram and use the latter to obtain a better estimate of the median within the median group. Find the mean for comparison.

Find also the inter-quartile range.

4. A small factory has 200 employees and the annual wage bill is distributed as follows, showing the number receiving each wage.

£500–£700	110	£2000	10
£700–£900	35	£3000	5
£900–£1100	15	£5000	1
£1500	24		

Calculate the mean. The median is clearly in the £500–£700 group. Draw a cumulative frequency curve to position it more accurately. Which form of average would you quote if you were: (a) a shop steward; (b) the managing director?

5. A check was made on the speeds, measured to the nearest 10 km/h, of 200 vehicles travelling along the Exeter by-pass.

Speed (km/h)	30	40	50	60	70	80	90	100	110	Total
Frequency	1	4	9	14	38	47	51	32	4	200

Draw a cumulative frequency diagram and use it to find:

(a) the median;   (b) the inter-quartile range.

6. Use the cumulative frequency diagram you drew in Question 5 to estimate the percentage of vehicles travelling:

(a) at less than 60 km/h;   (b) at more than 100 km/h;

(c) between 70 and 90 km/h.

7. What is the shape of the graph of the frequency function when:
(a) the median and the mean have the same value;
(b) the median and mean have smaller values than the mode?

8. Write down a set of five integers:
(a) whose mean is 5 and whose median is 3;
(b) whose median is 5 and whose mean is 3.

9. Is it better to quote the mean or median number of boys absent per day during a school term?

10. One brand of tyres has a mean life of 24000 kilometres and a median life of 32000 kilometres; another brand has both mean and median at 24000 kilometres. Which would you buy? Under what circumstances, if any, might you reverse your choice?

11. What is the significance of the point on a cumulative frequency diagram at which the slope is greatest?

Summary

Measures of position—averages

(i) The *mode* of a population is the most frequently occurring element in the population.

(ii) The *mean* of a population with N elements is

$$\frac{\text{the sum of the elements of the population}}{N}.$$

(iii) The *median* of a population is the middle element of the population when it is arranged in order of magnitude.

If there are N elements in a population, the median is the $\frac{1}{2}(N+1)$th.

(For large populations it can be taken as the $\frac{1}{2}N$th.)

Other measures of position

(i) The *lower quartile* is the $\frac{1}{4}(N+1)$th element from the lower end when the population is arranged in ascending order.

(ii) The *upper quartile* is the $\frac{3}{4}(N+1)$th element in this arrangement.

(For large populations, these can be taken as the $\frac{1}{4}N$th and $\frac{3}{4}N$th respectively.)

Measures of spread

(i) The *range* is the difference between the largest and the smallest elements of the population.

(ii) The *inter-quartile range* is the difference between the upper and the lower quartiles.

14
COMPUTERS AND PROGRAMMING

Dear reader, this notice will serve to inform you that I submit to the public a small machine of my own invention by means of which you alone may, without any effort, perform all the operations of arithmetic, and may be relieved of the work which has often times fatigued your spirit, when you have worked with the counters or with the pen. PASCAL

Any aid to computation such as the abacus or the slide rule has a right to be called a computer, but nowadays when people talk about computers they usually mean high-speed digital computers. These are machines that store numbers and instructions electronically and perform calculations automatically at a very high speed. Our aim in this chapter is to understand something of the powers of computers and the way in which they carry out their work.

Fig. 1. An Elliot 903 desksize computer. The tape reader is in the centre of the desk.

1. HIGH-SPEED DIGITAL COMPUTERS

As civilization has developed, the need to solve large numbers of complicated arithmetical problems has rapidly increased. To cross a stream in a dug-out canoe necessitates little calculation, but before we can bridge a river a kilometre wide it is necessary to carry out a considerable number of computations, and before sending a manned satellite into orbit an almost unbelievable number of computations must be carried out.

The most significant phrase in the last sentence is probably 'number of computations' for it is this, more than their complexity, which has prevented many problems from being solved. In the past when a scientist or engineer was faced with hundreds of computations he often had to abandon the problem because he did not have the time to carry them all out. Charles Babbage (1792–1871) saw very clearly that a device was wanted which could carry out relatively simple computations very quickly. His attempts to build such machines were unsuccessful largely because the engineers of his day were unable to make parts with the precision he required. During the last 25 years great advances in the understanding of electrical circuitry, and developments in the reliability of valves, transistors and relays, have made it possible to build electronic computers.

Before we look at the main parts of a modern computer, consider the way one might set about using a desk calculator to compute the total mass of the boys in your class.

To start with, one would need to find the mass of each boy in the form and store this information by writing it down on a piece of paper. These numbers are the *data* required for the computation.

Next, one would read a number from the paper, build it up on the setting register and wind it into the product register by turning the handle (see Figure 2).

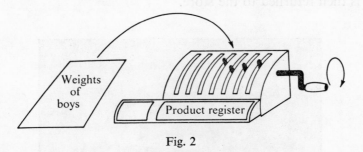

Fig. 2

This would be repeated until all the numbers had been added. The product register would then be storing a number corresponding to the total mass of the class and this could be noted. (What number would be stored in the counting register?) We can divide the solution of this problem into various steps as shown in Figure 3.

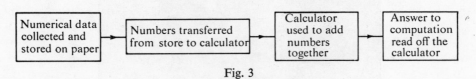

Fig. 3

Every step is controlled by the person operating the calculator.

The designers of modern computers have retained this basic pattern and Figure 4 shows the distinct parts into which a computer can be divided.

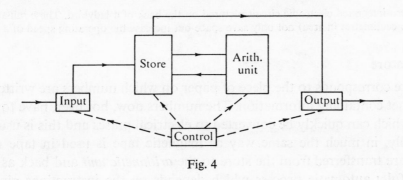

Fig. 4

243

1.1 The Arithmetic unit

This part of a computer corresponds to the desk calculator. It carries out all the arithmetical work at a very high speed (for example, it carries out 10,000 decimal additions a second) using transistorized circuits (see Figure 5) in which binary digits are represented by electrical pulses. Numbers are fed into the arithmetic unit as sequences of electrical pulses in binary form from the *store* and the result of the computation is then returned to the store.

Fig. 5. A micro-integrated electronic circuit pictured on the back of a ladybird. These minature circuits (0·01 square centimetres in area) not only save space but increase the operating speed of a computer.

1.2 The store

The store corresponds to the piece of paper on which numbers are written, or to a filing cabinet containing information. The numbers now, however, have to be stored in a way which can quickly be converted to electrical pulses and this is usually done magnetically, in much the same way as magnetic tape is used in tape recorders. Numbers are transferred from the store to the *arithmetic unit* and back as required. This is a fully automatic process which depends on the instructions given to the computer. These instructions, called the *program*†, must tell the computer in detail which numbers to operate on, what operations to perform, and where to store the result. The program is stored by the computer in the same way as the numbers. Once the data and the program have been fed into the store, the computer can be left to carry out all the computations required without any outside assistance. Since all the circuits are electronic, these computations are made at a very high speed.

Fig. 6. A magnetic tape backing store.

1.3   The control unit

This unit takes the instructions, one by one, from the store and issues the appropriate orders to the different parts of the computer. It acts rather like a foreman who conveys instructions that have been given to him by his superiors, to the workmen under his control. The superior in this case is the computer programmer, the person who wrote out the list of instructions to be followed.

† It is now common practice to use this spelling to denote a set of instructions to a computer, rather than 'programme' which, of course, is the spelling we use for the information sheet we buy at a theatre or at a football match.

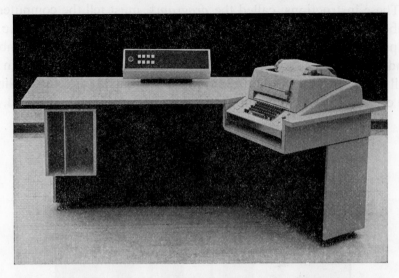

Fig. 7. The control console of an English Electric Leo Marconi computer.

Fig. 8. A paper tape punch in operation punching out results from a computer.

1.4   The input and output

Inside a computer numbers and instructions are represented by magnetic intensities or electric pulses. It is the job of the input and output units to convert the kind of instructions which we can write on paper into these forms. This is done in various ways but one of the easiest to understand is the use of patterns of holes punched in paper tape. Each letter of the alphabet and each digit is represented by a pattern of holes (see the 5-hole tape in Figure 9). The pattern for 'letter shift' indicates a change from the letter code to the number code or vice versa. This enables us to use the same pattern of holes in two ways.

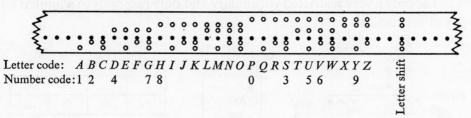

Letter code: A B C D E F G H I J K L M N O P Q R S T U V W X Y Z
Number code: 1 2   4   7 8   0   3   5 6   9

Fig. 9

The program is put onto tape using a tape punch which resembles a typewriter. The tape is then fed into the tape reader which uses photo-electric cells to convert the patterns of holes into electric pulses. Before the program is put onto tape, however, the instructions must all be written in a way that can be understood by the computer. In the next section, you will see how this is done.

The output is just the reverse of the input. Electric pulses corresponding to the results of the computation are used to drive a tape punch (see Figure 8) and the paper tape is then fed into a teleprinter which types out the results.

Exercise A

Projects

1. *Class activity*. Collect newspaper cuttings and magazine articles about computers and their uses, and display them in the classroom.

2. Write a short essay on one of the following topics:

(*a*) how computers work;   (*b*) the uses of computers;
(*c*) the historical development of computing aids.

3. Find out what you can about the following:

(*a*) punched cards;   (*b*) relays;
(*c*) magnetic core stores;   (*d*) analogue computers;
(*e*) data processing;   (*f*) Algol;
(*g*) line printer;   (*h*) teleprinter.

4. Write a message to a friend and code it using the 5-hole tape shown in Figure 9.

5. Work out the binary computations:

(a) $1011 + 111$; (b) 11001×1010;
(c) $1001 - 101$; (d) $10101 \div 111$.

2. PROGRAMMING

Programming Simon

Simon (see Figure 10) is a simple digital computer capable of carrying out the four operations: addition, subtraction, multiplication and division. Like most computers he has only a very restricted vocabulary and only responds to a limited number of types of instruction.

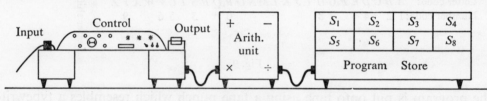

Fig. 10

To communicate with Simon, programs have to be written in a special language, Simpol, which can be punched onto paper tape and then fed into the computer. The store in Simon can hold as many instructions as are ever likely to be wanted, but there are only eight compartments for storing numbers. Each of these eight compartments has an address, one of S_1, S_2, ..., S_8, and stores only one number at a time.

There are three kinds of basic instructions that can be written in Simpol and these are illustrated in the following examples.

(1) Input 3·5 to S_3.

This instructs Simon to replace whatever number is in the compartment whose address is S_3, by the number 3·5.

(2) Replace S_5 by $S_2 + S_4$.

This instructs Simon to look at the numbers stored in S_2 and S_4, to add them together and then put the result in S_5. It has the effect of displacing whatever number was in S_5 before the instruction was carried out. S_2 and S_4, however, still contain the same numbers.

For example, suppose that before the instruction the stores held the following numbers: S_2, 20; S_4, 11; S_5, 99. Then after the instruction 'replace S_5 by $S_2 + S_4$' the stores would hold the numbers: S_2, 20; S_4, 11; S_5, 31.

This instruction can also be used with the same store repeated, for example,

$$\text{'replace } S_5 \text{ by } S_2 + S_2\text{',}$$
$$\text{'replace } S_5 \text{ by } S_5 + S_5\text{',}$$

or with the operations $-$, $\times$ and $\div$, for example,

$$\text{'replace } S_6 \text{ by } S_2 \div S_1\text{'.}$$

(3) Output the number in S_7.

This instructs Simon to punch out in tape the pattern of holes representing the number stored in S_7, and then to pass this through the teleprinter equipment to be typed out.

We can now write down a complete program for Simon.

Example 1

Write a program for Simon to find the average of the three numbers 7·6, 3·2 and 8·1. To find this average Simon must be given instructions to compute

$$\frac{7\cdot6+3\cdot2+8\cdot1}{3}.$$

The following is a suitable program:

(1) Input 7·6 to S_1 ⎫
(2) Input 3·2 to S_2 ⎬ These instructions read the data for the
(3) Input 8·1 to S_3 ⎪ computation into Simon's store
(4) Input 3 to S_4 ⎭
(5) Replace S_5 by S_1+S_2 ⎫ These instructions tell Simon
(6) Replace S_6 by S_5+S_3 ⎬ what calculations to make
(7) Replace S_7 by $S_6 \div S_4$ ⎭
(8) Output the number in S_7

Fig. 11

It is useful to check a program by using a table with one column corresponding to each store compartment used in the program and, acting as the computer, carrying out the instructions one at a time without actually making the calculations. This is known as 'dry checking' and it is a very necessary part of the art of programming (see Figure 12).

Numbers stored in Simon's store

Number of instruction	S_1	S_2	S_3	S_4	S_5	S_6	S_7
1	7·6						
2		3·2					
3			8·1				
4				3			
5					7·6+3·2		
6						7·6+3·2+8·1	
7							$\frac{7\cdot6+3\cdot2+8\cdot1}{3}$
8				The contents of S_7 are punched out			

Fig. 12

Notice that Simon can only add, subtract, multiply or divide two numbers at a time so that instructions (5), (6) and (7) cannot be replaced by a single instruction, although this may seem more natural.

The time taken by a computer to read in data is comparatively long compared with the time taken to perform an arithmetic calculation, so it is usual to arrange whenever possible that all the input instructions come together at the beginning of a program.

Exercise B

1. (a) How much of the program in Example 1 will need to be altered if we wish to find the average of 2·65, 4·72 and 3·68?

(b) Write a program for Simon to compute

$$\frac{326{\cdot}7}{68{\cdot}73}+\frac{29{\cdot}35}{0{\cdot}0876}.$$

2. Write down the computations Simon will carry out if given the following programs:

(a) Input 28·3 to S_1
Input 19·7 to S_2
Input 485 to S_3
Replace S_4 by S_1-S_2
Replace S_5 by $S_3\times S_4$
Output the number in S_5.

(b) Input 36·2 to S_1
Input 18·9 to S_2
Input 21·4 to S_3
Input 14·7 to S_4
Replace S_5 by S_1+S_2
Replace S_6 by S_3-S_4
Replace S_7 by $S_5\div S_6$
Output the number in S_7.

(c) Input 93·5 to S_1
Input 37·4 to S_2
Input 86·3 to S_3
Replace S_4 by S_1+S_2
Replace S_4 by S_4-S_3
Replace S_4 by $S_4\times S_4$
Output the number in S_4.

3. Write programs in Simpol to compute:

(a) $(3{\cdot}6\times6{\cdot}2)+(2{\cdot}8\div0{\cdot}94)$;

(b) $12{\cdot}6-\dfrac{4{\cdot}7\times6{\cdot}2}{13{\cdot}9}$;

(c) $6{\cdot}7^5$;

(d) $65{\cdot}1\div[23{\cdot}7\div(218\div189)]$.

In each case dry check your program.

4. (a) What is the minimum number of store compartments that are needed to find the average of three numbers?

[Hint: instead of instruction (5) in Example 1, the instruction 'Replace S_1 by S_1+S_2' could have been used. The effect of this is to lose what was in S_1 but it does not introduce a new store compartment.]

(b) Write out a program to find the average of the five numbers 2·3, 3·6, 4·2, 5·1 and 2·9 using as few store compartments as possible.

(c) Dry check your program.

5. Write a program to compute
$$4 \cdot 6 + 4 \cdot 6^2 + 4 \cdot 6^3.$$
It can be done using only two store compartments. Check your program carefully.

6. A boy wrote the following program in Simpol to compute the value of $(765 + 286)^2$ but unfortunately he made a mistake.

> Input 765 to S_1
> Input 286 to S_2
> Replace S_3 by $S_1 \times S_1$
> Replace S_4 by $S_2 \times S_2$
> Replace S_5 by $S_3 + S_4$
> Output the number in S_5

What does this program compute? Write a correct program.

3. PROGRAMS FOR FORMULAE

Consider the following program for computing $3 \cdot 4^5$ and the corresponding dry check:

		S_1	S_2
(1)	Input 3·4 to S_1	3·4	
(2)	Replace S_2 by $S_1 \times S_1$		3·4²
(3)	Replace S_1 by $S_1 \times S_2$	3·4³	
(4)	Replace S_1 by $S_1 \times S_2$	3·4⁵	
(5)	Output the number in S_1	Output 3·4⁵	

Fig. 13

This program shows clearly how the use of stores can be conserved by re-using store compartments containing numbers that are not required again. With many calculations, particularly in statistics, there is much data and it is vital that stores be used over and over again.

(a) How will the program have to be altered if we wish to find 62^5, $0 \cdot 0058^5$, or $32,671,853^5$?

This program is really a set of instructions for computing x^5 from x. Whatever number is fed into S_1 in the first instruction, it will be raised to the fifth power and printed out.

Once a program has been written to make one computation, then it can be used to make many others by adjusting the input instructions.

Example 2

Write a program to compute the volume, V, of a cylinder when its radius, r, and height, h, are known (see Figure 14).

The volume of the cylinder is given by the formula

$$V = \pi r^2 h,$$

Fig. 14

and a program to compute it is as follows:

(1) Input r to S_1 ⎫ These are fed in as numbers corresponding
(2) Input h to S_2 ⎬ to the dimensions of the cylinder
(3) Input π to S_3 ⎭
(4) Replace S_4 by $S_3 \times S_1$ This puts πr into S_4
(5) Replace S_5 by $S_4 \times S_1$ This puts πr^2 into S_5
(6) Replace S_6 by $S_5 \times S_2$ This puts $\pi r^2 h$ into S_6
(7) Output the number in S_6

Fig. 15

Note that although we can prepare a program in this way, Simon will only calculate with numbers—letters mean nothing to him; that is, we can, say, store 2, 3, or 6 in S_1, but not a symbol, say v, that *might* take any of these values. In other words, Simon cannot perform algebraic operations but only arithmetical ones.

(*b*) Compute the volume of a cylinder of radius 3·7 cm and height 5·9 cm by following through the program in Example 2 and using your slide rule for instructions (4), (5) and (6).

Exercise C

(Units have been omitted in most of these questions. This means that where they refer to measurements, the units set against the output will depend upon the data. Also, no conversion of units is required.)

1. (*a*) Write a program to compute x^8 from x using as few store compartments as possible.
   (*b*) What powers of x could be computed if only one store compartment were available?
   (*c*) Write a program to compute x^{21} from x using as small a number of instructions as possible.

2.

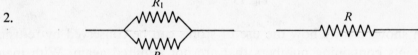

Fig. 16

Two resistances R_1 and R_2 in an electrical circuit (see Figure 16) can be replaced by a single resistance R where

$$R = \frac{R_1 R_2}{R_1 + R_2}.$$

(*a*) Write a program to compute R when R_1 and R_2 are known.

(*b*) Work out R, using your program, when $R_1 = 2$ and $R_2 = 6$. Check that this gives the same result as working R out from the formula directly.

3. The volume, V, of metal in a pipe whose external radius, R, internal radius, r, and length, l, are known (see Figure 17) is given by the formula

$$V = \pi l(R+r)(R-r).$$

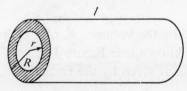

Fig. 17

(a) Write a program to compute V.

(b) Check your program by taking $R = 3.6$, $r = 3.4$, $l = 10$, and $\pi = \frac{22}{7}$.

4. In a pocket money survey made in a junior class it was found that x boys received A new pence a week, y boys received B new pence a week, z boys received C new pence a week and t boys received D new pence a week.

(a) Write a formula giving the total pocket money, T new pence, received weekly by the class.

(b) Deduce a formula giving the mean pocket money, P new pence, received weekly by a boy in the class.

(c) Construct a program for computing P when x, y, z, t, A, B, C and D are known.

(d) Compute the value of P when:

$$x = 5, \quad y = 13, \quad z = 8, \quad t = 4, \quad A = 15, \quad B = 25, \quad V = 30, \quad D = 50.$$

(e) How many boys in the class had (i) less, (ii) more pocket money than the mean?

5. (a) Write a program to compute y where

$$y = x^3 + px^2 + qx + r.$$

(b) Use a slide rule to find the value of y when

$$x = 2.4, \quad p = 3, \quad q = 5 \quad \text{and} \quad r = 16.$$

6. $\{(x, y): 2x + y = 7\}$ and $\{(x, y): 5x - 3y = 1\}$ can both be represented on graph paper by straight lines which intersect at the point $(2, 3)$. Sets of this kind are always occurring wherever mathematics is used but the numbers involved are not usually as simple as those in this example. The point of intersection can usually be computed, however, by using the fact that the intersection of the sets

$$\{(x, y): ax + by = c\} \quad \text{and} \quad \{(x, y): px + qy = r\}$$

is

$$\left\{ \left(\frac{cq - rb}{aq - pb}, \frac{ar - pc}{aq - pb} \right) \right\}.$$

(a) Show that this formula gives the correct point of intersection in the example given.

(b) Write a program to compute the point of intersection when a, b, c, p, q and r are given.

(c) Check that your program gives $(1, 2)$ when $a = 1$, $b = 1$, $c = 3$, $p = 3$, $q = {}^-1$ and $r = 1$.

(d) The statement of this question says 'can usually be computed'. Under what circumstances does this formula break down?

7. It can be shown that if x is an approximate square root of a number N, then a better approximation y is given by setting

$$y = \frac{x^2 + N}{2x}.$$

(a) Take $N = 12$ and let $x = 4$ be a first approximation to the square root of N. Use the formula to find a better approximation.

(b) Write a program to find y, given N and x.

(c) If the program is used for a second time, this time taking x to be the value obtained the first time for y, what can you say about the new value for y?

See how accurately you can compute $\sqrt{12}$ using your program several times. (Check your accuracy by squaring your approximation and seeing by how much it differs from 12.)

253

4. FLOW DIAGRAMS

So far in this chapter we have considered only programs that contained simple arithmetical instructions. With these it was possible to write out the details of a program without much difficulty. In practice, programs are often much longer and include instructions which can be expressed as questions. A programmer, therefore, usually starts by drawing a flow diagram to help him organize the way in which the computation is to be carried out. Flow diagrams, as you have seen already, are block diagrams showing the operations to be performed and the order in which these operations have to be carried out. As Example 3 shows, the use of flow diagrams need not be restricted to mathematical problems.

Example 3

Figure 18 is a flow diagram showing how to telephone a friend on a private, S.T.D.-type phone.

You will notice in this flow diagram that there are two kinds of blocks:

1. Rectangular blocks which contain operations to be carried out. These blocks have only one route leading from them.

2. Diamond shaped blocks containing questions that can be answered *yes* or *no*. These decision blocks have two alternative routes out, the route out depending on the answer to the question in the block.

Example 4

In a knitting pattern for a pullover the instructions for knitting part of the rib start as follows:

'Using the No. 10 needles cast on 65 sts.,
1st row Sl. 1, K. 1, * P. 1, K. 1 repeat from * to the last stitch, K. 1;
2nd row Sl. 1, * P. 1, K. 1 repeat from * to end of row.'

A flow diagram incorporating these instructions is shown in Figure 19.

This example (although probably unintelligible to most boys) shows clearly how the complicated operation of knitting a pullover can be broken down into very small steps which anybody can follow. A knitting pattern is in fact very similar to a computer program and this may explain why many girls make good computer programmers.

In both of the above flow diagrams there are lines which leave decision blocks and then re-enter the diagram at an earlier point. What is the effect of this? Lines like these are called *loops* and they play an important part in programming.

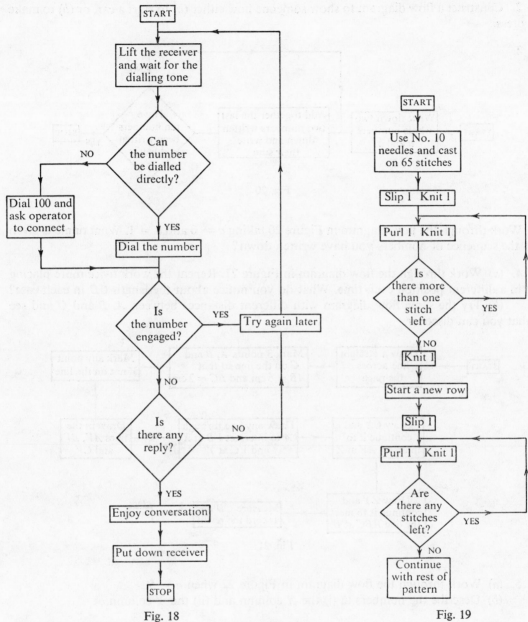

Fig. 18

Fig. 19

Exercise D

1. Draw flow diagrams to show what happens when you:

(a) get up in the morning;   (b) cross a road;
(c) visit a library;   (d) buy a new dress/suit;
(e) fly a kite;   (f) use a record player;
(g) mend a puncture;   (h) bake a cake;
(i) organize a party;   (j) take your turn in a game of Whist;
(k) sing a hymn with a refrain;   (l) look for a word in a dictionary.

2. Construct a flow diagram to show someone how either (*a*) to start a car, or (*b*) to make a dress.

3.

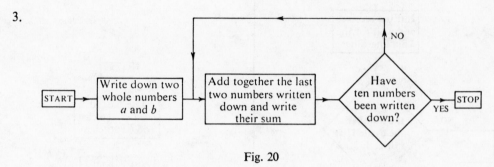

Fig. 20

Work through the flow diagram in Figure 20 taking $a = 0$ and $b = 1$. What name is given to the sequence of numbers you have written down?

4. (*a*) Work through the flow diagram in Figure 21. Repeat the work twice more placing *V* in a different position each time. What do you notice about the length *CD* in each case?

(*b*) Try the same flow diagram with different distances between *A*, *B* and *C* and see what you can discover.

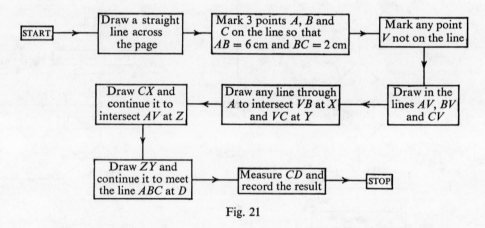

Fig. 21

5. (*a*) Work through the flow diagram in Figure 22 when $n = 5$.

(*b*) Describe the numbers in (i) the *X* column and (ii) the *Y* column.

6. Given that $\triangle A'B'C'$ is the image of $\triangle ABC$ under a rotation, construct a flow diagram to show how the centre of rotation can be found using a ruler and compasses.

7. A group of explorers arrive at the left bank of a river that has to be crossed. The only means of transport is a boat being rowed by two boys. If the boat can carry at most two boys or one explorer, how can the explorers cross the river? Draw a flow diagram to illustrate your solution.

*8. Construct a flow diagram to show how to find whether or not a number is prime.

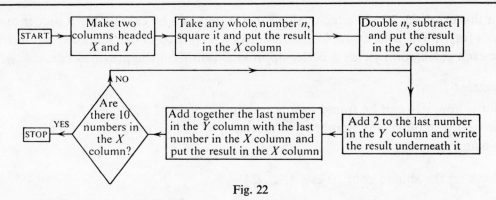

Fig. 22

*9. Construct a flow diagram to show the second player in a game of noughts and crosses how to avoid defeat.

5. REPETITION

'If at first you don't succeed, try, try again.'

This motto might well be the motto of most computers because so many of the methods used for computing results are repetitive. Many practical problems cannot be solved exactly and one must be satisfied with approximate answers. These latter are often found by methods that can best be described as 'organized trial and error'.

Example 5

A bridge is to be constructed across a river using reinforced concrete construction. The cost, £C, of building such a bridge is given approximately by the formula

$$C = 20,000 \left(\frac{12}{n}+n\right),$$

where n is the number of spans in the bridge. What number of spans will give the lowest cost? (Can you explain how this formula arises?)

This problem can be solved by systematically trying different values for n and finding which value of n gives the lowest cost. The costs corresponding to some values of n are shown in the table below.

n	$\frac{12}{n}+n$	C
I	13	260,000
2	8	160,000
3	7	140,000 ⎫
4	7	140,000 ⎭ Lowest cost
5	7·4	148,000
6	8	160,000

It can be seen from the table of values that the lowest cost can be achieved by building a bridge of either 3 or 4 spans. The formula is such that as n increases above 4 so does the cost C.

257

In this example, we see which value for n is required by calculating a sequence of values for C. The next example also requires a sequence of calculations, but in this case each calculation yields a better approximation than the previous one.

Example 6

Show how $\sqrt{24}$ can be found to any required degree of accuracy.

Stage 1. First take any number (for example, 4) and divide 24 by it. 24 divided by 4 is 6 and since

$$4^2 < 4 \times 6 < 6^2,$$

and taking the square root gives $4 < \sqrt{24} < 6$.

Stage 2. Next take 5, the mean of 4 and 6, and divide 24 by it. 24 divided by 5 is 4·8, hence,

$$4 \cdot 8 < \sqrt{24} < 5.$$

Stage 3. Take 4·9, the mean of 4·8 and 5, and divide 24 by it. 24 divided by 4·9 is approximately 4·898, hence,

$$4 \cdot 898 < \sqrt{24} < 4 \cdot 9.$$

Notice that at each stage this process produces two numbers between which $\sqrt{24}$ must lie. The difference between these numbers decreases at each stage and gives a measure of the accuracy obtained. For example, at the end of Stage 2, $\sqrt{24}$ is squeezed between 4·8 and 5 so we could say that

$$\sqrt{24} = 4 \cdot 9 \pm 0 \cdot 1.$$

At the end of Stage 3 we could similarly say

$$\sqrt{24} = 4 \cdot 899 \pm 0 \cdot 001.$$

(Books of Tables give $\sqrt{24} = 4 \cdot 899$ to 4 s.f. which confirms this result.)

To get a higher degree of accuracy the process can be continued.

We could find $\sqrt{24}$ to 2 s.f. by starting with 12 instead of 4 at the first stage. No matter which number we divide 24 by, the process will yield a better approximation to the square root.

This method, which is now widely used for computers, was first developed by Hero, a Greek mathematician who lived in the early part of the third century A.D.

Hero's method for finding an approximation to $\sqrt{N}$ can be expressed neatly as a flow diagram (see Figure 23).

Exercise E

Answer the following questions by 'trial and error' methods.

1. A shell is fired from an anti-aircraft gun. t s after the gun is fired, the height h m is given by the formula
$$h = 1000t(6 - t).$$
By computing the value of h when $t = 1, 2, 3, 4$ and 5 estimate the maximum height reached by the shell.

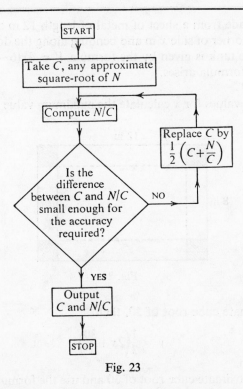

Fig. 23

2. The number of watts (units of power), P, developed by an engine is given by the formula

$$P = 750r^2(8-r),$$

where r is the speed of the engine in thousands of revolutions per minute.

(a) By taking $r = 1, 2, 3, \ldots, 7$, show that the maximum power is developed at approximately 5 thousands of revolutions per minute.

(b) Find, to the nearest kilowatt, the maximum power produced by computing P for values of r near to 5.

3. (a) Use Hero's method to find the square root of 42 to 3 S.F.

(b) What happens if you take a negative number as your first approximation?

4. Find, to 2 decimal places, the minimum value of the range of the function

$$x \to \frac{6}{x}+x+3;$$

given that it is the image of a point of the domain within $2 < x < 3$.

5. When an electric motor is connected to a battery, its power, P, is given by the formula

$$P = \frac{400R}{(R+5)^2}.$$

Motors are available in which $R = 2, 3, 4, 5, 6$ and 7. Which motor must be chosen to obtain maximum power?

*6. A water tank is made from a sheet of metal of length 12 m and width 8 m, by cutting out a square from each corner of side x m and bending along the dotted lines (see Figure 24). The volume V m³, of the tank is given by the formula $V = 4x(6-x)(4-x)$.

(*a*) Explain how this formula arises.

(*b*) Why must $x < 4$?

(*c*) By trying different values for x calculate the maximum value of the volume of the tank to slide rule accuracy.

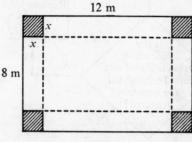

Fig. 24

7. If x is an approximate cube root of 30, then

$$y = \frac{1}{3}\left(2x + \frac{30}{x^2}\right)$$

is a better approximation.

Show that 3 is an approximate cube root of 30 and use the formula once to obtain a better approximation. Cube the approximation you obtain to see by how much it differs from 30.

15
LOCI AND ENVELOPES

So many paths that wind and wind.
ELLA WHEELER WILCOX, *The World's Need*

1. LOCUS

(*a*) Three boys lit a firework and immediately ran off at the same speed in different directions. Figure 1 shows their positions when the firework exploded.

Puzzle: Where did the firework explode?

B
•

C
•

A •

Fig. 1

To solve this we must find a point that is the same distance from each of *A*, *B* and *C*.

First of all, consider *A* and *B*. Copy Figure 1 and use your compasses to mark several points which are the same distance from A as from B. If you could mark all such points, what would the set of points form? Suppose we call this set of points p.

If q is a set of points that are the same distance from B as from C, what can you say about $p \cap q$?

Construct p and q and hence solve the puzzle.

The latin word *locus* (strictly meaning 'place' or 'position') is often used instead of the phrase 'set of points'. In the puzzle above we would say 'the locus of a point that is the same distance from A as from B is the mediator of AB', and so on.

(*b*) It is important to realize that a locus need not necessarily be a line or a curve; it can be a region or even a single point, an idea you have already met in linear programming.

Until Section 4, we shall consider only loci in 2 dimensions, that is, sets of points, within a plane.

Figure 2 shows the back garden of a house. The owner decides to plant an apple tree in the garden. It must be at least 10 m from the house and at least $7\frac{1}{2}$ m from the trunk of the existing tree, A.

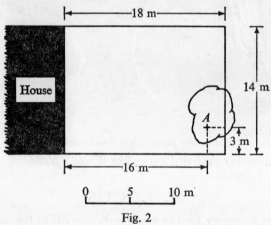

Fig. 2

Where can he plant it?

The set of all possible positions composes the locus of the tree and can be found by considering two simpler loci.

Suppose $\mathscr{E}$ = {points in the garden},
p = {points more than 10 m from the house},
q = {points more than $7\frac{1}{2}$ m from A}.

Make a plan of the garden on graph paper, using a suitable scale and indicate the sets $\mathscr{E}$, p and q. Label the set $p \cap q$. Where can the second tree be planted? Discuss the locus $p \cup q$ and describe it geometrically in words.

By labelling your diagram, mark also the locus of the tree if
(i) it is to be exactly 10 m from the house and at least $7\frac{1}{2}$ m from A;
(ii) it is to be exactly 10 m from the house and exactly $7\frac{1}{2}$ m from A.

262

Exercise A

1. State which of the following loci are straight lines, which curved lines and which regions:

(a) $\{(x, y): x+y = 7\}$;

(b) points at 5 cm distance from a point in a plane;

(c) the locus of the nib of your pen as you write a word;

(d) points on this page not covered with printers' ink.

2. (a) Figure 3 shows two half-lines, p and q, and a point Z that is equidistant from them. Copy the figure and mark on it by eye four or five further possible positions for the point Z. What does the locus of Z appear to be?

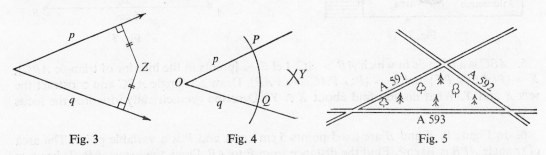

Fig. 3   Fig. 4   Fig. 5

(b) In Figure 4 the point Y has been constructed as follows. The point of a pair of compasses was put at O and an arc drawn cutting p and q at P and Q. The compasses were set to a different distance and, with centres P and Q, two equal arcs were drawn cutting at Y. What can you say about the symmetry of the figure as a whole? If OY is joined, what can you say about any point on OY in relation to p and q? Describe OY as a locus. Why is it called the *bisector* of $\angle POQ$?

(c) Figure 5 shows three busy main roads surrounding a common.

A caravanner wishes to put his caravan on the common but as far as possible from each road. Use your answers to (a) and (b) to help him find the best site.

3. In Figure 6, p represents part of a line, q represents part of a half-line and r represents a line segment AB. Copy the figure and sketch the locus of a point which is always 1 cm from (a) the line p; (b) the half-line q; (c) the line segment AB.

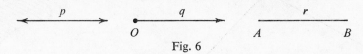

Fig. 6

4. The locus of points at which television reception from a certain type of transmitter is satisfactory is the interior of a circle of radius about 50 kilometres. Trace Figure 7 and draw in the locus of points having satisfactory reception if the transmitters are at the points A, B and C.

If only two transmitters are available, at which two of these points should they be placed in order to obtain the greatest coverage of land? Is this the main consideration in practice? Discuss the merits of the possible schemes.

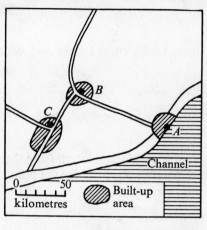

Fig. 7

Fig. 8

5. *ABC* is a triangle in which *AB* > *AC*. Let $\mathscr{E}$ = {points in the interior of triangle *ABC*}, *X* = {*P*: *PB* < *PC*} and *Y* = {*P*: ∠*PAC* < ∠*PAB*}. Draw a triangle *ABC* and construct the sets *X* and *Y*. What do you find about *X* ∩ *Y*? Describe geometrically in words the locus *X* ∪ *Y*.

6. In Figure 8, *A* and *B* are fixed points 5 cm apart and *P* is a variable point. The area of triangle *APB* is 10 cm². Find the distance from *P* to *AB*. Draw the locus of *P*. (It has two distinct parts.)

7. In Figure 9, *A* and *B* are fixed 10 cm apart and the perimeter of the triangle is 28 cm. Draw the locus of *P*. This can be easily done by making a loop of string 28 cm long and looping it around two drawing pins at *A* and *B*. A pencil, as shown, keeps the loop taut and draws the locus of *P*.

You will find that the locus is an oval curve called an *ellipse*. This is the curve you see if you shut one eye and look at a circle whose plane is not at right-angles to your line of sight. Describe its symmetries.

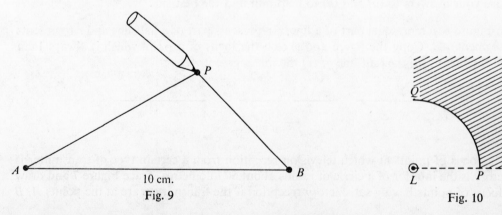

Fig. 9

Fig. 10

8. Figure 10 shows a photographer's lamp *L* and a screen which has the shape of a 90° arc, *PQ*, of a circle of radius 4 m. Describe the locus of a point in the shaded region using polar coordinates and taking the line *LP* as central direction.

2. INVESTIGATING LOCI

More difficult loci have to be drawn by finding a number of positions of the point under consideration. If appropriate, these may then be joined together by a smooth curve, a straight ruled line or, if they can be seen to occupy a region, the boundaries are identified and the region shaded in. We then try to find the name of the curve involved by comparing it with known curves.

Fig. 11

Interesting examples may be found by considering the beams from 'double-ended' searchlights. A double-ended searchlight is shown in Figure 11. The beam shines out horizontally in two directions 180° apart.

Two such searchlights are set up, one at A and the other at B on a horizontal plane, as shown in Figure 12. This figure also shows two beams; the beam from A makes an angle of 20° and that from B an angle of 40°, measured anticlockwise, with the half-line drawn from A to pass through B.

The point where the two beams cross can conveniently be called the point (20, 40). This is an ordered pair of numbers (why?) and 20 and 40 are the first and second coordinates of the point. This is a new system of coordinates. What systems have you met before? We shall find this system very handy for denoting points on a locus although there are drawbacks to the system which you will discover as we go along.

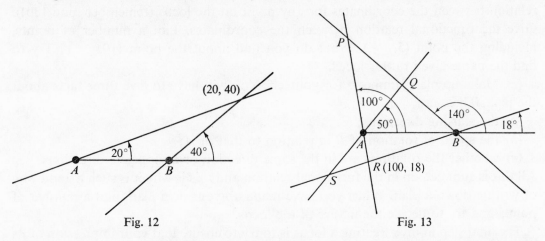

Fig. 12   Fig. 13

(a) In Figure 13 there are four other beams and their angles with AB have been marked. The point marked R is on the 100° beam from A and the 18° beam from B and so is marked (100, 18). Write down the coordinates of P, Q and S. What are the coordinates of A and B? What can you say about a point (θ, θ)? Discuss the co-ordinates of a point on AB between A and B. What about points on AB produced?

Why is this coordinate system less useful for general purposes than the Cartesian system?

(b) The operators of the two searchlights agree that they will rotate their beams according to pre-arranged plans. While A rotates at a steady speed, B will vary his rotation in relation to A's, for example, rotate at twice the speed, or keep his direction a fixed number of degrees different from A's. In fact they will agree on a function mapping A's angle onto B's angle.

Plan number 1. They decide that A will start in the 0° direction and B in the 60° direction and that they will rotate their beams at the same speed. After a few moments if A is in a direction θ°, in what direction is B shining? The function is θ → θ+60. Some of the points where their beams cross have coordinates (20, 80), (40, 100). Fill in the other coordinate of the point (160,   ). Is this a clock arithmetic? Write down the coordinates of three more points where their beams cross. Use your protractor to plot a number of points. What does the locus appear to be?

Plan number 2. This time A and B both start from the 0° position. The function they agree is θ → 2θ. Write down some points on the locus. Plot a number of them. Specify as carefully as you can what you think the locus is.

Plan number 3. Again A and B will both start from the 0° position. They will then rotate in opposite directions at the same speed. Without making an accurate drawing, try to say what the locus will be. Name some points on the locus and describe the function 'A's angle → B's angle.'

Plan number 4. The beams are rotated so that the locus passes through (40, 160), (60, 140), (80, 120), etc. Write down two further points on the locus. Write down the relation between the coordinates for any point on the locus (remember mod 180!). Give the functional relation between the coordinates. Plot a number of points, including the point (5,   ). What do you find about the point (10,   )? Try to find the name given to this locus.

(c) Make up plan number 5 for yourself. You will have to give three facts about the plan. These are:

(a) the starting directions;

(b) the speed of rotation of B in relation to that of A;

(c) whether the rotations are in the same direction or in opposite directions.

All this is summed up in the functional relation and this is why it is such a good way of writing down a plan. When you have made up your own plan, plot a number of points and try to decide the nature of the locus.

The final step in investigating a locus is to try to ensure that your impression of its nature is correct. A demonstration by experiment can only suggest the truth of something and can never be said to prove it beyond all doubt. We shall leave such proofs until later books.

Exercise B

In this exercise, A, B, C, ... are always fixed points, while P, Q, R, ... are variable ones.

D1. In Figure 14 the lines *AP* and *BP* rotate about *A* and *B* so that the angle at *B* is always twice the angle at *A* and is on the opposite side of *AB*. Plot the locus. Write down the coordinates of a number of points on the locus of *P*. Express this as a function using the notation of Section 2.

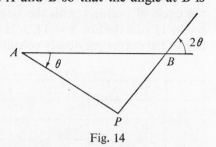

Fig. 14

2. (*a*) Mark two points *A* and *B* about 5 cm apart and towards the centre of a piece of paper. Stick a pin or drawing pin through each point. Cut a triangle *PQR* out of card, do not make it regular but it is best to avoid angles that are nearly 0° or 180°. Make each side of the triangle at least 5 cm. Place the triangle so that *PQ* rests against *A* and *PR* rests against *B* as shown in Figure 15. Mark a dot on the paper at the point occupied by the vertex *P*. Move the triangle to a new position, still keeping *PQ* against *A* and *PR* against *B* and mark the new position of *P*. Repeat many times keeping *P* on the same side of *AB*, and trace the locus of *P*. What do you find? Do you think the locus is part of a circle? Test it, stating your method (using your eye is not good enough!). Which of the searchlight loci does this remind you of? In what way is it different? Describe the locus if *P* can lie on either side of *AB*. What relation has *AB* to the new locus?

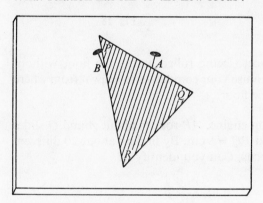

Fig. 15

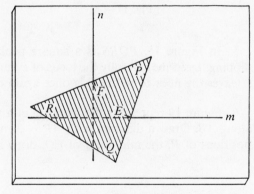

Fig. 16

(*b*) Draw two perpendicular lines *m* and *n* as shown in Figure 16. Mark two points *E* and *F* on the sides *PQ* and *PR* of the triangle that you used in part (*a*) making the lengths of *PE* and *PF* equal. Place the triangle on paper so that *E* lies on the line *m* and *F* lies on the line *n* as in Figure 16. Trace the locus of *P* in the first quadrant. Do you think that the locus is part of a circle this time? Sketch the remainder of the locus if *E* and *F* can lie anywhere on *m* or *n* and if *P* need not remain in the first quadrant. How are *m* and *n* related to the locus?

3. A ball is thrown horizontally and its position is recorded electronically at unit intervals of time, as positions on a grid. Some points on its path are (0, 0), (1, ⁻1), (2, ⁻4), (3, ⁻8), (4, ⁻16), etc. (Cartesian coordinates). Plot these points on graph paper using a suitable scale and trace the smooth curve representing the locus. It is part of what is known as a *parabola*.

18-2

4. Figure 17 shows a set of circles, all with centre at (2, 0). Copy the figure on squared paper and draw a few more circles of the set. Mark the points where the circle of radius 2 cuts the line $x = 2$, where the circle of radius 3 cuts the line $x = 3$ and so on (i.e. mark points equidistant from (2, 0) and the line $x = 0$). What is special about the intersection of the circle of radius 1 with the line $x = 1$? Construct also the points where the circle of radius $1\frac{1}{2}$ cuts the line $x = 1\frac{1}{2}$. Join the points together by a smooth curve. Does it resemble any of the curves previously considered in this chapter?

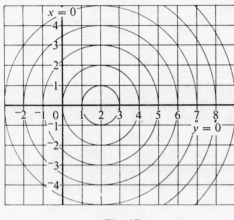

Fig. 17

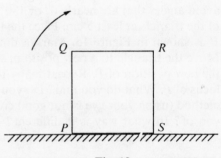

Fig. 18

5. In Figure 18, $PQRS$ is a square packing case being rolled across the floor without slipping. Describe carefully the locus of P and then use your compasses to draw it from where P leaves the floor to where P is once again on the floor.

6. Figure 19 represents the working of a piston engine. AP rotates about A and Q slides along AB. Draw a diagram with $AP = 3$ cm and $PQ = 9$ cm. By finding about 20 different positions of R, the mid-point of PQ, draw its locus, Can you identify it?

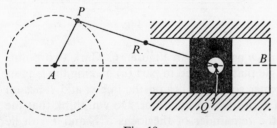

Fig. 19

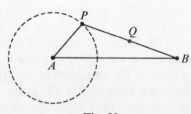

Fig. 20

7. In Figure 20, AP rotates around A and BP is a piece of elastic. Draw a diagram with $AP = 4$ cm and $AB = 9$ cm. Plot the locus of Q, the mid-point of PB. Join Q to the mid-point of AB and using ideas of enlargement determine precisely the locus of Q. Compare your experimental result with this theoretical locus.

D8. Figure 21 shows a section of the Kent coastline and two radio beacons F and F', at Dungeness and just south-west of Dover respectively.

(a) Complete a table, as shown below for a number of positions of P on the two parts of the curve in the diagram.

	FP (cm)	$F'P$ (cm)	Difference (cm)
P_1	1·8	5·8	4
P_2			
.			
.			

(b) Describe in your own words the locus that the curve represents. The curve is called a *hyperbola*.

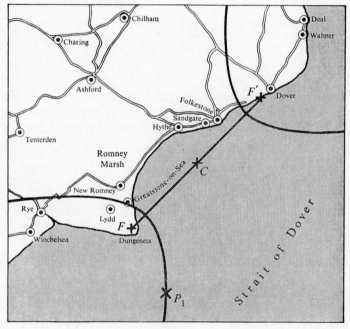

Fig. 21

(c) If signals were sent out simultaneously from F and F', what would be noticed about the difference in their times of arrival at any point on this hyperbola? What would be the locus of a point at which the difference in times of arrival had a second constant value, t s? What would be the locus of points at which $t = 0$ s? How many extra stations are necessary for a ship's captain to get a precise radio beacon 'fix'?

The ellipse

A method of drawing this curve has already been given in Exercise A, Question 7. Here are three further methods. Discuss ways of finding out whether they do, in fact, give the same curve.

9. Draw a circle with radius 5 cm and centre (0, 0), as in Figure 22, and draw a number of lines such as QQ' parallel to $x = 0$. On QQ' mark points P and P' such that $PR = \frac{3}{5}QR$, and $P'R = \frac{3}{5}Q'R$. Sketch in the complete locus of P.

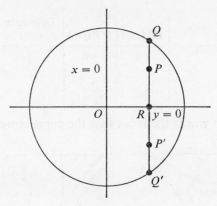

Fig. 22

10. On the edge of a piece of paper mark P, Q and R such that $PQ = 3$ cm and $QR = 2$ cm. Keeping Q on $y = 0$ and R on $x = 0$, as in Figure 23, mark sufficient positions of P to draw its locus. If $\angle OQR = \theta$, show that the coordinates of P are $(5 \cos \theta, 3 \sin \theta)$.

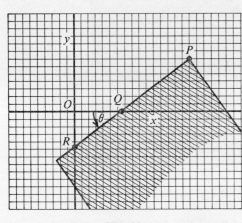

Fig. 23

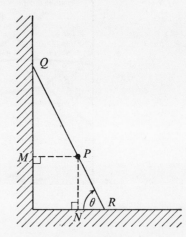

Fig. 24

11. Figure 24 represents a ladder 8 m long leaning against a wall. A man starts to climb the ladder and when he reaches P, 3 m up the ladder, it slips. Using a scale of 1 cm for 1 m, draw various positions of the ladder as it slips and also draw one or two in which the ladder is closer to the vertical than is shown in Figure 24.

Hence draw the locus of the man's feet, that is the point P, from the vertical to the horizontal position of the ladder. Using tracing paper, or otherwise, draw the reflections of this locus in the wall and the ground, thus getting a complete ellipse.

Find, in terms of θ, the lengths PM and PN and compare them with the coordinates of P in Figure 23.

270

Summary

Locus is the word used for a set of points (plural *loci*). A locus may consist of a straight or curved line or lines, a plane, a region in two or three dimensions, or a single point or set of isolated points.

3. ENVELOPES

In the first section we considered sets of points. A corresponding idea is to consider sets of lines or curves. A striking example is shown in Figure 25. If you have done some curve stitching with coloured thread or wool, you will already be familiar with this idea. A pinboard, with pins either arranged in a square lattice or in a circle, also helps one to produce attractive results.

Fig. 25

(*a*) Figure 26 shows a circle with 24 points equally spaced around it. Lines are drawn joining 0 to 6, 1 to 7, 2 to 8, ... What can you say about the lengths of these lines? They appear to form another smaller circle inside. Discuss the relation between the lines and this new circle. We say that the lines *envelop* the circle or that the circle is the *envelope* of the lines. What would happen if lines were drawn joining

0 to 9, 1 to 10, 2 to 11, ...?

What would happen if lines were drawn joining

0 to 12, 1 to 13, 2 to 14, ...?

Can a set of lines envelop a point?

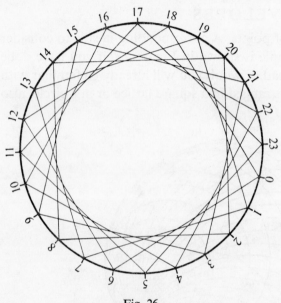

Fig. 26

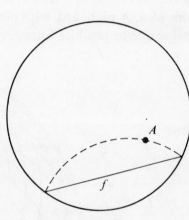

Fig. 27

Notice that we are using arithmetic mod 24 on the set {0, 1, 2, ..., 23}. Figure 26 has been constructed using the function $x \to x+6$, e.g. 2 is joined to $2+6 = 8$, and 21 is joined to $21+6 = 3$.

(*b*) Paper folding enables us to obtain an envelope quickly. The folds do not show up very well and it is best to run over them in pencil. Cut a circle out of tracing paper or use a circular filter paper. Mark a point A inside the circle and fold the paper over so that the circle passes through A, as shown in Figure 27. This gives the fold f. Repeat this about 15 times around the circle. What shape do the folds envelop?

(*c*) Figure 28 shows how a pinboard and elastic bands or thread may be used to form envelopes. The curves in this case are parabolas.

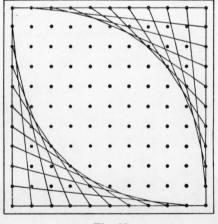

Fig. 28

272

Exercise C

1. In Figure 29, *AP* rotates about *A* and *AP* = 8 cm. The angle between *AP* and the line *l* is always 30°. Draw the envelope of *l*. Explain why it is a circle and find its centre and radius.

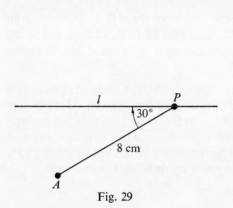

Fig. 29

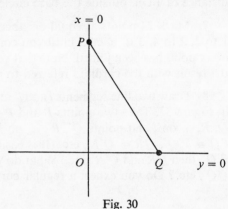

Fig. 30

2. In Figure 30, *PQ* = 4 cm, *P* is always on $x = 0$ and *Q* is always on $y = 0$. (Imagine a slipping ladder.)

Draw the complete envelope of *PQ*. It has four 'branches' and is called an *astroid*.

3. In Figure 31, *P* is the point $(h, 2)$ and is always on $y = 2$; *Q* is the point $(k, ^-2)$ and is always on $y = ^-2$. Draw the envelope of *PQ* if $hk = 12$, by taking, say, 14 suitable values of *h* from $^-12$ to 12 inclusive. (In the figure, *P* is at $(4, 2)$ and *Q* at $(3, ^-2)$; thus $hk = 4 \times 3 = 12$.)

4. Draw the envelope of *PQ* in Figure 31 if $h + k = 12$. What do you find?

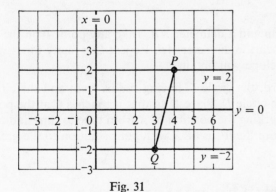

Fig. 31

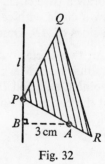

Fig. 32

5. Draw a line *l* and mark a point *A* 3 cm from *l* as in Figure 32. Place a set square with *P* on *l* and *PR* passing through *A*. Draw several positions of the line *PQ*, hence constructing its envelope. This is a parabola.

(You will have to turn the set square over for positions of *P* below *B*.)

6. Figure 25 shows the envelope of a set of circles. It can be drawn by marking a point *A* on a base circle, then taking another point *P* on the circle and drawing a circle with centre *P*

273

and radius PA (it will, of course, pass through A). This is repeated using a succession of different positions of P on the base circle. The final result looks more artistic if these positions are equally spaced. The envelope is called a *cardioid* which means heart-shaped.

Draw a similar envelope but, instead of taking a point A on the base circle, mark it at a distance of 1 cm. outside the base circle. Do you find that this envelope is also a cardioid?

7. Mark 24 points at equal distances round a circle and label them 0, 1, 2, ..., 23. Join 1 to 2, 2 to 4, 3 to 6, etc., until you come to 11 to 22, then join 12 to 0, 13 to 2, etc., until every point has been joined. Note that you have been considering $x \to 2x$ (mod 24). Compare the result with the cardioid referred to above.

8. Draw two line segments l and l' making an angle of about 40° with each other as shown in Figure 33. Take two points P and P'—one on l, the other on l'—as shown. Mark points Q, R, ... on l and points Q', R', ... on l' putting Q, R, ... at irregular intervals but making $PQ = P'Q'$, $QR = Q'R'$, etc. (It is easiest to use a pair of compasses marking first PQ and $P'Q'$, then QR and $Q'R'$, etc.) What do you think will be the envelope of the line joining PP', QQ', etc.? Do you expect a regular curve? Test your guess by drawing the envelope.

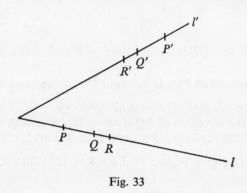

Fig. 33

9. Draw a base circle of radius 3 cm and a diameter AB. Take any point P on the circle and draw a circle with centre P to touch the diameter AB. Repeat this many times with P on both sides of AB. Describe the envelope you obtain.

10. Cut two circles out of cardboard, the circle C having radius 6 cm and the circle D having radius 3 cm. Mark a point X on circle D. Place D so that it touches C at the point X and, keeping C still, roll D round C, marking the position of X from time to time and taking care that the circles do not slip. Compare the locus of X with your solution to the previous question.

4. LOCI IN THREE DIMENSIONS

(*a*) In two dimensions the locus of a point P such that $AP = BP$, where A and B are fixed points, is the mediator of AB. We write this locus $\{P: AP = BP\}$.

If A and B are fixed in space and P can vary in three dimensions, how many mediators could be drawn? Altogether what do they form? We shall still write this locus $\{P: AP = BP\}$ but $\mathscr{E}$ is now different. Describe $\mathscr{E}$. In the rest of this section the universal set for P will be the whole of space.

(*b*) Describe in words the locus

$$\{P: AP = BP = CP\},$$

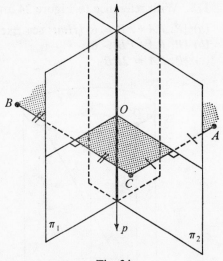

if C is a third fixed point not collinear with A and B. Describe the planes π_1 and π_2 in Figure 34 using set notation. (Note that they are really infinite planes, though they have to be shown finite.) Describe $\pi_1 \cap \pi_2$ using set notation. Describe the line p in set notation. What relation does any point on it have to the points A, B, C?

(*c*) If the shaded plane passes through A, B, C and if p meets it at O, what can you say about O in relation to the triangle ABC? Why is p at right-angles to the shaded plane? Describe another plane, not shown in the figure, which will contain p.

Fig. 34

How many spheres can be drawn through A, B and C? Where will their centres lie?

Exercise D

1. With reference to Figure 34 describe the following 3-D loci:

    (*a*) $\{P: PA = 1\}$;   (*b*) $\{P: PA < PC\}$.

2. What can you say about the locus of
(*a*) a chair on the big wheel at a fair;
(*b*) a control line model aeroplane;
(*c*) a child sliding down a helter-skelter?

3. What is the locus of points 1 m away from

    (*a*) a line l;   (*b*) a line segment AB.

4. Let l be a line in a plane π. If $X = \{P: P \text{ is 2 cm from } \pi\}$, and $Y = \{P: P \text{ is 3 cm from } l\}$, describe $X \cap Y$.

5. Let π be the infinite plane of which your paper is a part. If c is a line perpendicular to π and $X = \{P: P \text{ is 10 cm from } c\}$, identify X and $\pi \cap X$.

Sketch $\pi \cap X$ if c makes an acute angle with π.

6. Let

    $X = \{P: P \text{ is 4 cm from a plane } \pi\}$

and

    $Y = \{P: P \text{ is 5 cm from } A,$

           where A is a fixed point in $\pi\}$.

Describe (*a*) X; (*b*) Y; (*c*) $X \cap Y$.

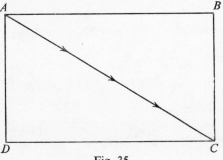

7. Figure 35 represents the label from a cocoa tin. Sketch the path, in 3 D, of Fred the fly if he crawls from A to C when the label is on the tin. Name some familiar objects that possess this shape.

Fig. 35

D8. With reference to Figure 34 and given that $AB = 4$, describe the following loci:

(a) $\{P: PA+PB = 6\}$ [*Hint*: see Exercise A, Question 7];

(b) $\{P: PA+PB > 6\}$;

(c) $\{P: PA = 2PB\}$.

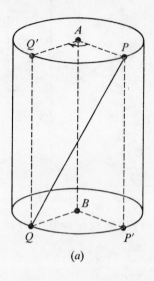

(a)   (b)

Fig. 36

9. *Project.* Figure 36(a) represents a circular cylinder. Points P and Q move on the top and bottom edges of the cylinder respectively, in such a way that PAQ' is a constant angle. The envelope of the line segment PQ may be inferred from Figure 36(b). A model to illustrate this may easily be made by constructing two congruent circular discs of hardboard and drilling a number of holes equally spaced round their edges. Shirring elastic is then threaded through the holes as shown. The discs may be mounted on a wooden axle, made from dowelling; alternatively Mecanno wheels and rods may be used. A surface of this nature is called a *ruled surface*. Other examples of ruled surfaces are the 'hyperbolic paraboloid' roofs of some modern buildings.

D10. Construct a paper cube of side 5 cm. Pierce it along a line of symmetry with a long needle and spin it. Repeat with other lines of symmetry. Try to predict the envelopes you will notice and to account for them when you have made your observations.

276

PUZZLE CORNER

Now you see it, now you don't.

1.

```
.   .   .

.   .   .

.   .   .
```

Draw 4 straight lines which will pass through the 9 dots without taking your pencil off the paper or tracing out any line twice.

2. Remove 3 matches from the 15 shown in Figure 1 so that only 3 squares are left.

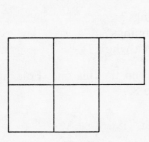

Fig. 1

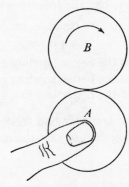

Fig. 2

3. There are 8 coins in a row, alternately head and tail. A move consists of moving 2 adjacent coins without altering their positions relative to each other. e.g. from

HTHTHTHT to HTH   THTTH

is a possible move.

In four moves rearrange the coins so that the heads are together and the tails are together.

4. One 10p piece A is held fixed. Another B rotates around it (see Figure 2). How many revolutions does B make about its own centre in returning to its original position?

5. Arrange the Kings, Queens, Jacks and Aces of a pack of playing cards in 4 rows and 4 columns so that there is only one in each suit and denomination in each row and column. How many essentially different arrangements are there?

6. Find the smallest set of 20 consecutive numbers none of which is a prime.

7. I am thinking of a whole number less than 1 million. You may ask me 20 questions to which I shall reply 'yes' or 'no'. How would you find the number?

8. What is the greatest sum of money in coins one can have without being able to change a 50p piece?

9. Two trains, both travelling at 50 km/h, start simultaneously from 2 stations *A* and *B*, 100 km apart. Frank the fly starts at the same time from station *A* and flies at 100 km/h towards station *B*. When he meets the train from *B* he is frightened and turns back towards *A*. He flies backwards and forwards between the trains until they meet and he is finally squashed.

How far has the fly flown? (Don't worry about the fate of the trains.)

10. Is it possible to drill a square hole for, say, the clock key shown in Figure 3? If so, design a tool.

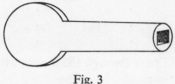

Fig. 3

11. When New South Wales played Victoria at Sydney in 1906–07, C. G. Macartney and M. A. Noble had the following bowling analyses:

| *1st innings*: | Macartney 2 for 43 | Noble 1 for 32 |
| *2nd innings*: | Macartney 4 for 6 | Noble 6 for 21 |

Who had the better bowling average for the first innings?
Who had the better bowling average for the second innings?
Who had the better bowling average for the match as a whole?

12. Have you ever had trouble in folding a map? Then try this one. Fold up the map shown in Figure 4 so that the numbers are in order 1 to 8.

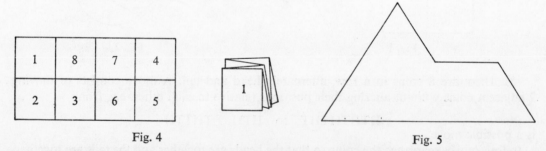

| 1 | 8 | 7 | 4 |
| 2 | 3 | 6 | 5 |

Fig. 4   Fig. 5

13. You will remember from Book 1 that regular pentagons do not tessellate. However, the 5-sided figure shown in Figure 5 does tessellate.
Arrange four of these to form a similar shape.

14. There are 2 glasses: one containing 10 spoonfuls of wine and the other 10 of water.
A spoonful of wine is taken from the first glass, put in the second glass, and mixed round. Then a spoonful of the mixture is taken and put back in the first glass.
Is there now more wine in the water than water in the wine?

15. The maths lesson should finish at 3.15 p.m., but the teacher always keeps the class until the hour hand and minute hand of his watch are exactly together.
What is the time then?

16. Each letter in the following addition stands for a number. What are the numbers?

$$\begin{array}{r} S\ E\ N\ D \\ M\ O\ R\ E \\ \hline M\ O\ N\ E\ Y \end{array}$$

17. The square in Figure 6(a) measures 8×8 cm. It is rearranged to give a rectangle measuring 5×13 cm (Figure 6(b)). Its area was 64 cm², and is now 65 cm². Where does the extra square centimetre come from?

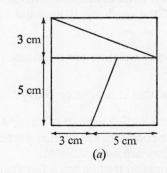
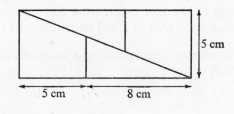

(a)   (b)

Fig. 6

18.

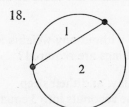
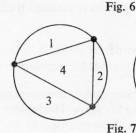
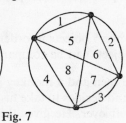
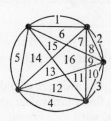

Fig. 7

When 2 points on a circle are joined, 2 regions are formed.
When 3 points on a circle are joined, 4 regions are formed.
When 4 points on a circle are joined, 8 regions are formed.
When 5 points on a circle are joined, 16 regions are formed.
When 6 points on a circle are joined, ? regions are formed?
(N.B. Avoid 'losing' regions because of triple intersections.)

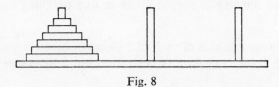

Fig. 8

19. Legend has it that at the creation of the world, three columns were erected in the floor of the temple of Benares (see Figure 8). On one of the columns were placed 64 pure gold discs of diminishing size. The priests were instructed to reassemble the discs in the same order on

279

one of the other pillars, but obeying the rules that only one disc at a time could be moved, and no disc could ever be placed on one of smaller size. It was said that when this task was completed, the world would come to an end.

If they transfer one disc per second, when will the end of the world come?

[*Hint*: experiment with 3, 4 discs, and try to find a relation between the number of discs and the number of moves.]

20. Each letter in the following multiplication represents a number. What are the numbers?

$$T W O \times T W O = T H R E E.$$

21. Assume that the earth is a perfect sphere 40 000 kilometres in circumference. A telephone line is erected around the equator so that it forms a circle concentric with the equator. If the length of the wire exceeds the circumference of the earth by 30 m, would there be enough space for a man to crawl under the wire?

22. How many weighings (using a balance without any weights) are necessary to detect the false coin out of 9 coins:

   (*a*) given that it is heavy;   (*b*) not given that it is light or heavy?

23. In order not to quarrel about 'fair shares' when dividing a piece of cake, Alan and Barbara have a system: Alan cuts the cake into what he considers are 2 equal portions, and Barbara then chooses which portion she wants. Thus they are both satisfied.

Devise a process for 5 people so that each person is satisfied that he has a fair share of the cake.

24. It is required to arrange 5 objects in order of mass. A balance without any weights is available so that pairs of objects can be compared. How many weighings are required?

25. On a desert island, 3 men and a monkey gather coconuts all day, and then sleep.

The first man wakes up, and decides to take his share. He devides the coconuts into 3 equal shares, with one coconut left over. He gives the extra one to the monkey, hides his share and goes to sleep. Later the second man awakens and takes his third from the remaining pile; he too finds one extra and gives it to the monkey. The third man does likewise. In the morning the men wake up and find they can divide the coconuts exactly into 3 piles with 1 coconut over for the monkey.

Find the minimum number of coconuts originally present.

26. 12 bags each contain 20 gold coins and each gold coin has a mass of 1 kg. However, one bag contains forged coins, each of which is 50 grams lighter than it should be.

How would you find the bag of forged coins in one weighing on a weighing machine (coin-in-the-slot type)?

27. In an electric toaster one side of each of 2 pieces of bread is toasted at the same time. Two hands are needed to insert or remove each slice, but 2 slices can be turned over at the same time.

The time to toast a side is 0·50 min; the time to turn over a slice is 0·02 min; the time to remove a toasted slice and place it on a plate is 0·05 min; the time to pick up a slice and place it in the toaster is 0·05 min. It is required to toast 3 slices on both sides. The bread starts on a plate, and the toast must be returned there. What is the shortest possible time?

28. When a motorist comes to a road junction he finds that the sign-post has been knocked down and all that he can discover is that one road leads to Exeter and the other to Bristol. Nearby is a house in which 2 brothers live: one always tells the truth, the other always lies. The motorist asks one question. He does not know which brother replies, but from the answer he knows which road to take. What question does he ask?

29. When the crackers were pulled at John's Christmas party there were 3 blue paper hats and 2 red. John then played a game with his friends. Three of them sat in a line so that A could see B and C, B could see C, and C could see no one. He placed a hat on each of their heads, not allowing them to see their own or the 2 hats that were left over. He then asked A if he knew what colour his hat was. A said 'No'. B was asked if he knew the colour of his hat. He said 'No'. C could see no hats, but gave the right answer when he was asked. What colour was his hat? (C, incidentally, was a logician!)

30. In this cross-number, a, b and c are positive integers.

1	2	3	4
5		6	
7	8	9	
10			

Across
1. $2a^2bc$
5. $3c-1$
6. bc
7. $3a(b^3-2c^2)+b$
9. $a-b+4c$
10. $c(a^3b+ac-1)$

Down
1. $2bc^2$
2. $2b^2$
3. $\frac{1}{2}(3c-1)$
4. c^3
8. $\dfrac{c^2-3b}{\sqrt{a}}$
9. $3a^2$

REVISION EXERCISES

SLIDE RULE SESSION NO. 7

Give all answers as accurately as you can.

1. $2 \cdot 16 \times 1 \cdot 62$.
2. $3 \cdot 03 \times 2 \cdot 53$.
3. $2 \cdot 45^2$.
4. π^2.

5. $0 \cdot 607 \times 0 \cdot 112$.
6. $2 \cdot 16 \div 1 \cdot 62$.
7. $3 \cdot 03 \div 2 \cdot 53$.

8. $2 \cdot 45 \div 8 \cdot 1$.
9. $\pi \div 3$.
10. $0 \cdot 607 \div 0 \cdot 112$.

SLIDE RULE SESSION NO. 8

Give all answers as accurately as you can.

1. $\sqrt{10 \cdot 5}$.
2. $\sqrt{4100}$.
3. $\sqrt{0 \cdot 98}$.
4. $\sqrt{0 \cdot 098}$.

5. $8 \cdot 86^3$.
6. $0 \cdot 112^3$.
7. $\pi \times 7 \cdot 4^2$.

8. $24 \cdot 6 \times 19 \times 0 \cdot 07$.
9. $\dfrac{1 \cdot 21 \times 1 \cdot 06}{1 \cdot 12}$.
10. $(25 \cdot 2 \times 16 \cdot 1) + \left(\dfrac{1 \cdot 72 \times 0 \cdot 85}{0 \cdot 74}\right)$.

S

1. If $44^2 - 41^2 = 3p$, state the value of p.

2. If $n(X \cup Y) = 25$, $n(X \cap Y) = 5$, and $n(Y) = 14$, draw a Venn diagram to illustrate these data, and find $n(X)$.

3. Calculate x and y if $\qquad \begin{pmatrix} x \\ y \end{pmatrix} = \begin{pmatrix} 2 & 1 \\ 3 & -1 \end{pmatrix} \begin{pmatrix} 1 \\ 3 \end{pmatrix}$.

4. State the probability that a throw of a die will result in a score of 3 or more.

5. When p and q are positive numbers, $p * q$ denotes the positive number $\sqrt{(pq)}$. Find the value of $24 * (4 * 9)$.

6. The numbers of the principal farm animals in Great Britain are (to a sufficient degree of accuracy): cattle 12 million, sheep 30 million, pigs 6 million. A pie chart is to be drawn to illustrate the proportions of the three kinds of animal. State the angle of the sector which represents pigs.

7. State a fraction whose value lies between $\frac{1}{2}$ and $\frac{4}{9}$.

8. State the number $0 \cdot 07346$ correct to three significant figures.

T

1. Find the value of ab/c, where $a = 10^6$, $b = 10^7$, $c = 10^{-3}$.

2. If $a * b$ denotes $a + 2b$, calculate $3 * 2$ and $2 * 3$.

3. What do the results of Question 2 show about the nature of the operation $*$?

4. Is it always, sometimes or never true that $X \cap Y \subset X \cup Y$?

282

5. Give the interquartile range of the numbers 4, 6, 7, 9, 10, 15, 19.

6. Write $(p+2q)^2$ without brackets.

7. If $\mathscr{E}$ = {quadrilaterals}, P = {quadrilaterals with point symmetry}, and Q = {quadrilaterals with line symmetry}, draw a quadrilateral that is a member of $P' \cap Q$.

8. Write down an ordered set of five integers whose mean is 4 and whose median is 3.

U

State the letter corresponding to the correct answer, or answers.

1. The statement $(x+3)^2 = x^2+6x+9$ is true for:
(*a*) all values of x; (*b*) only two values of x;
(*c*) only one value of x; (*d*) no value of x.

2. The statement $(x+3)^2 = x^2+4x+6$ is true for:
(*a*) all values of x; (*b*) only two values of x;
(*c*) only one value of x; (*d*) no value of x.

3. (See Figure 1.) The fraction

$$\frac{\text{area of triangle } AMX}{\text{area of triangle } CDX}$$

is equal to: (*a*) $\frac{1}{2}$; (*b*) $\frac{1}{3}$; (*c*) $\frac{1}{4}$; (*d*) none of these.

4. (See Figure 1.) The fraction

$$\frac{\text{area of triangle } CDX}{\text{area of parallelogram } ABCD}$$

is equal to: (*a*) $\frac{1}{3}$; (*b*) $\frac{1}{4}$; (*c*) $\frac{1}{6}$; (*d*) none of these.

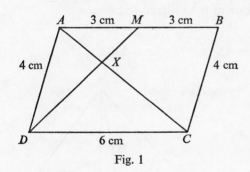

Fig. 1

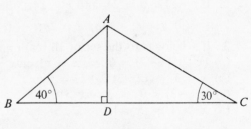

Fig. 2

5. (See Figure 2.) If AB is 5 cm long, then the length AC, in cm, is
(*a*) $5 \sin 40°$; (*b*) $5 \sin 40°/\cos 60°$;
(*c*) $5 \cos 40°/\cos 60°$; (*d*) $5 \cos 40° \cos 60°$?

6. In a certain district 70% of the families own a TV set, and 30% of the families own cars. Which of the following statements are *not necessarily* true, but *could* be true?
(*a*) All families have either a TV set or a car.
(*b*) Most car owners have a TV set.
(*c*) Fewer than half the owners of TV sets have cars.
(*d*) If the number of car owners increased by 50% of the present number, there would be more car owners than TV owners.

7. The distance between two parallel planes is 6 cm. The locus of a point equidistant from these planes and 3 cm away from a line in one of these planes is:

(*a*) a single point;   (*b*) a single line;

(*c*) two lines;   (*d*) none of these.

8. In Figure 3 the angle *BHC* is equal to:

(*a*) θ;   (*b*) 2θ;   (*c*) $180° - \theta$;   (*d*) $360° - \theta$.

9. The value of $\sqrt{4840}$ is:

(*a*) 22;   (*b*) 220;

(*c*) between 69 and 70;   (*d*) none of these.

10. The length and breadth of a rectangle are measured as 6·4 cm and 3·1 cm correct to the nearest tenth of a centimetre. It follows that the smallest possible value for the perimeter, correct to the nearest tenth of a centimetre, is:

(*a*) 18·6 cm;   (*b*) 18·8 cm;

(*c*) 18·9 cm;   (*d*) 19·0 cm.

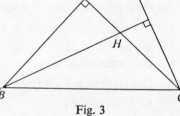

Fig. 3

V

Say which statements are true and which are false.

1. A triangle *ABC* in which no two sides are equal is given a clockwise turn equal to the angle *A* about the vertex *B*. Then:

(*a*) the angle between the old and new directions of *AC* is *A*;

(*b*) the angle between the old and new directions of *BC* is *B*;

(*c*) *B* is an element of the mediator of *AA'*, where *A'* is the new position of *A*;

(*d*) no side of the new triangle is parallel to a side of the original triangle.

2. If $p = 12_5$, $q = 24_5$ and $r = 24_{10}$, then:

(*a*) $q < r$;   (*b*) $q = 2p$;   (*c*) $p + q = 42_5$;   (*d*) $5q = 240_5$.

3. If *x* belongs to the set of all real numbers, then:

(*a*) $(x+1)(x-2) = 0 \Leftrightarrow x = {}^-1$ or $x = 2$;

(*b*) $x = 3 \Rightarrow (x-3)(x+1) = 0$;

(*c*) $x(x-3) < 0 \Rightarrow 3 > x > 0$;

(*d*) $x^2 > 1 \Rightarrow x > 1$.

4. Figure 4 shows a regular octahedron.

(*a*) The solid has exactly eight faces, six vertices and eight edges.

(*b*) The angle $ACE = 60°$.

(*c*) $EC = AF$.

(*d*) There are exactly four distinct routes from *A* to *B* along the edges of the solid and passing through just two other vertices.

5. If *x*, *y*, *z* are positive numbers such that $x = y^2$ and $z = 1/y$, then:

(*a*) $x > y$ for all $y > 1$;   (*b*) $y > 1 \Rightarrow z < 1$;

(*c*) $z = 3 \Leftrightarrow x = 9$;   (*d*) $x = 1/z^2$.

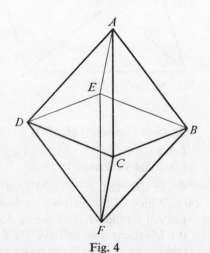

Fig. 4

6. If **P** denotes reflection in $y = 0$, and **Q** denotes reflection in $x = 4$, and if Z is the point $(^-1, 3)$, then:

(a) $\mathbf{P}(Z) = (^-1, ^-3)$; (b) $\mathbf{Q}(Z) = (^-1, 1)$;
(c) $\mathbf{PQ}(Z) = (^-9, 3)$; (d) $\mathbf{PQ} = \mathbf{QP}$;
(e) $\mathbf{P}^2 = \mathbf{I}$ (where $\mathbf{I}$ is the identity transformation).

7. It is given that $T = (3W - a)/2a$. Then:

(a) $T = (3W/2a) - \frac{1}{2}$; (b) $T = 0$ when $a = 3W$;
(c) $W = \frac{2}{3}aT + a$; (d) if $a = W$, then $T = 1$.

8. (a) 35% of 140 is 49;
   (b) 400 is the number of which 140 is 35%;
   (c) 175 is 35% more than 140;
   (d) 50% more than 50% less than 140 is 105;
   (e) 50% less than 50% more than 140 is 140.

9. For all values of the letters:

(a) $(x+y)^2 = x^2 + y^2$; (b) $\dfrac{3a+4b}{3a+5c} = \dfrac{1+4b}{1+5c}$;

(c) $\dfrac{3a+4b}{3a+5b} = \dfrac{4}{5}$; (d) $4s^2 - 9t^2 = (2s-3t)(2s+3t)$;

(e) $\dfrac{m^2 n - n^2 m}{kmn} = \dfrac{m-n}{k}$.

10. (a) 'Isosceles' is a wrong spelling of a kind of triangle.
    (b) Since $\sqrt{169} = 13$, then $\sqrt{1690} = 130$.
    (c) A boy cycles from P to Q averaging 30 km/h. He returns, averaging 20 km/h. Then his average speed for the whole trip must be 25 km/h.
    (d) If $M \times N = 0$, then $M = 0$ or $N = 0$ (where M and N are numbers).
    (e) For any three sets A, B and C, $(A \cap B) \cap C = A \cap (B \cap C)$.

W

1. It is given that $\mathscr{E} = \{x: ^-10 \leqslant x \leqslant 10\}$, $Q = \{x: ^-5 < x \leqslant 3\}$,
   $P = \{x: ^-10 < x < 10\}$, $R = \{x: 3 \leqslant x < 5\}$.

Write down expressions for (a) P'; (b) $Q \cap R$; (c) $Q \cup R$; (d) $Q \cap P'$.

2. In a factory containing ten sewing machines, observations were made to find the number of machines inactive for complete days because of the absence of the operator. The results were:

Number of inactive machines	0	1	2	3	4	5	6	7	8	9	10
Number of days (frequency)	17	13	8	4	1	5	0	3	0	0	0

Provided it could be divided among several machines, how long should be allowed for some sewing that would take one machine 260 working days to complete?

3. All quadrilaterals that are members of the set $\{R\}$ have property D. Is it necessarily true that quadrilaterals that have the property D are members of the set $\{R\}$? Give an example to illustrate your answer.

4. A tray is carefully measured with a ruler and the dimensions recorded to the nearest centimetre as; length 60 cm, width 45 cm.

285

(a) State the possible limits of the true length.

(b) State whether it is true or false that the perimeter could be as little as 206 cm.

(c) What is the least possible area of the tray?

5. The point P moves on the line AB (see Figure 5). A transformation maps P onto the point P' such that P is the mid-point of OP'. Copy the figure and draw on it as much as you can of the locus of P'. Mark the transforms C', D' of C and D and state their coordinates.

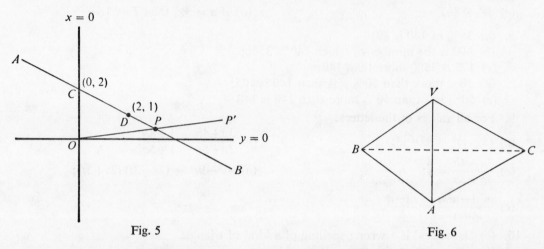

Fig. 5   Fig. 6

6. In the pyramid shown in Figure 6, the face VAB is equilateral with sides of 6 units; $CA = CB = 10$ units; $VC = 8$ units.

(a) State which angles formed by adjacent edges are right-angles.

(b) State the position of any plane of symmetry of the pyramid.

(c) Copy the figure and, adding extra lines if necessary, mark angles which are:

(i) the angle between the planes VAB, CAB (mark this x);

(ii) the angle between the planes VBC, VAC (mark this y).

7. (See Figure 7, which is not drawn to scale.)

(a) State which of A or B has the greater x coordinate.

(b) Calculate the difference between their y coordinates.

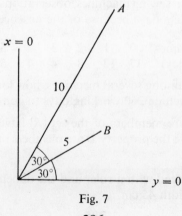

Fig. 7

286

8. The triangles in Figure 8 are all equilateral, and $AB = 2$ cm.

(*a*) Name the solid of which *ABCDEF* is a net.

(*b*) With which point does *C* coincide when the net is folded up?

(*c*) Calculate the total surface area of the solid. (The answer may be given in a form which includes a square root.)

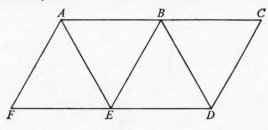

Fig. 8

X

1. (*a*) Add 35_6 and 14_6, giving the answer in the same base.

(*b*) Express 230_n in terms of n.

(*c*) State two factors of 230_n.

2. (*a*) Express $0 \cdot 26666\ldots$ correct to three decimal places.

(*b*) Express $0 \cdot 026666\ldots$ correct to two significant figures.

(*c*) If $x = 0 \cdot 26666\ldots$, write down the value of $10x$ and from these two values obtain the value of $9x$. Hence express x as a fraction in its simplest terms.

3. The bearing of *B* from *A* is 040°; the bearing of *C* from *A* is 060°; and the bearing of *B* from *C* is 290°.

(*a*) Draw a diagram showing the relative positions of *A*, *B* and *C*.

(*b*) State the size of $\angle ABC$.

(*c*) State the bearing of *A* from *C*.

4. Copy Figure 9 and

(*a*) draw on your diagram the locus of points which are within the triangle and are equidistant from *AB* and *BC*;

(*b*) shade the set of all points which are nearer to *BC* than to *AB* and which are less than 1 cm from the point *A*.

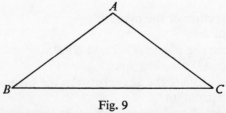

Fig. 9

5. (*a*) Simplify $A \cap (B \cup B')$.

(*b*) If $\mathscr{E} = \{\text{animals}\}$, $D = \{\text{dogs}\}$ and $F = \{\text{fat animals}\}$, write a sentence equivalent to the statement $D \cap F' \neq \emptyset$.

6. In Figure 10, ABC and $A'B'C'$ are congruent triangles, and $BCC'B'$ is a straight line.
(a) Describe a single transformation that would map A, B, C onto A', B', C' respectively.
(b) What can you state about the relation between the lines AA' and CC'.

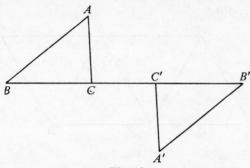

Fig. 10

7. (a) Let
$$\mathbf{M} = \begin{pmatrix} 1 & -2 \\ 3 & 1 \end{pmatrix} \quad \text{and} \quad \mathbf{N} = \begin{pmatrix} 2 & 1 \\ 0 & 1 \end{pmatrix}.$$

Find $\mathbf{MN}$ and $\mathbf{NM}$. Are they equal?
(b) $ABCD$ is a parallelogram. If the coordinates of A, B, C are $(0, 0)$, $(2, 1)$ and $(3, 3)$ respectively, what are the coordinates of D?

8. A boy very much wanted a mongrel puppy. His parents said he could have it if it could be trained within a school holiday (30 days). To persuade them, the boy asked mongrel owners he knew how long they had taken to train their dogs. These are the answers in days:

20	31	45	18	28	17	23	30	35	42	21	37
24	26	34	18	27	16	12	33	23	27	26	

He decided to find the mean and the median and to show the answer more favourable to his argument. He then decided to show some measure of scatter or deviation. He worked out the inter-quartile range.
Draw a cumulative frequency diagram and mark on it the mean, median and quartiles. Briefly state the boy's argument to be allowed to keep the puppy.

Y

1. $ABCDV$ is a pyramid. $ABCD$, 8 cm square, is its base; and V is 6 cm vertically above the centre of the base.
(a) Draw an oblique projection of the pyramid.
(b) Calculate the length of BV.
(c) State the angle between the planes AVC and BVD.
(d) Is it true that BV and AD are skew lines?
(e) State how you would calculate the angle between the planes BCV and $ABCD$, but do not actually carry out the calculation.
(f) P is a point 27 cm from B and 19 cm from A. Is there a single plane containing the three points P, B and A?

2. Graph the function $x \rightarrow x^2$ for $x = -3, -2\frac{1}{2}, -2, ..., 2, 2\frac{1}{2}, 3$. Join the points with a smooth curve and hence estimate the value of $\sqrt{5}$.

3. A football moves from A to E by passes described by the following vectors:

$$\mathbf{AB} = \begin{pmatrix} 4 \\ 3 \end{pmatrix}, \qquad \mathbf{BC} = \begin{pmatrix} -3 \\ 4 \end{pmatrix}, \qquad \mathbf{CD} = \begin{pmatrix} 2 \\ 0 \end{pmatrix}, \qquad \mathbf{DE} = \begin{pmatrix} 5 \\ -1 \end{pmatrix}.$$

Calculate the vector $\mathbf{AE}$, and indicate the ball's motion on a diagram. Calculate the length of $\mathbf{AE}$.

4. 240 sweets are to be divided between four boys, Alan, Brian, Colin and David, in the ratio $4:3:2:1$ respectively. Find each boy's share, and express them as percentages of Brian's share.

5. Two dice are made in the shape of regular tetrahedra and have the numbers 1, 2, 3, 4 inscribed on their four faces. Make a table to show all the possible combinations of the scores of the two hidden faces when the dice are thrown together. What are the probabilities of the total scores being: (a) 2, (b) 5, (c) 9?

6. Draw a perspective picture of a match-box, showing one of the black sides, one of the ends, and the top, on which is printed the name HI-LITE. Show clearly any vanishing points you use. Also draw an oblique projection of the match-box from the same point of view.

7. On a photograph of the west front of a cathedral, the width appears as 3·7 cm and the height as 4·3 cm. If the actual width is 46 m, what is the actual height? Also, if the area of glass in a window is 10 m², what is the area of the window as shown in the photograph?

8. In a mathematics exam, a boy scored 30% on the first paper, which was marked out of 180. How much must he score on the second paper, which is marked out of 150, if he is to get at least 50% overall?

Z

1. If $x - y = 7$ and $y \geqslant 3$, what can you say about x?

2. 10022 is a number in the base of three, and the same number is represented as 155 in another base. What is the base?

3. Let A be the point $(3, 0)$, B the point $(6, 5)$ and C the point $(3, 5)$. If the line through C parallel to BA meets the line $y = 0$ at D, what are the coordinates of D?

4. An angle less than $360°$ has a negative cosine and a positive sine. State the limits between which it lies.

5. In the following table, y is proportional to a power of x, but one value of y is in error.
(a) What is the power of x?   (b) What is the error?

x	5	10	15	20	25
y	11	48	99	176	275

6. The following table shows the heights, to the nearest centimetre, of a sample of 124 seedling fir trees:

Height	33	36	39	42	45	48	51	54	57	60	63
Number	5	9	14	18	20	17	18	13	6	3	1

Find the mean, mode, median and quartiles.

7. A bookshop buys books from a publisher at a price which is 30% less than the price marked on the books. Write down a formula for the profit the shop expects to make on a book marked at x new pence, and another formula for the price it pays for such a book.

8. On the C scale of a slide rule, the distance between the 2·5 mark and the 4·0 mark is x cm. What is the mark on this scale which is $2x$ cm to the right of the 2·5 mark?

INDEX

addition, of displacement vectors, 30; of matrices, 30–2
additive identity, 187
algebra, of transformations, 16–19
angles, 114–20; between a line and a plane, 115, 120; between two planes, 116, 120; between two skew lines, 114, 120
Archimedes, 67, 72
arcs of a network, correspondence between edges of a polyhedron and, 98–102; relation connecting nodes and regions with, 98
area, bounded by a circle, 74–6, 87; of curved surface of a cylinder, 83, 87; and matrices, 209–12; of parallelogram, 202; of a sector, 81, 87; under shearing, 196, 202–5; of triangle, 203
area scale factor, 212
arithmetic, clock, 186, 189
arithmetic unit of computer, 244
associativity, of matrix addition, 32
astroid, 273
average, mode and mean as measures of, 232, 239

Babbage, Charles, 242
brackets, 174–9

cardioid, 274
Cavalieri's Principle, 213
chord, 82
circle, 67–87
circumference of a circle, 70–2, 87
class interval, in frequency functions, 228, 229
classes, in frequency functions, 228
clock arithmetic, 186, 189
closed sets, 184–6, 190
code of letters and numbers for computer, 247
collinear points, 112, 120
colouring polyhedra, 103–4
column matrices, 28, 32; combination of, with row matrices, 32–6
column (or displacement) vectors, 28, 30, 42
combination, of column and row matrices, 32–6; of transformations, 13–15, 26
commutativity, of matrix addition, 32; of transformations, 14
complementary sets, 181–2, 184
composite functions, 155–6; inverse of, 162–3
computers, and programming, 241–60
cone, circular, volume of, 215
congruence, direct and opposite, 14, 22
contours, 49–50
control unit, of computer, 245
coordinates, for points on loci, 265–6

coplanar points, 112, 120
cosine, see sine and cosine
cube root, 260
cuboids, shearing of, 212–13
cumulative frequency, 236–9
cumulative frequency diagram, 237
cylinder, area of curved surface of, 83, 87; shearing of, 213; volume of, 83–4, 213, 215, 251–2

data, for computer, 243
diameter of a circle, 68
directed networks, 89
displacement (or column) vectors, 28, 30, 43
displacements, central and sideways, 150; sine and cosine as, 142–4, 150–1
distance, between a point and a plane, 118, 120
domain of a function, 156, 159
dominance matrices, 92–5
dry checking of computer programs, 249

edges of a polyhedron, correspondence between arcs of a network and, 98–102; relation connecting faces and vertices with, 98
ellipse, 264, 269–70
envelopes, 271–4
equations, functions and, 165–79; graphical solution of, 168; graphs of inequalities and, 124–30
Euler's relation for polyhedra, 98–101

faces of a polyhedron, correspondence between regions of a network and, 98–102; relation connecting edges and vertices with, 98
Fermat, P., 4
flow diagrams, for composite functions, 155, 156; in computer programming, 254–7; for finding inverse functions, 162, 164; for solving equations, 165–7
formulae, 170–4; computer programs for, 251–3; rearrangement of, 170
frequency, cumulative, 236–9; of an oscillation, 148
frequency functions, 226–32; normal, 229
frequency tables, 226–9; finding mean from, 232
function machine, 154–5, 158
functions, 154–79; composite, 155–6, 162–3; frequency, 226–32; inverse, 160–5; matrices describing, 159–60, 161; notation for, 154–7; as relations, 159, 160; self-inverse, 163–4; sine and cosine, 141–6, 150–1; transformations as, 155, 156

geometry, three-dimensional, 110–20
gradient, mathematical, 60; at a point on a curve, 57, 61; rate of change as, 53, 61; of a road, 50–2, 60

graphs, of equations and inequalities, 124–30; of frequency functions, 229–30; solution of equations by, 168; of solution sets, 121–4
grouped frequency tables, 229; finding mean from, 233

half-lines, 110
half-planes, 111, 127
Hamiltonian path, 108
Hero, 258
hyperbola, 269
hyperbolic paraboloid, 276

identity, and inverse, 180–94
identity elements, 186–90
identity matrix, 48
identity transformation, 18
images, of points in shearing, 197–201; of transformations, 16, 17; under functions, 167
incidence matrices, 105–9
input and output of computer, 247
infinity, symbol for, 113
inter-quartile range, 240
invariant line, in shear, 196–201
inverse, and identity, 180–94
inverse elements, 190–1
inverse functions, 160–5
inverse matrix, 48
inverse operations, 192
inverse pairs, 191–2
inverse relations, 96, 158–60
inverse transformations, 20–2
isometries, 12–26; direct and opposite, 14

knitting pattern, as computer program, 254, 255

Latin square, 10
limaçon, 152
linear programming, 130–4
line segments, 110
lines, 110, 120; intersecting, 133; parallel, 113; perpendicular to a plane, 115, 120; skew, 112, 113, 114, 120
loci, 261–71; in three dimensions, 274–6
loops, in computer programming, 254

machines, function, 154–5, 158; matrix, 46, 48
matrices, 27–48; addition of, 30–2; area and, 209–12; column, 28, 32; combination of row and column, 32–6; compatible for multiplication, 39, 106; describing functions, 159–60, 161; dominance, 92–5; identity, 48; incidence, 105–9; inverse, 48; multiplication of, 32–42, 105–6; orders of, 28, 32; relations and, 95–7, 159–60; route, 88–92; row, 28, 32; shearing, 205–9; square, 28, 30; and transformations, 42–8; transposes of, 96, 159, 160; zero, 32

matrix machine, 46, 48
mean, 232–5, 239
median, 235, 236, 238, 239
mid-interval of a class, 233
misrepresentation, by statistics, 224–6
mode, 232, 239
Moebius band, 108
multiplication, of matrices, 32–42, 105–6
multiplicative identity, 187

networks, 88–109; connected, 100, 101; directed, 89; and polyhedra, 98–102
node-sum of a network, 102
nodes of a network, correspondence between vertices of a polyhedron and, 98–102; relation connecting arcs and regions with, 98
normal frequency functions, 229–30
notes (musical), frequencies of, 148

odds, 9
one-dimensional 110
'one-way stretch', 208
operation tables, 185–6
order of a matrix, 28, 32
oscillation, frequency of, 148; periodic time of, 146

Pappus, 85
parabolas, 267, 272, 273
parallelogram, area of, 202
Pascal, Blaise, 4
Pascal's triangle, 11
pendulum, construction of, 147
perimeter, of a sector, 81
periodic time of an oscillation, 146
permutations, 192–3
π (pi), 72–4
planes, 111, 120
points, 110; collinear and coplanar, 112, 120
polyhedra, colouring of, 103–4; networks and, 98–102
population, for frequency function, 228
position vectors, 43
potato printing, 12–13
powers of a transformation, 18
prism, volume of, 213, 215
probability, 1–11; expected, 6–9; experimental, 4–6
programs for computer, 245, 248–53
projection, of a line onto a plane, 115
pyramid, volume of, 213–15
Pythagoras, theorem of, 204–5

quartiles, 236, 237–8, 240

radius of a circle, 68
random selection, 9–11
range, of a function, 156, 161; in a population, 235–6, 240

INDEX

rate of change, 49–61; as gradient, 53, 61; at an instant, 55–61

rays, 110

reflections, 14; combination of, 22–6

regions of a network, 111; correspondence between faces of a polyhedron and, 98–102; relation connecting arcs and nodes with, 98

relations, functions as, 159, 160; inverse, 158–60; and matrices, 95–7, 159–60

repetition, in computer methods, 257–60

rotations, 14

route matrices, 29–30, 88–92

row matrices, 28, 32; combination of, with column matrices, 32–6

ruled surface, 276

Schlegel diagrams, 98, 99, 100

section, 49

sector of a circle, 80–3, 87

segment of a circle, 80–3, 87

self-inverse, 190

self-inverse functions, 163–4

sets, closed, 184–6, 190; complementary, 181–2, 184; solution, 121–4; sub-, 181, 184; union of, 182–4; universal, 180–1, 184

shearing transformation, 195–218; area under, 196, 202–5; constructions for, 199–201; matrix for, 205–9; in three dimensions, 212–18

'Simon' digital computer, 248–51

'Simpol', language used by 'Simon' computer, 248

sine and cosine, definition of, 142–4

sine and cosine function, 141–6, 150–1

skew lines, 112, 113, 114, 120

slide rule, calculation of squares with, 76–8, 87; of square roots with, 78–80, 87

solution sets, graphs of, 121–4

sphere, volume of, 60

spread, in a population, 235–6; measures of, 240

square matrices, 28, 30, 32

square roots, 77–8; calculation of, with slide rule, 78–80, 87; Hero's method for finding, 258–9

squares, calculation of, with slide rule, 76–8, 87

statistics, 224–40

store, in computer, 245

subject of a formula, 171

subsets, 181

symbols for: is a complement of, 181, 184; contains, 181; implies, 166; implies and is implied by, 166; infinity, 113; less than or equal to, 122; is a member of, 182, 184; is a subset of, 180, 182; union of sets, 182, 184; universal set, 180, 184

symmetry, of a circle, 69–70

tangent, as gradient at a point on a curve, 57, 61

Theorem of Pythagoras, 204–5

three dimensions, loci in, 274–6; shearing in, 212–18

transformations, algebra of, 16–19; combination of, 13–15, 26; as functions, 155, 156; identity, 18, 20; inverse, 20–2; and matrices, 42–8; powers of, 18; *see also* reflections, rotations, shearing, translations

translations, 14; combination of, 19, 26

transposes of matrices, 96, 159, 160

trial and error, organized, 257–60

triangle, area of, 203

Tsu Chung Chieh, 73

two-dimensional, 111

'two-way stretch', 209

union of sets, 182–4

universal sets, 180–1, 184

vector notation, for combined translations, 19

vectors, column (or displacement), 28, 30, 42; position, 43

Venn diagrams, 184

vertices of a polyhedron, correspondence between nodes of a network and, 98–102; relation connecting edges and faces with, 98

volume, of circular cone, 215; of cylinder, 84, 87, 213, 215; of prism, 213, 215; of pyramid, 213–15; of sphere, 60; of solids under shearing, 212–15

waves, 146–53

zero matrix, 32